HUNTING *the* NORTHERN CHARACTER

TONY PENIKETT

HUNTING
the
NORTHERN
CHARACTER

PURICH
BOOKS

Purich Books, an imprint of UBC Press
2029 West Mall
Vancouver, BC, V6T 1Z2
www.purichbooks.ca

26 25 24 23 22 21 20 19 18 17   5 4 3 2 1

Printed in Canada on paper that is processed chlorine- and acid-free,
with vegetable-based inks.

Library and Archives Canada Cataloguing in Publication

Penikett, Antony, author
Hunting the northern character / Tony Penikett.

Includes bibliographical references and index.
Issued in print and electronic formats.
ISBN 978-0-7748-8000-8 (hardcover). – ISBN 978-0-7748-8002-2 (PDF). –
ISBN 978-0-7748-8003-9 (EPUB). – ISBN 978-0-7748-8004-6 (Kindle)

1. Canada, Northern – Politics and government.
2. Canada, Northern – Social conditions.
3. Canada, Northern – Environmental conditions. I. Title.

FC3956.P43 2017   971.9   C2017-903749-8
                                                     C2017-903750-1

Canadä

UBC Press gratefully acknowledges the financial support for our publishing
program of the Government of Canada (through the Canada Book Fund), the
Canada Council for the Arts, and the British Columbia Arts Council.

Printed and bound in Canada by Friesens
Set in Caslon, Univers, and Minion by Artegraphica Design Co. Ltd.
Substantive editor: Barbara Pulling
Copy editor: Matthew Kudelka
Proofreader: Kristy Lynn Hankewitz
Indexer: Pat Buchanan
Cover designer: Michel Vrana

To my late brother, Stephen Richard Penikett,
Arctic and Antarctic aviator

Contents

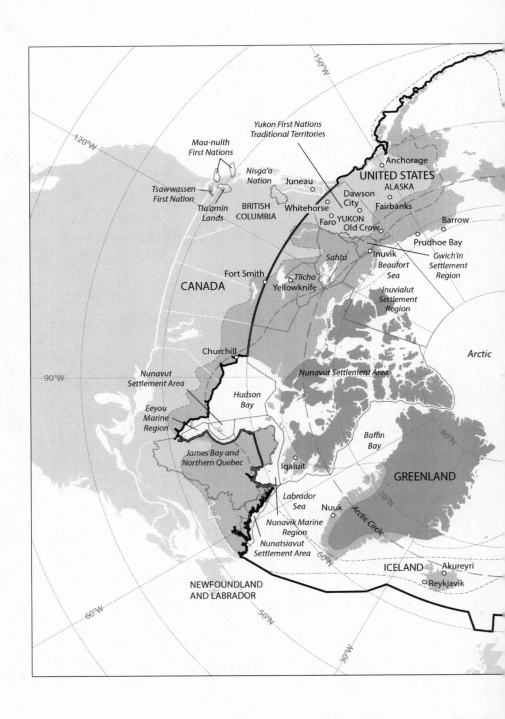

Yukon First Nations
Traditional Territories

Maa-nulth
First Nations

Nisga'a
Nation

Juneau

UNITED STATES
Anchorage

ALASKA

Tsawwassen
First Nation

Tla'amin
Lands

BRITISH
COLUMBIA

Whitehorse

Dawson
City

Fairbanks

Faro

YUKON

Old Crow

Barrow

Prudhoe Bay

Inuvik

Sahtu

Beaufort
Sea

Gwich'in
Settlement
Region

Fort Smith

Tlicho

CANADA

Yellowknife

Inuvialut
Settlement
Region

Arctic

Churchill

Nunavut Settlement Area

Nunavut
Settlement Area

90°W

Hudson
Bay

Baffin
Bay

Eeyou
Marine
Region

80°N

James Bay and
Northern Quebec

Iqaluit

GREENLAND

Labrador
Sea

Nuuk

70°N

Nunavik Marine
Region

Arctic Circle

Nunatsiavut
Settlement Area

60°N

ICELAND

Akureyri

NEWFOUNDLAND
AND LABRADOR

Reykjavik

60°W

50°N

30°W

120°W

150°W

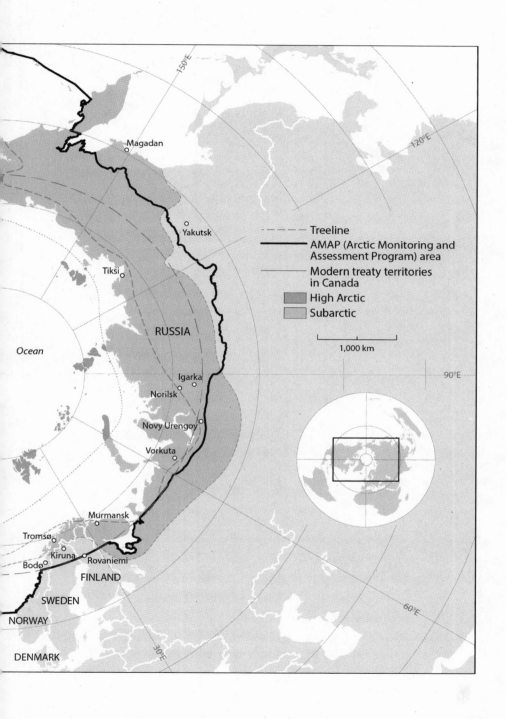

Treeline

AMAP (Arctic Monitoring and Assessment Program) area

Modern treaty territories in Canada

High Arctic

Subarctic

1,000 km

Magadan

Yakutsk

Tiksi

RUSSIA

Ocean

Igarka

Norilsk

Novy Urengoy

Vorkuta

Murmansk

Tromsø

Kiruna

Bodø   Rovaniemi

FINLAND

SWEDEN

NORWAY

DENMARK

150°E

120°E

90°E

60°E

30°E

Prologue

During his time in Ottawa as member of Parliament for the Northwest Territories, Wally Firth used to carry a compass in his pocket. Every so often during a political discussion, he would take it out and stare at it. When challenged to explain what he was doing, Firth would say, "Just checking to see which way is north."

That love of his northern homeland, that deep sense of the North's distinctiveness, was something Firth never failed to communicate. He understood very well that many of his southern counterparts saw the Arctic as barren and remote and empty. As Firth's campaign manager for his upset win in 1972 (he was the first Indigenous politician from the North to gain a seat in the House of Commons), I learned much from him. Firth had little formal education, but in his forty years he had lived through enormous change. In his work as a trader for the Hudson's Bay Company, as a radio "pronouncer" for the CBC, and as an organizer and pilot for the Indian-Eskimo Association of Canada, he had been a leader in many of those changes.

National leaders like to drone on about "the northern identity" and "the Arctic character," but what exactly are they talking about? Over the past several generations, communities around the circumpolar North have undergone major transformations. Northern residents have lived through the Cold War, decades of Indigenous land rights struggles, the booms and busts of resource megaprojects, environmental and social

1

stress, and now, increasingly, the cruel consequences of climate change. The insecurities suffered by northern communities in the course of these changes far outweigh those experienced by their southern counterparts. At the same time, the decolonization processes also under way in the Arctic have been profoundly liberating.

Colonial mindsets have a long history. The Vikings on Greenland stabbed a "Skraeling" to see if the Inuk in question would bleed and prove himself human. In Russia, the oppression of Indigenous peoples – reindeer herders, hunters, and fishers – started centuries ago. During the Second World War and afterwards, nation-states moved Arctic Indigenous people around like pawns on a circumpolar chess board, forcing them off their lands, abusing their children in residential schools, and dragging them through years of grinding land and political rights negotiations. While all this was taking place, national governments aided outside developers in plundering northern resources.

Over the past four decades, land treaties and devolution agreements have localized the distribution of resource revenues, jobs, and business opportunities to some degree, but nation-states continue to control vast lands and the resources under northerners' feet. Presidents, prime ministers, deputy ministers, and diplomats now appreciate that the Arctic is a contested space. Renewable resource harvesters in the North face conflicts with powerful non-renewable resource ventures from the south and, increasingly, overseas. For many Arctic residents, climate change is a raging ghost, chasing game off hunting grounds and unsettling community foundations. The absurdities of arbitrary colonial divisions have outlived the reality that thousands of mixed-race northerners and their blended families do not fit neatly into the federally created boxes of Indigenous and settler, Status and non-Status Indian, US-recognized tribal government and Alaska Native Corporation. Northern residents recognize that the Arctic is the site of fierce circumpolar geopolitics, but what they seek is to become masters in their own homes.

Ólafur Ragnár Grimsson, former president of Iceland, observes that it is in the federal states – the United States, Russia, Denmark, and

Canada – that capital cities exist at the greatest physical and psychological distance from the Arctic regions. Indeed, the Canadian government often seems baffled by the North; it has half a ministry for Indigenous Affairs and a second half for Northern (read "settler") Affairs. Canadian prime ministers travel north often enough, but like most tourists, they prefer to make flying visits in the summer season. Barack Obama was the only sitting American president ever to visit Alaska. Nordic leaders live closer to the High North, but their Arctic citizens nevertheless question whether those leaders speak for them. Russia has invested heavily in its Arctic economy, but since the end of the Cold War, its northern population has been in sharp decline.

It astonishes northerners how little national capitals actually know about northern places and peoples. Everybody recognizes the American eagle, the Russian bear, and the Canadian beaver, but how well acquainted are southerners with symbols such as Alaska's willow ptarmigan, Greenland's left-handed polar bear, or the Nordic reindeer? South and North stand worlds apart.

Yet out of sight of New Yorkers, and far from the minds of Copenhagen's citizens, Indigenous and non-Indigenous leaders together are forging new Arctic realities. The often painful interactions among the three main actors – Indigenous villages, Arctic cities, and nation-states – have fundamentally altered the contours of the northern character.

▪■▪

My fascination with the North began as a child, when I received a little grey hardback called *Lars in Lapland* as a Christmas gift from my schoolteacher grandmother. The title page featured a line drawing of a little boy in Sámi costume and a reindeer with sleigh bells around its neck. This little book ever after pointed me northward.

Most writers on the North, even the excellent ones, approach the Arctic from a southern perspective, as outsiders looking in. In this book I aim to offer a northern perspective – not *the* Arctic view, but a view based on my own northern experience. After many years as a territorial legislator and later as a mediator, mentor, and negotiator dealing with Indigenous and northern issues, I count myself as something of an insider. As well, like most northerners – or residents of any colony or peripheral area – I have often bristled at my status as an outsider, since residing in the North meant that I was far from the inner circles of policy-makers in Ottawa and Washington. In the words of the immortal science fiction writer Isaac Asimov, we existed in Terminus and they thrived in Trantor.

My links to northern lands go beyond my experiences in public life. They include an intricate web of family and personal relationships, ties knotted in my case through years of on-the-ground work in Alaska and all three Canadian territories: Yukon, the Northwest Territories (NWT), and Nunavut. Since that first childhood encounter with Lars and his reindeer, I have visited Lapland and met Sámi herders in Finland, Sweden, and Norway. In Alaska, the NWT, and Yukon, I have admired the reindeer's wild counterpart, the caribou. Once, along the Dempster Highway, I stood on a mountainside while hundreds of migrating members of the Porcupine Caribou Herd milled around me.

I have also learned practical lessons on more recent Arctic assignments: as a facilitator for the Arctic Governance Summit at Tromsø; as moderator for a Canada-UK Colloquium titled "The Arctic and Northern Dimensions of World Issues" at Iqaluit; as chair of the ten-year External Review Team for the University of the Arctic (UArctic); and as an adviser for the Arctic Security Project organized by the University of Toronto's Munk School of Global Affairs and the Walter and Duncan Gordon Foundation. In the years since my time in government, I have had hundreds of conversations with other public policy practitioners in the eight Arctic states and beyond. All of these experiences have contributed to my education in Arctic issues.

During my years in and around the North, I have been lucky enough to see the advent of a new northern consciousness. I have witnessed – and sometimes participated in – Aboriginal rights struggles, ongoing devolution talks, and northerners' rising demands for a fair share of the benefits from northern resources. I have marked the growing recognition that Arctic communities are cornerstones of sovereignty and security, and I have watched new forms of Arctic governance emerge, along with the fierce efforts of reactionaries to undo any steps towards modernity.

For some time, northern and Aboriginal communities have been pursuing their own foreign policies, with or without the sanction of national governments. Circumpolar initiatives have flourished, with conferences on everything from agriculture to education and health. Northerners are keen to strengthen east–west links that will counter the south's domination, and new institutions reflect this growing feeling of community across the Far North. With a unique demographic that is half Indigenous and half non-Indigenous, northern Canada has been the primary laboratory for many reconciliation initiatives, including Aboriginal self-government, circle sentencing, consensus legislatures, wildlife co-management, and the blending of scientific and Indigenous knowledge.

But stereotypes persist. Many southerners still imagine the Arctic as they see it in the media. TV dramas can leave viewers with false impressions. Southern reporters flock to Indigenous villages to capture the "traditional" while ignoring the modern Arctic cities where most northerners live. "North Poll," an *Up Here* magazine survey conducted in February 2011, found that a majority of Canadians believe penguins live in the Arctic and that people in the northern climes live in igloos.

People who should know better don't help the situation. A Norwegian scientist declared at a meeting I attended in northern Finland that "Eskimos know nothing about polar bears." A Finnish scholar informed me that he did not "believe in" traditional knowledge. A Swedish diplomat told an NWT Dene audience – one that included residential school survivors – that they should give up their Athabaskan tongues in favour of the universal language, English. Stories can define nations, but fiction cannot serve as the foundation for good public policy.

In my youth, the North listened while the South talked. To a large extent, through the efforts of northerners themselves, that has changed. The story I want to tell in this book is about an Arctic that Oslo, Ottawa, Moscow, and Washington often refuse to see. This is a book not about northern stereotypes but about the events that have shaped and are reshaping the northern character in the twenty-first century. Here, in a hopeful account of accommodations between village chiefs and regional legislators and their prospects for reconciliation with nation-states, is my hunt for an Arctic identity the world does not yet know.

CONTOURS

1

Who, What, Where?
Arctic Peoples and Places

*When tundra tourists wonder aloud if they are lost,
the guide grins. "No. We are here, right here."*

Most politicians, like most citizens of the eight Arctic states – Canada, the United States, Norway, Finland, Russia, Denmark (including Greenland and the Faroe Islands), Iceland, and Sweden – have never spent time in the Arctic. Instead, they base their impressions largely on mass media news reports or film and television entertainments. Misleading headlines tout an impending "Arctic Gold Rush" or a "New Cold War." A survey conducted in 2015 by EKOS Research Associates found that the majority of Canadians believe that their country has military bases along the Northwest Passage and that there are roads connecting all Nunavut communities.[1] Who is planting such ideas in their heads?

The situation is the same south of the border. The vast majority of *New York Times* readers will never visit the Arctic. That stops them from appreciating how newspaper stories, even those filed by conscientious reporters, distort the northern character and landscape. On a broader scale, reportage about Indigenous land claims and climate change has etched pictures of the Arctic's isolated villages and endangered wildlife onto the global consciousness. Yet even the sharpest of these images blur at the edges.

How do those who've never seen the Arctic envision its residents? Do they imagine Charlie Chaplin in "The Gold Rush"? Or the Kenidi family from the CBC TV series *North of 60*? Each generation may favour a different hero, from Robert J. Flaherty's Nanook to the latter-day stars of the reality TV show *Ice Road Truckers*, but almost without exception, these iconic figures are the creations of southerners. As we now know, *Nanook of the North* was part documentary and part fiction, subject to the same manipulations applied by reality TV. Television series play out in thirty- or sixty-minute time slots, and political commentary is broadcast in ten- or twenty-second sound bites. But history, and life, unfold on an entirely different timetable.

Popular TV dramas such as the CBS series *Northern Exposure* and CBC's *Arctic Air* are full of distortions. Broadcast in the 1990s, *Northern Exposure* dramatized the cultural clashes between a transplanted New York physician and the quirky residents of a fictional Alaskan village. That show, filmed in Washington State, had a loyal following in the south, but many Alaskans disliked its false representations of their state. The jobs of the show's main characters, for example, contrasted sharply with the state's actual leading occupations as listed by the Alaskan Department of Labor in 2012: 10,000 cashiers, 6,000 office workers, and 5,000 employees, each in the construction labour, food service, and janitorial sectors. According to the department's statistics, only a few hundred people in Alaska still pursued the traditional primary occupations of fishing, forestry, and hunting and trapping. Similarly, Statistics Canada reported in 2012 that there were 10,000 public employees in the Northwest Territories, and the NWT private sector boasted comparable numbers of the kinds of jobs that are found in every southern town.[2]

Arctic Air was a short-lived series about bush pilots shot mainly in and around Vancouver. The series – "set" in Yellowknife, NWT – starred Indigenous heartthrob Adam Beach and attracted a million viewers in 2012. But no real bush airline operations could survive on *Arctic Air*'s diet of romance and adventure. Icelandic Canadian anthropologist and explorer Vilhjalmur Stefansson used to quip that when it came to Arctic travel, "adventure was a sign of incompetence."[3] Aleqa Hammond, Greenland's former prime minister, echoes that thought: "Greenland has a small population of roughly 58,000 people, of which non-

Greenlanders or nonindigenous people are approximately 10,000. Our rate of growth is very low, and there is a reason for this. We live in the midst of the world's smartest animals – the polar bear and the Arctic fox. To live well, we exercise precaution, we plan our activities very carefully, in particular on stormy, snowy days, when we are immersed in darkness."[4]

Countries reveal much about their cultures in the stories they tell about themselves, but stories about the northern regions by northerners have a hard time breaking into prime-time TV. My father was once a northern doctor, but he would not have recognized himself or his patients in *Northern Exposure*. Nor would my bush pilot brother, Stephen Penikett, have seen himself as a character in the Canadian TV drama *Arctic Air*. Steve led a life full of hard work, incident, and human tragedy. An aircraft maintenance engineer as well as a commercial pilot, he started flying the Arctic skies in his youth and went on to a legendary career that took him around the world.

It's not that the North lacks for beauty and drama, but neither is of the sort that translates into television entertainment. Steve once put me in the second seat for a Twin Otter trip along Canada's Arctic coast. We cruised for hours under the canopy of a perfect blue sky, over a landscape of endless white. Steve is gone now, and the endless white is going too. When a real bush pilot dies, there's no string-section soundtrack or slow fade to black. The last time I saw my youngest brother, he lay in a coma, hooked up to a battery of machines, one controlling his breathing, another monitoring his blood, a third draining fluid from his lungs. Steve loved machines, but he liked having them under *his* control. On October 2, 2013, a super-bug took Steve's life.

An alcohol-fuelled Sunday-afternoon farewell held in an airport hangar featured many tales about Steve the aviator. Steve's wife, Laura, now an Air Canada pilot, described how Steve had once talked her through a crash landing in Nanaimo from his seat in a Calgary bar, where he was "at lunch." A colleague recounted the story of a company aircraft leased to some Central American deadbeat. Journeying down to reclaim the plane, Steve – who detested time-wasting bureaucracy

– encountered nothing but official obstruction, so before dawn he climbed the airport's perimeter fence, fired up the plane and, below radar, flew it out of the country.

Rosemarie Kuptana, former president of Inuit Tapirisat of Canada, wrote to me that she remembers Steve as the aviator who held up a scheduled flight so that a young Inuk, just off the jet from Edmonton, could make it home to Sachs Harbour for Christmas. Yukon flyer Rick Nielsen told me that he credits Steve for both the success and the explosive growth of Kenn Borek Air, arguably the most famous and best operator of Twin Otter "bush" aircraft in the world.

Handling 5 million passengers a year, the Anchorage airport is one of North America's busiest. Many Alaskans proudly carry private pilot's licences, but modern runways are hardly overwhelmed by bush pilots or fly-in doctors. Rather, thanks to late-twentieth-century land claims settlements, there is a whole new generation of northern airlines owned by the Arctic Aboriginal shareholders they serve: Air North, Canadian North, and First Air, to name a few.

Northerners, who survive by being flexible and adaptable, also strain the usual occupational and class categories. A union carpenter working on housing projects during the short summer construction season may, for the long winter months, become a cabinet-making entrepreneur. Many people work year-round at a variety of part-time jobs: as substitute teachers, contract researchers, children's piano instructors, desktop publishers. "Full employment" in Edmonton is not the same as being "fully employed" in Whitehorse. Any way you look at it, the Far North's managers, teachers, and social workers now outnumber the bush pilots and trappers. But it is hard to picture TV producers luring southern audiences with a TV series about territorial bureaucrats.

The cultural tensions between the metropolitan imagination and northern realities are rarely reported on. But what is the "true North"? For a start, in the twenty-first century, the Far North is melting ice, shifting ground, contested space. Romantic (and sometimes moronic) misrepresentations do more than just annoy northerners; they also confound understanding between South and North. They divide national capitals and northern regions, and the remote recipients who feel the brunt of this top-down misinformation have few ways to correct the record.

Hapless media shaping means that harried policy-makers may frame issues to fit outdated images of the Arctic and its peoples. Spare the Arctic any political leader who models him or herself on historical figures such as Sam Steele, Bishop Stringer, or even Sir John Franklin, much less the fictional characters from Jack London's *White Fang* or John Wayne in *North to Alaska*. Such mythic Arctic headspaces are ungovernable. The true North has outlived and outgrown them. Political decisions about the Arctic in the next few decades will have repercussions well beyond Far North regions, growing to encompass the whole world. So it is essential that fact- and science-based policies and Indigenous local knowledge underpin the decisions governments make, not fable or fantasy.[5]

The need for clarity of vision has never been greater. In *The World in 2050*, UCLA geographer Laurence C. Smith posits that four global forces – demography, resource demands, globalization, and climate change – will dramatically alter the statistics of Arctic populations in the twenty-first century. Smith argues that these four global pressures will transform the northern quarter of our planet, making it a place of greater human activity, strategic value, and economic importance. He projects population increases of 76 million people for Nordic and North American countries, with most of the growth concentrated in the United States and Canada.[6] He predicts that the eight nations of the Arctic Rim will grow prosperous and powerful, while the equatorial world will suffer water and energy shortages, combined with crowded cities. No one knows if Smith's predictions will come to pass, but in the face of great change, northerners and southerners alike will need to get to know the North better. Northerners know their homelands better than anyone, of course, but the pace of change in the Arctic and Subarctic demands lifelong learning and relearning.

Then

The North opened up for me as a young man with a move south from Dawson City to Whitehorse in 1970. In May of that year, I showed Dick North, an Alaskan journalist, the storyboards for a film I fancied making, and Dick shared with me his own notes on the story of the so-called Mad Trapper. During ten August days at my family's cabin on the North Fork of the Klondike River, I wrote the first draft of a Mad Trapper screenplay. After we handed the draft to a typist, Dick proposed that we celebrate over a beer in Dawson's Downtown Hotel. "One beer," I agreed.

As we stumbled out of the bar at 2:00 a.m., Dick suddenly remembered that he'd once met a film producer from London, England, and from a phone booth near the Midnight Sun Café, he called David Cobham. We caught Cobham on a rare day at the office. Dick pitched him hard: "I've got this kid here with a script, and I want to put him on a plane to London."

The posh but polite tones of Cobham's reply had a sobering effect: "Dick, Dick, send the script if you must, but I beg you, please, do *not* send the kid."

Around the same time, the managers at a nearby asbestos mine declared my labour surplus to their needs – a decision I suspect was linked to my energy as a union shop steward. The miners responded by nominating me to run for a seat in Yukon's territorial legislature. So after my night on the town with Dick North, I flew not to London but to Old Crow, Yukon's northernmost community, for a day of campaigning for the forthcoming election. I'd planned to fly back that evening, but a snowstorm blew up and kept me in the Gwich'in community for the best part of a week.

I arrived back in Dawson on Election Day, September 8, 1970. My brother Steve met me at the airport and handed over an airmail letter, which I pocketed until after the polls had closed. Alone that night at my "victory headquarters," I opened the letter. David Cobham had written to say that he liked my script, and he offered to meet me at a Montreal hotel on October 5 to negotiate a contract – as it turned out, against a backdrop of Canadian soldiers patrolling the streets in response to Quebec's October Crisis.

Upon my return to Yukon, facing the unemployment line, I packed my bags and decamped for Whitehorse, where the manager of the Travelodge, spotting me hanging out in the lobby, offered me $2 an hour to fill in for a missing front desk clerk. At 4:00 p.m., when it became clear that the evening clerk had also blown his shift, the manager asked me to stay another eight hours. I worked there for two years but was allowed an hour off every day for my part-time job as the host of a talk radio show on local station CKRW.

One evening in 1972, Wally Firth, a Métis bush pilot who was involved in organizing Native groups north of 60, including the Indian Brotherhood of the Northwest Territories (later the Dene Nation), the Yukon Native Brotherhood, and the Yukon Association of Non-Status Indians, stopped by my post at the Travelodge for a chat. He asked if I would be his campaign manager.

"What are you running for?"

"The NWT seat in parliament."

"Which party?"

"NDP," he said.

"Okay," I replied, and handed in my notice to the Travelodge.

A few days later, I stopped in for a drink at Whitehorse's Gold Nugget Lounge. Whitehorse is a capital city, but it is also a small town, and the politically active people all know one another. As my eyes adjusted to the dark of the bar, Erik Nielsen, Yukon's veteran Conservative MP, waved me over. After introducing me to his companion, Bud Orange, the retiring Liberal MP for the NWT, Nielsen casually asked me, "How would you like to manage my campaign?"

"Sorry, I'm going over the mountains to work for Wally Firth," I told him.

Orange laughed. "Native people will never vote for one of their own," he advised.

Firth and I moved into our headquarters, a fur warehouse in Yellowknife's Old Town, and got to work. Firth had an American Express card, and I had a Visa. Over the next few weeks, both cards were seriously overused. At the time, the NWT was the largest riding in Canada: 2.1 million square kilometres, with few roads. While Firth flew his borrowed Cessna from community to community, gathering crowds outside co-op stores by playing his fiddle and telling a political story or two, his team of canvassers knocked on doors in Fort Smith, Hay River, Inuvik, Pine Point, and Yellowknife. Firth and his crew campaigned against the proposed Mackenzie Valley Pipeline, arguing that the project should be put on hold until northern land claims were settled. My steelworkers' union was a financial supporter of Firth's campaign, as were other unions. First Nations activists, public servants, and teachers came out in numbers to support the cause.

For me, the worst moment came in the final week of the campaign at a Yellowknife Chamber of Commerce all-candidates debate, when the moderator asked Firth his views on the "money supply" question. The Liberal candidate, a Harvard-trained economist, had been eloquent on M1, the metric for a nation's supply of cash, chequing, and deposit accounts. The Tory candidate also acquitted himself well enough. But Firth seemed stumped.

"Mr. Firth," the moderator intoned.

I was listening to CBC Radio's coverage of the debate as I drove around Yellowknife, checking campaign sign locations. In the silence that followed the moderator's question, I parked the pickup truck and held my breath.

"Mr. Firth," the moderator pressed.

As Wally's silence continued, I died a little.

The moderator raised his voice. "How would you handle that one, Mr. Firth?"

After a beat, Wally replied, "I could just about handle that ... with a shovel." And the crowd roared. Firth won the seat handily, and the Liberals, returned to government with a slim minority, soon after appointed Judge Thomas Berger to hold an inquiry into the Mackenzie Valley pipeline project.

That year on Boxing Day, BBC TV aired *The Mad Trapper*. It was not a great movie, but the residuals kept me in coffee money for years. I went back to hunting for votes after the federal election, knocking on doors by the thousand in Whitehorse and across the Yukon Territory, this time on my own behalf. I eventually won election to City Council and then, for five terms, to the Territorial Legislature as the NDP MLA for Whitehorse West. I went on to serve two terms as premier of the territory and, later, once I moved south, seven years as a provincial public servant.

Now

The script I'd written for *The Mad Trapper* was a mostly true story about the biggest manhunt in northern history. In 1932, the RCMP, aided by two-way radio and aircraft, chased an outlaw from the Rat River across the mountains to the Eagle River, Yukon, where he died in a shootout with the police. The exact nature of his crimes, the accuracy of the "Mad Trapper" diagnosis, and even the man's name ... all remain a mystery. I've long had this nameless anti-hero in the back of my mind.

In "The Spell of the Yukon," Robert Service wrote that the value of the Klondike's gold lay not in the hoarding of bullion but in the finding of it. The *hunt* was the thing. During the 1960s, young Yukoners looked for "gold" in all the wrong places: asbestos mines, copper mines, silver, zinc, and lead mines. Mining booms are like sugar highs; they inevitably lead to excruciating busts. Before a miner could even make his stake, the mine in question might close, and there was no alchemy in the mined-out ghost towns, which even by then outnumbered Yukon's living communities.

Service's truth also holds for Yukon's second industry, the trapping of tourists. In the 1960s and '70s, a Dawson City hotel bar was *the* place to make a deal or find a job. When a miner drank too much, it was often the hotelier's job to pack him off to a room where he could sleep until the morning after. There was a time when tourists came north to Alaska and Yukon seeking the land of Robert Service, Jack London, and Pierre Berton. Nowadays, they come to see the Arctic environment and encounter Indigenous cultures. Huge tour companies own many northern hotels, luring clients from around the world and keeping them captive on company boats and buses and in company restaurants.

Highway hunting is a long-honoured local tradition in the North. Many of the moose and caribou harvested in the territory in fact die mere metres from the willow ditches and dusty shoulders of Yukon's excellent roads. A number of these kills should, strictly speaking, count as accidents or vehicular slaughter, since no firearm was involved, but the Yukon hunter does not normally brag about putting "road kill" on the supper table, so the published data may not be reliable. In any event, the hunter in question might not have been actively hunting at the time. Moose seldom signal before crossing the road, and if they cross on the opening day of hunting season, what can a trucker do? In another scenario, a highway hunter may have been looking for a moose, but, coming round a bend, found a bull caribou browsing by a culvert. A driver dreaming of moose stew or caribou ribs might run smack into a grouse or a ptarmigan instead. Indigenous hunters, who have no truck with romantic European notions about "big game," the conquest of nature, or the glorious chase, are likely to accept the highway hunt as something more analogous to shopping for groceries at a convenience store: at odd hours, you take what you can get.

Setting aside government neglect, mass media astigmatism, and the myopia of the Arctic states – each tends to view its own northern region as *the* Arctic – let it be said that northerners are prone to a blinkered vision of themselves. How well do they know themselves? Sometimes northerners get snared in historical traps of their own making. Irate citizens once threatened to lynch a Whitehorse editorialist for criticizing the Sourdough Rendezvous' can-can dancers, beloved champions of Yukon's Gold Rush heritage. It took Carolyn Anne Moore, a young scholar, to remind everyone that the Klondike's can-can dancers were launched by a government tourism campaign in the 1960s. They were artifacts of modern marketing, not Yukon history.[7]

In another instance, while Yukon legislators were debating a wolf cull program, a self-identified "Aboriginal traditional knowledge" expert went on the radio to demand a return to the "traditional" practice of invading wolf dens to sever cubs' tails for the handsome bounty the government paid in the 1950s. Sam Johnston, Tlingit chief and speaker of the Yukon Legislature, was appalled. Tlingit law and tradition prohibited the killing of the young of any species, Johnston protested – especially for money.

Once upon a time, much of the non-Indigenous world regarded the Arctic as a frozen wasteland. The 2004 Arctic Climate Impact Assessment (ACIA) report shocked that world into recognizing the Arctic as a rapidly changing environment, as well as a place of increasing political significance.[8] The Arctic landscape has lately suffered major disruptions, including shoreline erosion from winter storms, infrastructure upheavals from permafrost melts, and surprising wildlife dislocations. As the polar ice cap melts, the Arctic has become strategically important, and great powers and global corporations are now casting a covetous eye on the Arctic's previously inaccessible natural resources.

The imminent arrival of this latest rush of gold seekers and oil drillers, with their promises of jobs and business opportunities, often heightens local fears of social disruption and environmental degradation. Summer tourists in growing numbers cruise the Arctic coastline, bus the highways, and hike mountain trails. Beyond the competing narratives of southern scientists, media centres, and northern storytellers, in the contested spaces of today's Arctic, one hears a multitude of voices: of villagers and city dwellers, land stewards and mine managers, hungry people and contented bureaucrats, those who have come for the boom times and those who stay on through the busts. In the hunt for the northern character, all of these voices must be considered.

Where

Bullish North American politicians have expanded the area considered to be the Arctic. Under the terms of the 1984 Arctic Research and Policy

Act (ARPA), US government leaders had Arctic Alaska take in all of the United States' Bering Sea. The Canadian government's Arctic covers everything above the 60th parallel, in particular Yukon, the NWT, and Nunavut. However, this framework is problematic, since the 60th parallel demarcation excludes Nunavik, Quebec, and Churchill, Manitoba; both are Inuit homelands and polar bear habitats.[9] This boundary also misses many communities in the northernmost areas of Canadian provinces that are far more remote and poorly served than their territorial counterparts.

When nationalists throughout the polar region worry about sovereignty, border disputes, and land boundaries, they sometimes overlook one fact: the Arctic is mainly a marine area, with the Arctic Ocean at its centre. According to geographers, the region encompasses the polar area north of the Arctic Circle at 66°33'39"N. Climatologists focus on the highest latitudes, where summer temperatures never rise above 10 degrees Celsius. Scientists argue over whether the Arctic's southern boundary should be based on the southernmost extent of permafrost, the northern treeline, or the distribution of flora and fauna.[10]

Even Indigenous peoples do not all agree about Arctic boundaries. Inuit, who generally live north of the treeline, consider themselves a unique Arctic people and may accord Subarctic status to their Dene neighbours, who dwell to the south of that line, along with thousands of non-Indigenous northerners. Yet because the treeline crosses the NWT in a northwesterly direction, there are deep-rooted Dene communities living north of the Arctic Circle and Inuit villages lying to the south of it.

Residents of the circumpolar North often use the terms *Arctic*, *Far North*, and *High North* interchangeably. This comes simply from feeling at home in the entire region. For northerners who feel ignored and disrespected by distant governments, it is empowering to embrace a distinct regional identity, one shared with the Arctic areas of other nation-states. When northerners transit from the Subarctic to the Arctic, they cross an invisible line, one that most hardly notice, if they notice it at all. For all the flaws of official designations, northerners have come to accept the political boundaries of the Arctic United States (Alaska) and Arctic Canada (the three northern territories). Rovaniemi may not look like a southerner's idea of an Arctic community, but as the capital of Finnish Lapland it counts as one. Tromsø was once a fishing village; now it is home to the Arctic University of Norway.

Who

Indigenous Peoples

First and foremost, the Arctic remains the homeland of ancient Indigenous nations, whose cultures and political systems have, to varying degrees, survived the arrival of colonizing powers and the subdividing of their traditional territories. In Alaska and northern Canada, these include the Inuit (a word meaning "people") and the Athabaskans (also known as Dene, or "people"); in Scandinavia, Sámi fishers and reindeer herders; in Greenland, Inuit fishers and hunters; and in Russia, numerous distinct Aboriginal communities. Nowhere else in North America or Europe do Indigenous people play such pivotal roles in the economic and political life of their regions. Remarkably, these Arctic peoples thrived for centuries in one of the planet's harshest environments. The Dene, Inuit, and Sámi languages survived even the imposition of alien education systems and remain vital elements of their people's cultural lives.

Inheritors of what anthropologists describe as Thule culture, the Inuit migrated across the Arctic from western Alaska around 1,000 CE. In Nunavut, 84 percent of the population is Inuit, with a median age of 24.7 years.[11] The Dene have lived in the Far North of the North American continent for thousands of years. They live mainly to the south of the Inuit and are members of the Athabaskan language group, the largest Indigenous linguistic family in North America; thirty-two Athabaskan dialects and languages are still in use in Alaska, Yukon, and the NWT, as well as in the northern communities in Canada's four western provinces.

Most northern Canadian communities have fewer than 500 residents, reflecting the tendency of Indigenous populations to treasure traditional village life. Villagers may not feel completely at home in the region's cities, with the result that town-and-country tensions have added to the predictable political conflicts between settler cities and Indigenous villages. Another hard truth is that the national capitals of the Arctic federal states exist at alienating physical and psychological distances from many Arctic communities, large and small. In recent years, Arctic voices have started to talk back to the southern centres of power, and it is largely Indigenous village voices that have caught the southern public's ear.

The Arctic's ancient societies deserve their reputation for astonishing resilience, especially in the face of new insecurities: global warming, globalization, and resource extraction booms and busts. Over the past few years, Arctic Indigenous peoples' struggles have caught the attention of world media, and the resulting headlines have helped deliver remarkable political change. Yet their newly won media attention and political power cannot disguise the fact that Indigenous people now constitute a minority of the Arctic's population.

Settlers

The Arctic Human Development Reports (AHDR) detail demographic data for the populations of the circumpolar regions. Its first edition, in 2004, neatly distinguished between Indigenous and non-Indigenous populations, and the 2015 report found that more than 85 percent of current Arctic residents are settlers.

Many settlers come north looking for work and plan to leave once they have built their "stake." Others have lived in the North for generations. Thanks to the presence of substantial mixed-race populations across the Far North, northerners – a category that includes *all* northern residents, whether Aboriginal or settler – may view the Indigenous/settler differentiation as somewhat muddy. Also, data collectors sometimes include transient workers in their population counts. That said, the North has plenty of long-term residents who initially planned to stay only one summer. The Alaska Constitution expressly promotes settlement and settlers: "It is the policy of the State to encourage the settlement of its land and the development of its resources by making them available for maximum use consistent with the public interest."[12]

In the Whitehorse coffee shops of my youth, local sages mocked CBC North reporters who fed stories to the national news about colourful local characters, grizzled prospectors, mad trappers, and high-kicking can-can dancers in a bid for permanent network jobs. Southern reporters often forgo the banalities of small Arctic cities, with their brand-name retailers and fast-food outlets, for the supposedly exotic charms of isolated Indigenous communities. Yukoners may joke about the "northern colour" items on the national news, but they are not amused. Blinkered thinking has caused most reporters to miss one very important story: for four decades, while the forces of climate change and globalization have raged around them, leaders and legislators from Indigenous *and* settler communities in the North have been designing and redesigning Arctic institutions to radically transform the architecture of Arctic governance.

However long they peer at the tiny black dots representing settlements on maps of the "great white North," southerners might be surprised to hear that most northerners live in cities. Almost half of the Canadian Far North's 107,000 residents live in two urban centres, Whitehorse (pop. 27,889 in 2013) and Yellowknife (pop. 19,234 in 2011). Both Alaska and the Russian Arctic boast cities with more than 250,000 inhabitants, although the populations of Murmansk and Anchorage, which are full of working-age adults, rise and fall with resource booms and busts. Murmansk, the Arctic's largest city, is Russia's far northern ice-free port for fishing, naval, and merchant fleets. A metropolis of deteriorating Stalin-era apartment blocks, Murmansk suffered a post-Soviet population drop from 500,000 in the 1980s to 300,000 in 2015, although energy developments and increases in Arctic shipping have recently revived its boomtown status.[13] Anchorage is home to more than 300,000 people, which is 40 percent of Alaska's population, and 60 percent of Iceland's inhabitants live in and around Reykjavik (pop. 199,289 in 2012). Iqaluit in Nunavut and Nuuk in Greenland are relatively large population centres, as are Fairbanks, Juneau, Kiruna, Norilsk, Rovaniemi, and Tromsø.

Nation-States

Each Arctic state has its own distinct characteristics; that said, the Arctic nations have found common environmental, social, and scientific interests. In 1996 those common interests led to the creation of the Arctic Council, first proposed by Canadian prime minister Brian Mulroney in a speech in Saint Petersburg in 1989. The eight Arctic states are full members of the Arctic Council. Under an innovative international arrangement, six Indigenous peoples' organizations have also joined the Arctic Council as "Permanent Participants."

Canada's legendary northern-ness may largely be a deliberately constructed self-image. Even though 40 percent of the country's land mass lies in the Arctic and Subarctic regions, 75 percent of Canadians live within a few kilometres of the US border.[14] Canada has the second-longest Arctic coastline after Russia, yet it has no Arctic port, having sold the Port of Churchill to private American interests in 1997. The new owners are now selling the port to a consortium of First Nations.[15] The Canadian government's Arctic policy, which is currently under review, includes a five-point strategy: exercise Arctic sovereignty; protect the region's environmental heritage; improve and devolve Northern governance; conduct world-leading Arctic science and technology; and help the North realize its true potential as a healthy, prosperous, and secure region.[16]

When it purchased Alaska from Russia in 1867 for $7.2 million, the United States became an Arctic nation. Alaska achieved statehood in 1959 and by 2013 had a population of 740,000. The state is rich in energy resources, and its beautiful wilderness attracts shiploads of cruise passengers every summer. As a result of their 1971 land claims settlement, Alaskan Native peoples are now the state's largest private landowners. In his Arctic policy, former US president Barack Obama made it clear that Alaska was important to national security, but also that his government was interested in addressing the region's social and environmental needs. His four stated goals were to advance US security interests; to pursue responsible Arctic stewardship; to strengthen international cooperation; and to engage in a consultation process with Alaskan Aboriginal groups.[17] As of this writing, nobody knows what the Trump administration intends to do in the Arctic, but early indications point to pro-oil and anti-environmental agendas. Whether Arctic populations will have any influence at the White House remains to be seen.

Almost half of the Arctic's 4 million residents live in Russia, a militarily powerful state with an energy-based economy similar in size to Canada's and an uncertain future as a democracy. Under Stalin, the Soviet Union shifted its economy towards the East and the North to focus on resource extraction, processing, and fabrication. Stalin forced millions to labour in Arctic gulags where hundreds of thousands died. The worst of these brutal labour camps were the Kolyma gold mines; there, prisoners worked outside in temperatures as low as −50 degrees Celsius. Industrial and military developments from the Soviet era have left serious environmental as well as social scars. Since the end of the Cold War and the demise of the Soviet Union, there has been a mass exodus from the Russian Arctic. Since 1989, Chukotka, for example, has lost most of its population. Russia has one of the lowest birth rates in the world, and northern fertility rates are even lower. Yet according to Valeriy A. Kryukov, even today, the Arctic produces 11 percent of Russia's national income.[18] And President Vladimir Putin has long favoured aggressive Arctic resource development. Federal Russia has twenty-one republics, fifty-four *krais* or *oblasts,* four autonomous *okrugs,* one autonomous *oblast,* and two federal cities. A 2014 law designated the following territories as part of the "Arctic Zone": Murmansk Oblast, Nenets Autonomous Okrug, Chukchi Autonomous Okrug, Yamalo-Nenets Autonomous Okrug, the cities of Vorkuta and Norilsk, and selected areas of Yakutia and the Arkhangelsk region.[19]

The Finns have inherited some of the characteristics of their northern land, which their ancestors farmed and logged under harsh conditions. Finland lost its Arctic coastline after the Second World War, but it still builds world-class icebreakers. During the Winter War of 1939 and 1940, under army commander Carl Gustaf Emil Mannerheim, the Finns famously fought off an invading Soviet army. Because Russia has based much of its nuclear arsenal close to the Finnish border, Finland has chosen to stay out of NATO, but in 1995 it did join the European Union. At the end of the Cold War, the "Finnish initiative" led to the creation of the Arctic Environmental Protection Strategy and, ultimately, the creation of the eight-nation Arctic Council.

For many years, Sweden had a reputation as Europe's iconic social-democratic state. However, Swedes have recently been electing many conservative and anti-immigrant candidates. Nowadays, North Americans seem to know Sweden mainly for IKEA and crime novels. Sweden was an early supporter of the Finnish initiative.

The envy of its Nordic neighbours, Norway, with a population of over 5 million, is Europe's largest oil producer. It is also known for environmentally controversial export of fish farm operations that threaten wild salmon fisheries, the Oslo Peace Accords, and an $890 billion sovereign wealth fund dedicated to the creation of a post-oil economy. During the nineteenth century, widespread poverty caused 800,000 people – one-third of Norway's population – to immigrate to North America, along with one million Swedes.[20] In the twentieth century, Norway became the first nation in the world to ratify International Labour Organization (ILO) Convention 169, a legally binding international instrument dealing specifically with the rights of Indigenous peoples. Since the end of the Cold War, Norway and Russia have increasingly cooperated and exchanged technologies. Like Sweden, Norway was an early supporter of the Finnish initiative.

Unless one counts as "Indigenous" the Vikings who have populated this island nation for a thousand years, Iceland is the only Arctic state without an Indigenous population. Settlers arrived there in 874, and archeologists recently discovered a Viking longhouse at Stöðvarfjörður in East Iceland. Today, the world knows tiny Iceland for its banking collapse, its fishing economy and, of course, its soccer team. The country's 99 percent literacy rate reflects a tradition dating back to the Viking sagas.[21] Every year in October, Reykjavik hosts a global gathering called the Arctic Circle, which is attended by corporate and government leaders, experts, entrepreneurs, and environmentalists, along with a few northern and Indigenous representatives.

Denmark, a constitutional monarchy, attends the Arctic Council on its own behalf and also as a "federal" state representing the autonomous Faroe Islands and Greenland. Erik the Red may be Greenland's iconic hero, but 89 percent of Greenlanders are Inuit. With approximately 58,000 residents, Greenland is both the largest island in the world and the least populated Arctic jurisdiction. Throughout history, its population has risen and fallen in response to the island's changing climate. Although Greenland has long been economically, culturally, and politically connected to Denmark and Europe, its closest neighbour is Baffin Island in Nunavut, whose Inuit residents are distant relatives. Having achieved self-government with responsibility for everything except defence and foreign affairs, Greenland may be in transition from European colony to Inuit nation-state. At one time, Danes made it illegal for men of certain occupational classes in Greenland to marry local women. Now Greenland, on its way to a future independent of Denmark, may become the first nation-state in the Northern hemisphere with an Indigenous government.

In the 1990s, the Faroe Islands, Denmark's other autonomous Arctic possession, suffered a collapse of its fishing economy and a significant outflow of population. During the early years of the twenty-first century, the Faroese population – descendants of Nordic and Scottish settlers – has grown very slowly.

Do the North and the South really have different agendas? Indeed, they do. A 2012 Institute of the North survey revealed that Alaskan respondents considered the environment and the economy to be priority issues in the Arctic.[22] According to surveys conducted by both the Institute of the North and EKOS Research Associates, northern populations in Alaska and the three Canadian territories shared a deep concern about the inadequacy of public infrastructure: housing, schools, and roads. A 2010 EKOS survey found that all eight Arctic states were publicly debating security issues. Arctic residents further insisted that neither Canada nor the United States had adequate disaster response, search-and-rescue, or police services for Indigenous communities. In a study funded by the Gordon Foundation in 2015, most Canadians expressed an understanding that the Arctic contains great resource wealth but is environmentally fragile. But even if southern populations recognize some of the legitimate concerns of northerners, nation-states and national leaders have substantially different priorities.

2

Pawns
The Cold War

*Governments drew lines on a map and forced people
to move to one side.*

I n 1983, Robin Sears, deputy secretary general of the Socialist International, told me that a French Socialist Party politician famously declared that France's South Pacific nuclear tests were perfectly safe. To this, former Australian prime minister Gough Whitlam famously replied, "If they're so bloody safe, why don't you test them in Paris?"

As a territorial legislator, that's what I should have said about Ottawa in 1983 when the federal government assured Arctic citizens, chiefs, and legislators protesting cruise missile tests over the northern territories that the tests were totally risk free. It would have been a characteristically northern retort, but hesitation caused me to miss the moment.

Publicly, Prime Minister Pierre Trudeau defended the northern missile tests as an essential demonstration of Canada's commitment to NATO. "We'd be pretty poor partners of an alliance if we didn't do that," the *Christian Science Monitor* quoted him as saying.[1] The article claimed that Trudeau had allowed the cruise missile tests because he'd been persuaded that northern Canada resembled the Siberian landscape.[2] At the height of the Cold War, military planners saw the Arctic as a frozen emptiness that bombers and missiles could easily traverse, and the US brass had calculated that the vast, snow-covered terrain would make it difficult for Soviet radar to track American activity.

Both Trudeau and his successor as prime minister, Brian Mulroney, approved the use of Canada's northern territories as testing grounds for

American cruise missiles. Mulroney valued his close relationship with US president Ronald Reagan, and both Mulroney and Trudeau treated the territories as *terra nullius*, an empty space occupied by no one, or at least no one who much mattered.

Cruise missile protests persisted throughout the 1980s. Both Dene Nation chiefs in the NWT and members of the territorial legislature complained loudly about their lands becoming a rocket range. To these complaints, the feds responded with contemptuous indifference, citing the imperative of making Canada secure.

For many northerners, however, the tests contributed little to their sense of security – quite the opposite. Cold War antagonisms had turned their homelands into a potential nuclear battleground. Northern residents realized that the US nuclear umbrella did not protect them from Russian bombers but instead made it more likely that all hell would rain down on their heads. Had the Cold War turned hot, American missiles and Russian bombers would have blown each other to pieces midway between the two states: in other words, over the northern territories.

US Arctic expert Oran Young nicely captured this anxiety when he wrote:

> The testing of weapons (for example, the recent American program of testing Cruise missiles in the Canadian Arctic) constitutes an unwelcome intrusion from the perspective of local residents and heightens the desire of Native peoples to protect themselves through the assertion of sovereign rights ... Even more concretely, military exercises carried out in the Arctic are not only capable of producing costly disruptions, they are also indicative of an extraordinary disregard for the concerns of local residents.[3]

This "disregard" for Arctic citizens didn't begin with the Cold War. In the 1930s, when Catholic priests arrived in Inuit communities, their mission was to go to war with the shamans, whom Wade Davis described in a 2014 article as "the cultural pivot, the heart of the Inuit relationship to the universe."[4] The feds encouraged the priests to set up residential schools and kidnap Indigenous kids from their families. Andrei Golovnev and Sergei Kan, in "Indigenous Leadership in Northwestern Siberia," write that in Russia, colonization of the North took place in three stages: "(1) the military invasion, (2) the persecution of pre-Christian rituals and shamans and the promotion of secular elders and chiefs, and (3) co-opting of the indigenous leaders."[5]

The Second World War

The Second World War took millions of lives, and people everywhere celebrated its end. But the war was also occasion for human rights abuses on the home front. After Japan bombed Dutch Harbor (Unalaska) in Alaska's Aleutian Islands in 1942, the United States, without any evidence of their disloyalty, evicted the islands' Indigenous population.[6] Like Canadians and Americans of Japanese descent, the Aleut were interned. The military transported people to camps in southeast Alaska, 1,500 miles from their homes.

Given only an hour to pack one bag before climbing aboard a troopship, 881 Aleut landed at five overcrowded camps, including a former gold mine and a rotting cannery. The internees from a treeless Bering Sea territory were held in crowded, cold, and unhealthy conditions, without adequate housing or running water, at unfamiliar rainforest locations. And when the Alaskan Aleut returned to their homes after the war, they discovered that American troops occupying the Aleutian Islands had looted their Russian Orthodox churches. Ten percent of the camp residents had died while interned, and the Aleut, already a fragile community in terms of numbers, blamed the US Department of the Interior and the territorial government for this loss.[7] The Japanese had bombed Dutch Harbor, not the Aleut, but the Aleutians had paid the price, suffering greatly during the war and bearing the psychological scars of their experience.

During the 1940s, Sahtu Dene labourers at Port Radium, the world's first uranium mine, on the NWT's Great Bear Lake, packed leaky gunnysacks of material associated with the production of the bombs that would be dropped on Hiroshima and Nagasaki in August 1945. Work at the mine continued for years afterwards, and the Déline First Nation chiefs feared that the labourers, who spoke of material hot enough to blacken the silver coins in their pockets, had been exposed to gamma rays and radon gas. The early deaths of many workers earned Déline the reputation of being a "village of widows."[8] As scientist David P. Stone writes, while a Canadian government study showed no unusual cancer rates for the community, "the Port Radium story is a sad lesson on the anxiety and concerns that can be caused when industrial activities provide little or no environmental and health information to local residents and when such sites are abandoned with inadequate or no remediation."[9] Why were the Déline not told about the risks? Did Canada's wartime leaders not recognize that the residual distrust might damage the Déline chiefs' relations with Canada's federal state? Such is the outrage of being considered nobodies on nobody's land.

Even in the years before the war, the Arctic security situation had cried out for political agreements among neighbouring Arctic nation-states. By the 1940s, US soldiers in the Far North threatened to outnumber Canada's Arctic residents. In 1941, Denmark and the United States signed an agreement making the latter responsible for defending Greenland for the duration of the war. In 1942, as part of the Northwest Staging Route (a network of airstrips, airports, and radio stations), US Army engineers built the 2,700 kilometre Alaska Highway across southern Yukon from Dawson Creek, British Columbia, to Delta Junction, Alaska. The construction project ploughed across southern Yukon had a predictably disruptive effect on the lives of Indigenous communities along the way.

The Cold War

With the launch of the Atomic Age, as George Orwell predicted, a "Cold War" enveloped the world.[10] The carnage of the Second World War brought about a new world order during which the two superpowers, the United States and the Soviet Union, crafted a new kind of war. The United States professed its faith in capitalism and democracy; the Soviet Union pushed the contrary ideology of communism as the path to world peace. Berlin became a divided city in a divided country, with massive armies facing each other across a divide that Winston Churchill in 1946 would call "the Iron Curtain."[11] Other nations, too, divided into east and west. In San Francisco in October 1945, representatives of forty-five states convened to form the United Nations (UN). That group opted to leave enforcement to a Security Council, whose five permanent members (China, France, United Kingdom, the United States, and the Soviet Union) each held a veto over military action.

In the middle of the Bering Strait between Alaska and Siberia, two islands straddle the International Dateline: Little Diomede and Big Diomede (Ostrov Ratmanova). Little Diomede belongs to the United States, Big Diomede to Russia. Although a trail across the sea ice would make it theoretically possible for a person to walk the 3.5 kilometres between the islands, the Yup'ik on Little Diomede were separated from their Soviet cousins for the duration of the Cold War.

The Yup'ik were not alone in this experience. In distant corners of the circumpolar world, the Cold War wounded many Indigenous communities – the Inuit in Canada and Greenland, the Sámi in Norway and Russia, the Aleut in Alaska, and the Sahtu Dene in the Northwest Territories. None of these communities knew what had hit them, and none had seen it coming. Superpower enmity trumped even community and family unity.

In 1950, US Air Force General Hap Arnold predicted: "If there is a Third World War the strategic center of it will be the North Pole."[12] The Cold War turned the Far North into a near-battleground and dislocated many Indigenous communities. Because no Indigenous nation had a seat in the UN General Assembly, the Arctic's Indigenous peoples had no voice at all. When the two superpowers targeted traditional Arctic homelands as potential nuclear war zones, nobody in Moscow or Washington or Oslo or Ottawa cared what the Indigenous peoples thought. Their chiefs became the invisible pawns of contending states.

In the end, the two superpowers never faced each other directly, although they came close to it over the Berlin Blockade, the Korean War, and the Cuban Missile Crisis. Until 1989, proxies, satellite states, and Third World "client" states did much of the Cold War's dirty work. The US-led North Atlantic Treaty Organization (NATO), formed in 1949, bound the United States, Canada, and ten European countries in an alliance to collectively defend one another. In response, the Soviet Union and its Eastern Bloc states sought to enhance their global power by creating the Warsaw Pact in 1955. NATO would also pull Iceland, Norway, and Denmark (and therefore Greenland) into the Cold War conflict. In 1957, Canada and the United States signed the North American Aerospace Defense Command (NORAD) Agreement as a continental air defence system under their shared command. Over time, the United States made Canada its partner – albeit a junior one – in both NATO and NORAD.

Arctic communities living in Third World conditions often suffered the insecurity of being caught between these superpower manoeuvrings. The great "empty" space between Canada and Russia – the Arctic – soon emerged as a strategic focus for both superpowers.

The anthropologist and explorer Vilhjalmur Stefansson insightfully noted that if a Canadian prime minister or an American president had been banished to the Arctic in their youth, as Stalin was, perhaps the two countries would have shown more interest in northern development, as Russia had done. Canada and the United States might then have been strategically prepared for an Arctic future.[13] As it was, Arctic residents had no say in the Cold War policies of the great powers, and it would be decades before they won a voice in decisions about Arctic development.

The Postwar Years

The whole world listened in 1947 as US president Harry S. Truman declared that the US military would combat all communist takeovers. That same year, China emerged as a communist state. In 1949, physicist Patrick

Blackett published *Fear, War, and the Bomb*, a protest against the folly of nuclear war; it became a bestseller and was translated into eleven languages. The following year, in 1950, the Korean War ignited, adding more fuel to the Cold War fire.

The Soviets tested an atomic bomb in 1949; a few months later, the Americans moved "Fat Man" atomic bombs to the US Air Force base in Goose Bay, Labrador.[14] These two events placed the Canadian Arctic firmly on the strategic front line. Arctic airspace had become the shortest route between the population centres of the United States and Russia. To track Soviet bombers, the United States began building a 10,000 kilometre Distant Early Warning (DEW) Line of radar stations across Alaska and Canada's Arctic. The DEW Line radar would supposedly give the United States several hours' warning in the event of an attack, but it won few friends among local Indigenous people.

In *Arctic Dreams,* Barry Lopez describes one Tuktoyaktuk resident's reaction to the DEW Line. When a radar station went up along the man's dogsled route on the coast, he stopped to see what it was. "The military men welcomed him not as a resident of the region but as a figure of Arctic fable," Lopez writes. They enthusiastically fed his dogs a stack of raw steaks. Each time the man came, they pounded him on the back and fed his dogs piles of steak. Their largesse seemed so odd and his rapport with them so unrealistic that he stopped coming.[15]

These two worlds – the distant outposts of empire and Indigenous people on their home territory – coexisted in the Arctic, but communication failures persisted. The paths of the soldier on the frontier and the hunter following game may have crossed, but rarely did they converge. At the time, it would have been completely out of character for northerners to articulate their confusion to outsiders.

Canada's High Arctic islands also became pieces in the defence-versus-sovereignty game. In 1953, soon after being elected US president, Dwight Eisenhower pledged to reduce military spending while remaining committed to diplomat George Kennan's strategy of "containing" Soviet expansion.[16] But events in the German Democratic Republic and elsewhere that year heightened American concerns about communism.

Over the next few years, a series of international upheavals entrenched Western fears of the "Red" menace, and the tit-for-tat behaviour of the superpowers and their clients continued.

In 1957 the Soviet Union launched the Sputnik satellite. For the Americans, this signalled that it was close to being able to send Intercontinental Ballistic Missiles (ICBMs) over existing US air defence systems. This made Canada's leaders highly anxious. They didn't particularly want such a large foreign presence, but they acknowledged the common threat and realized they had no good alternatives to cooperating with the Americans, who placed even more military equipment on Canadian soil.

The Canadian Arctic's vast size and tiny population led policy-makers in Ottawa to worry about challenges to Canadian sovereignty in the region. As the Americans continued to expand their presence in the Arctic, Canada arbitrarily relocated seventeen Inuit families from their homelands in northern Quebec to two High Arctic outposts, Resolute Bay and Grise Fiord.[17] Historian Shelagh Grant writes that "the Inuit, who had never lived that far north, called the hamlets 'Qausuittuq' (the place where the sun never sets) and 'Auyuittuq' (the place where the ice never melts)."[18] Critics later accused Canada of treating the Inuit deportees as "human flagpoles" to buttress its Arctic sovereignty claims.[19]

At one point in the early 1950s, strategists in Washington actually recommended to the Truman administration that it buy the island of Greenland from Denmark. In 1953, under Eisenhower, with almost no notice to the residents concerned, the US government removed Inuit villagers from Thule, Greenland, 1,200 kilometres north of the Arctic Circle, to make way for a huge airbase there. The Danes allowed this; however, they, like the Norwegians, refused to allow American bases and nuclear weapons on their home soil. Nevertheless, Arctic Norway could not insulate its citizens from Cold War complications.

As noted earlier, the Iron Curtain divided communities, leaving some Arctic residents in the Eastern Bloc and their neighbours in the West. In the autumn of 1944, the retreating German army had scorched the earth, homes, and infrastructure in the counties of Finnmark and Tromsø in northern Norway. Consequently, when Soviet troops advanced, the locals greeted them as heroes. As Sámi scholar Camilla Brattland recalls, "this shaped relations with the Soviet Union after the war, not least also due to the fact that forty-five Norwegians from Kiberg in Finnmark were trained in intelligence by the Red Army during the war." In correspondence, Brattland has told me that these forty-five people were treated as traitors (partisans) after the war. The Iron Curtain so completely divided the Sámi communities and generated such strong suspicions in Finnmark along the border between Norway and the Soviet Union that years passed before normal relations were restored. The Sámi have since strengthened their community within an internationalist strategy of building multilateral relationships.

In preparation for a Third World War in the Far North, the Soviet Union based hundreds of submarines along the Arctic Coast. This huge fleet guarded the frontier from the Bering Sea to the Kola Peninsula and the White Sea coast. Having chased off the area's Indigenous population, the Soviets tested dozens of nuclear weapons at Novaya Zemlya, with little regard for long-term effects of radiation. Initiatives like these, prompted by immediate strategic considerations, have had lasting effects everywhere in the Arctic, especially for Indigenous communities.

In 1957 the US Atomic Energy Commission dreamed up Project Chariot, a mad scientist's scheme to use five nuclear devices to blast a hole big enough to create a deep-water port near the Alaska Inupiat community of Port Hope. Not until 1960 did the feds show up to tell the Inupiat that the project was perfectly safe.[20]

Northern peoples had no seats in the war rooms during the early Cold War years; but neither could they ignore the missile-rattling on the radio news or the bomber flights overhead. Constant war talk unsettles noncombatants, and if they live near the prospective battleground, it also fosters an almost permanent sense of unease and uncertainty, along with a before-the-storm kind of quiet. For those who lived through this period, Cold War events formed a backdrop reality in the Arctic, one constituted by moments of high drama and anxiety followed by cooling-off periods and lingering insecurities. Northerners raised in such circumstances may never shake those anxious feelings.

Many remember the 1960s for sex, drugs, and great music, but that decade also saw the construction of the Berlin Wall; the Cuban Missile Crisis, which brought the world to the brink of nuclear war; American bombing raids on Communist North Vietnam, and Czechoslovakia's Prague Spring, a democratic moment that collapsed when Soviet tanks rolled in. The ongoing Cold War had very real consequences for northern residents.

On January 21, 1968, a USAF B-52 carrying four hydrogen bombs experienced trouble near the Thule Air Base in Greenland.[21] A cockpit fire forced the crew to bail out, and one of them died. The plane crashed on the sea ice at North Star Bay, spilling radioactive plutonium. The American military collected contaminated snow and ice for disposal in the United States and cleaned up the area, but they could not locate one of the plane's nuclear weapons. Greenland was still a colony of Denmark, and the following year, the Danish Institute for Clinical Epidemiology found that the incidence of cancer among workers at the base was considerably higher than for those who had arrived before the accident. In 1987, surviving clean-up workers sued the United States.

Many northern towns became military bases during the Cold War. In Alaska, as the United States prepared its air bases, bombers, and nuclear weapons to target the enemy across the Arctic expanse, towns boomed as a result of the need to house thousands of troops. The Cold War put several centres on war-room maps: Eielson near Fairbanks, Alaska, and Keflavik near Reykjavik, Iceland, but also Whitehorse, Inuvik, Iqaluit (Frobisher Bay), and Churchill, all in Canada.

With a view to fostering rapprochement with Beijing and bringing about a superpower realignment, US president Richard Nixon travelled with Henry Kissinger to China in 1972 for meetings with Mao Zedong. Before Kissinger became Nixon's national security advisor and, later, secretary of state, he taught at Harvard, where he published an influential volume, *Nuclear Weapons and Foreign Policy*.[22] In it he argued that fears about thermonuclear war and "mutually assured destruction" were strategically limiting for the United States. His book examined the case for limited nuclear war, which would require perfectly rational military leaders on both sides – something Kissinger admitted would be hard to arrange, even if the war were fought in a relatively underpopulated area such as the Arctic.

Kissinger's view troubled game theorist Anatol Rapoport: "What appears to Americans as 'limited war' appears as total war to the people against whom it is waged."[23] It all depended from which end of the cannon one viewed the conflict.

With the contours of their homelands long planted in their minds, Indigenous hunters followed the seasons for fish and game. Indigenous observers observed the new arrivals as they came and went. They watched these outsiders bulldoze their way through the bush, building roads and runways and pushing aside local people who got in their way. Most outsiders, for their part, caught only glimpses of the lives being lived around them: a Native child bending to pick up kindling in the forest, a hunter snowshoeing across a frozen creek, a family walking in single file beside a road. Some brought their racist attitudes with them, and in northern mining camps, one might hear diamond drillers refer to Indian chiefs as "bush niggers" or "Navajos." The landscape appealed to some of the outsiders, though, and they did not mind the winter cold. Some of them settled in the Far North.

In those early Cold War days, wary and watchful "Natives" and war-weary, disdainful "whites" lived in the mostly separate realities of bush and town. Individuals from both sides of the cultural divide did get to know one another. Some became friends. Others got married. In 1959, I remember hearing the popular country song "Squaws along the Yukon Are Good Enough for Me" by Hank Thompson on my radio. But white males who "shacked up" with Indigenous women might still be condemned at the time as "squaw men." The children of such relationships suffered from being neither Indian nor white and were condemned by federal officials as "nobodies," the children of flawed parents. Generally, Natives and non-Natives lived worlds apart. The character of their relationship was that of familiar strangers, although over time something quite different started to happen.

When the Cold War ended, the Arctic's East and West became reconnected and Indigenous peoples around the circumpolar Arctic were able to assert themselves. On October 1, 1987, Soviet head of state Mikhail Gorbachev travelled to the port city of Murmansk on Russia's northwestern Arctic coast, where he gave a remarkable speech calling for the Arctic to become a zone of peace. Against the loud chorus of Reaganite rhetoric about totalitarianism and Soviet expansion, Gorbachev spoke of a new era: "Reykjavik [the site of his meeting with President Reagan the year before] indeed became a turning point in world history; it showed a possibility of improving the international situation." But, he warned, "it would be irresponsible on our part to underestimate the forces of resistance to change."[24]

After accusing the Americans of accelerating the arms race in order to bankrupt the Soviet Union, Gorbachev spoke of the Arctic's importance, not only for its polar ocean but also for its unique positioning, which united three continents through one geographic point. Gorbachev was thus anticipating the case – later put forward by China, India, Korea, and others – that the Arctic Ocean should be treated as a global common instead of being divided up among the eight Arctic states. Directly addressing Arctic security issues, Gorbachev said:

> The community and interrelationship of the interests of our entire world is felt in the Northern part of the globe, in the Arctic, perhaps more than anywhere else. For the Arctic and the North Atlantic are not just the weather kitchen, the point where cyclones and anticyclones are born to influence the climate in Europe, the USA and Canada, and even in South Asia and Africa. One can feel here the freezing breath of the Arctic strategy of the Pentagon. An immense potential of nuclear destruction concentrated aboard submarines and surface ships affects the political climate of the entire world and can be detonated by an accidental political-military conflict in any other region of the world.[25]

Gorbachev invited the Arctic countries to begin an open dialogue about their pressing security issues, both present and future, asking that all nations consider possibilities other than war. He proposed joint energy initiatives, scientific exchanges, and a conference on coordinating Arctic research. And, remarkably, he raised questions related to the interests of northern Indigenous populations and to environmental protection, urging his listeners to protect the tundra, the forest tundra, and northern forest areas. Finally, Gorbachev proposed opening the North Sea Route along the Arctic Coast to foreign ships, with Russia providing icebreaker services. "Such are our proposals. Such is the concrete meaning of Soviet foreign policy with regard to the North," he finished. Although some critics found his speech self-serving, others thought it signalled the imminent end of the Cold War. For our purposes, we might even read Gorbachev's speech as predicting a new Arctic identity.

Ever mindful of its painful history with the Soviet Union, Finland quickly stepped into the opening created by Gorbachev. The next day, Finnish president Mauno Koivisto welcomed the Soviet leader's speech as "show[ing] a far-reaching spirit of cooperation with regard to security and cooperation questions in the northern regions."[26] In 1989, Koivisto authorized his foreign minister, Kalevi Sorsa, and his environment minister, Kaj Barlund, to canvass Finland's Nordic neighbours about cooperating on an initiative to breathe life into Gorbachev's environmental agenda. The Finns recognized an urgent need for a cooperative circumpolar environmental program, and so the Finnish Initiative was born. As former Harvard and Queen's University professor Tom Axworthy has explained to me, the Finnish Initiative's focus on the environmental leaves of Gorbachev's olive branch helped raise the importance of this issue for the Arctic regions. On the heels of Gorbachev's Murmansk speech, what would become the Arctic Environmental Protection Strategy (AEPS) represented the next big step.

During the Washington Summit of December 1987, Gorbachev and Reagan agreed to dismantle US and Soviet arsenals of intermediate-range nuclear missiles. In November 1989, the Berlin Wall came down and the Cold War was all but over. Fans of Ronald Reagan declared that he had "won" the Cold War, but it was Mikhail Gorbachev who articulated a compelling vision for an Arctic peace.

John English notes in his book *Ice and Water* that "on the day Gorbachev spoke in Murmansk, the UN Environment Programme reported that the ozone layer depletion in the Antarctic was the greatest ever, and scientific research had shown that human-made chlorofluorocarbons were the cause."[27] Ozone was also impacting the Arctic. Former Norwegian prime minister Gro Harlem Bruntland's UN World Commission on Environment and Development had issued its report, *Our Common Future*, a few months before Gorbachev's speech, in March 1987, and the Arctic audience welcomed its central idea of sustainable development. Also issued that year was a two-part document titled *Yukon 2000*, a bottom-up economic planning process launched by Yukon's NDP legislators. That *Yukon 2000*, tabled by a small territory in the northwest corner of Canada, echoed many of Bruntland's ideas showed just how small the world had suddenly become.

A Zone of Peace?

Can the Arctic truly become a zone of peace rather than a battleground? Inevitably, some residue of the Cold War remains. Mikhail Gorbachev warned in 2015 that ongoing East–West conflicts had the potential to erupt, and he blamed the conflict in Ukraine on American post–Cold War "triumphalism."[28]

The Arctic remains, so far, a safe space for Russia and the United States to maintain an intergovernmental relationship. In the circumpolar world, Indigenous communities, regional governments, and scientists readily cooperate with one another. However, former US defense secretary William J. Perry warns that nuclear terrorism and the threat of a nuclear winter still hang over the world.[29] A new Cold War – or even a hot war – could still happen.

Dozens of Soviet nuclear submarines based near Murmansk have been decommissioned, but Cold War stockpiles of weapons still exist and continue to present a military and environmental threat. All the while, suspicions between Americans and Russians persist. In moments of high political tension (such as when Russia invaded Crimea in 2014), many northerners remember the days of constant Cold War anxiety, and this has added to the normal distrust of distant governments.

In the Far North, travellers repeatedly look behind them to see where they have been, not just so that they can find their way home but also to get their bearings on the way ahead. After the alienation, division, and marginalization created by the Cold War, Arctic peoples took a deep breath, located themselves, and began to move forward. The Yup'ik of Little Diomede were finally able to reconnect with their relatives on the Soviet coast. In 1988, Congress finally legislated reparations for the surviving Aleut internees. Sámi families on the Norwegian–Russian border began a period of healing. Inuit of Canada and the United States joined their Greenland cousins in 1977 in creating the Inuit Circumpolar Conference (now the Inuit Circumpolar Council). In both Canada and Greenland, the Inuit eventually sued their national governments over their forced relocations. Greenlanders embarked on the long march to home rule and self-government. In Alaska and the Canadian territories, Indigenous groups that had been ignored, forcibly displaced, and infantilized by law and governments began the struggle to redefine themselves as Arctic peoples, reclaim their hereditary lands, and assert their right to govern their own communities.

3

Born in the Northern Bush
Indigenous Government

*At the ice hole, a young hunter learns that with quiet
come the fish.*

I n 1867 the United States purchased Alaska from Russia without consulting the territory's Aleut, Athabaskans (Dene), Inuit, Tlingit, or
Yupik inhabitants. A hundred years later, when oil companies announced a plan to build an 800-mile pipeline from Prudhoe Bay to
Valdez, William L. Iggiagruk Hensley, a young Iñupiaq leader, politely
informed them that their pipeline route crossed Native land. Subsequent negotiations involved much backroom bargaining, lobbying, and
political posturing, largely in the halls of Congress. Eventually, Congress agreed to a treaty that gave Alaskan natives almost $1 billion and
44 million acres (180,000 km²) of land.[1]

On December 18, 1971, President Richard Nixon telephoned William
Hensley, who had made more than 120 trips to Washington to tangle
with senators and congressmen over a resolution to the Alaska Native
land claim. "I want you to be among the first to know that I have just
signed the Alaska Native Claims Settlement Act," the president told
Hensley.[2] ANCSA became the first modern northern treaty. In time,
there would be more than twenty such documents covering the northern
40 percent of Canada's land mass.

Acres of Land

Twentieth-century treaties and governance agreements negotiated with
the Arctic's Indigenous communities in Alaska, Canada, and Greenland

have fundamentally changed the character of the North, yet southerners generally know nothing about them. In the Canadian North, modern treaties have returned to the Dene, Inuit, and Tlingit hundreds of thousands of square kilometres of land, in an era when federal governments have made little progress on land rights issues in southern Canada.

Idle No More, a grassroots protest movement supported by First Nations, Métis, and Inuit, as well as non-Indigenous social media activists, sprang up in Canada in December 2012. Triggered by the federal Conservative government's Bill C-45, an omnibus budget bill that protesters claimed would threaten treaty rights and environmental protections for Aboriginal hunting and fishing grounds, the movement soon targeted larger projects. These included the Alberta Oil Sands and massive pipeline projects aimed at moving oil and gas to Canada's West Coast, across BC lands claimed by numerous First Nations. Idle No More advocates believed that Ottawa, by neglecting Indigenous rights and treaty obligations, was unapologetically embracing American energy corporations, Chinese mining giants, and pipeline megaprojects.

First Nations chiefs have repeatedly had to fight for their limited treaty rights at negotiating tables, in the courts, and in legislative battles. As constitutionalist John Whyte once observed to me, Aboriginal treaty-making in Canada displays a repeated pattern of innovation followed by betrayal. Similarly, US federal policy has swung back and forth between erasing a way of life and letting Native Americans protect their tribal traditions. North America's Indigenous peoples thus find themselves caught in a situation that resembles a Mobius loop.

Idle No More protests in every major Canadian city, north and south, became this generation's way of shouting "Enough! No more repeats!" Yellowknife-Dene political scientist Glen Coulthard neatly summed up the goals of Idle No More for me as a struggle for land and jurisdiction. Land-use conflicts between governments and Indigenous groups exist right across the country. Treaty negotiations drag on in BC; in every other province, frustrated First Nations are struggling to negotiate self-government accords and to litigate tribal governance issues. These endless negotiations with the feds, involving the negotiation and implementation of Indigenous land treaties, the role of settler legislators in making and breaking those treaties, and proposals for a third-order Aboriginal self-government (an Arctic innovation that has failed to put down roots in southern Canada), warrant more discussion.

Treaties: A Brief History

Aboriginal leaders have long claimed that, for the most part, neither Canada nor the United States purchased or even rented Aboriginal ancestral homelands; nor did their colonial predecessors – Britain, France, Holland, Portugal, and Spain. Instead, European settlers expropriated the lands of North and South America and enslaved the Indigenous populations. Each nation provided its own justification. Spain and Portugal pointed to Pope Alexander VI, who gave the New World to their kings after Christopher Columbus returned from his first voyage. Other European powers claimed a right of conquest. In his 1689 essay "Of Property," English Enlightenment thinker John Locke contended that by mixing their labour with the soil, settlers acquired property rights: "Thus this Law of reason makes the Deer, that Indian's who hath killed it; 'tis allowed to be his goods who hath bestowed his labour upon it, though before, it was the common right of every one."[3]

During the eighteenth century, European states competing for control of the Americas sought to bind their allies and trading partners among the Indigenous nations with treaties of peace and friendship. The British and the French, for example, offered friendship pacts with tribes such as the Malecite of the Saint John River Valley and the Mi'kmaq of Nova Scotia. At the beginning of the eighteenth century, Indigenous peoples were still the majority of North America's population; by the beginning of the nineteenth, Europeans outnumbered them.

When French forces fought the British on the Plains of Abraham in 1759, they counted the Ottawa Nation as their firm ally. After the French defeat, however, Ottawa war chief Pontiac, angered by legions of British squatters occupying his tribal lands, began to marshal an army of resistance from the tribes of the western Great Lakes.[4] In May 1763,

Pontiac's armies captured nine British forts. Stunned by Pontiac's military genius, the British decided to repair their relationship with the Indian tribes.

The Royal Proclamation of 1763 promised that henceforth the Crown would obtain Indian lands for settlement only through treaties publicly negotiated with the chiefs of Indian nations. Through this proclamation, Britain formally recognized Aboriginal title to ancestral lands *and* Aboriginal government of those territories.[5] The negotiation of four hundred land treaties in Canada and the United States followed this proclamation, as colonists settled the West. Unfortunately, colonial governments soon violated most of these treaties. In his book *Red Skin, White Masks*, Glen Coulthard defines these colonial actions as "structured dispossession."[6] Moviegoers might recognize them as "ethnic cleansing" or "organized crime."

Like those negotiated in the United States over the same period, these colonial-era treaties can now be read as documenting the surrender of Indian lands and the herding of First Nations onto marginal lands called Indian reserves – reserves that condemned their residents to isolation, hunger, and poverty. Many first citizens regarded these treaties as sacred covenants binding for "as long as the sun shone and the river flowed" – as a marriage, if you like, between the state and the tribe.[7] In contrast, federal authorities too often treated these agreements as termination contracts, something more like a divorce or a "here's your land and money, now off you go" separation.

By the late nineteenth century, "the West was won" and Indian tribes no longer posed a military threat to settlement. At that point the US government lost interest in treaty-making. After 1871 the United States signed no Indian treaties for a century, until Congress adopted the Alaska treaty in 1971. With the signing of Treaty 11 in 1921, Canada also stopped negotiating treaties. Yet whenever there was a major frontier resource development pending, governments used treaties to extinguish Aboriginal title. When Canada wanted to build the transcontinental railway across the prairies, for example, it wrote the Numbered Treaties and asked illiterate chiefs to sign them.

Furthermore, between 1927 and 1951, Canadian law prohibited Indians from hiring lawyers to press land claims. In 1953, with House Concurrent Resolution 108, the US Congress resolved to abrogate all treaties with Native people and to abolish federal supervision over tribes. That policy operated until 1996, by which time 109 tribes had been terminated and a million acres of Indian land had been lost.[8] For years afterwards, non-Indigenous writers and artists portrayed American Indians as a defeated and disappearing population.

Settler Legislators

In Alaska and the Canadian territories, settler legislators helped shape modern northern agreements. In the nineteenth century and early in the twentieth, nobody questioned that Indian treaties involved only tribes, chiefs, and the federal authorities. Late in the twentieth century, however, in both Alaska and Canada's northern territories, local non-Indigenous or settler populations gained a voice in treaty negotiations. Ultimately, hard work and compromises by both Indigenous leaders and regional legislators would help federal governments achieve resolution. But in the 1970s, when modern land claims negotiations got under way in the Canadian Arctic, a settler backlash erupted.

In June 1969, Prime Minister Pierre Trudeau and his Indian affairs minister, Jean Chrétien, published a White Paper that proposed terminating the Indian Act and the special legal relationship between Aboriginal peoples and the Canadian state. Aboriginal leaders reacted angrily to what Harold Cardinal in his book *The Unjust Society* called "cultural genocide."[9] But the White Paper's ideas struck a chord with those opposed to treaty-making with Indian nations, and the opposition aroused by Indigenous claims seemed to cross party lines. Prominent Liberals liked to quote a speech by Pierre Trudeau given at the Seaforth Armoury in Vancouver on August 8 of that year:

> We won't recognize aboriginal rights. We can go on adding bricks of
> discrimination around the ghetto in which Indians live, and at the

same time helping them preserve certain cultural traits and certain ancestral rights. Or we can say you are at a crossroads – the time is now to decide whether the Indians will be a race apart in Canada, or whether they will be Canadians of full status ... Perhaps the treaties shouldn't go on forever. It's inconceivable, I think, that in a given society one section of a society should have a treaty with the other section of society. We must all be equal under the laws and we must not sign treaties amongst ourselves. Indians should become Canadians as all other Canadians. This is the only basis on which I see our society can develop as equals. But aboriginal rights, this really means saying, "We were here before you. You came and cheated us, by giving us some worthless things in return for vast expanses of land, and we want to reopen this question. We want you to preserve our aboriginal rights and to restore them to us." And our answer – our answer is no. We can't recognize aboriginal rights because no society can be built on historical might-have-beens ... We will be just in our time. That is all we can do. We will be just today.[10]

Canada's west coast had long been a theatre of resistance to Indigenous rights claims. In 1867, Joseph Trutch, chief commissioner of lands and works for the Crown colony of British Columbia, wrote: "The Indians have really no right to the lands they claim, nor are they of any actual value or utility to them, and I cannot see why they should either retain these lands to the prejudice of the general interests of the Colony, or be allowed to make a market of them either to the Government or to Individuals."[11] One hundred years later, Mel Smith, constitutional adviser to BC premiers and an admirer of Trudeau's 1969 position, argued that Indian claims in BC had been settled, without treaties, by the creation of Indian reserves. Smith went on to write a bestselling book, *Our Home or Native Land*, attacking Indian claims.[12] Political scientist Tom Flanagan, a former adviser to Conservative prime minister Stephen Harper, wrote another bestseller, *First Nations? Second Thoughts*, in which he proposed a return to the policy of assimilation: "In order to become self-supporting and get beyond the social pathologies that are ruining their communities, aboriginal people need to acquire the skills and attitudes that bring success in a liberal society, political democracy, and market economy. Call it assimilation, call it integration, call it adaptation, call it whatever you want: it has to happen."[13]

Trudeau's thinking appealed to many northern settlers, but by 1973 the prime minister's perspective had begun to change. The shift arose as a result of the Supreme Court of Canada's divided decision in *Calder* regarding whether the Nisga'a Nation still held Aboriginal title to the Nass Valley in northwestern BC. Nisga'a chiefs claimed a partial victory; BC legislators and government lawyers insisted that the Aboriginal side had lost. Regardless, Trudeau observed that "maybe you have more rights than we thought you did."[14] As a constitutional lawyer himself, Trudeau understood that the Supreme Court had reopened the question of Aboriginal rights and title, at least for Canada.

In the three decades between the Nisga'a chiefs' filing of the *Calder* case in 1968 and federal ratification of the Nisga'a treaty in 1999, much changed, both in the United States and in Canada. Federal negotiators were dispatched to areas without treaties: northern Quebec, BC, and the northern territories.

The Cree and Inuit of northern Quebec, the province of Quebec, and the Government of Canada signed the first modern treaty in Canada, the James Bay and Northern Québec Agreement, in 1975. The treaty has provided the beneficiaries with 14,000 square kilometres in community lands; extensive fishing, hunting, and trapping grounds; $225 million in compensation; a Cree family income plan for wildlife harvesters; and the right for people to use their native tongue as their official language. The treaty took less than four years to negotiate – a rush job, driven by Hydro-Québec's urgent need to pour concrete for massive dams in the James Bay watershed. The speed with which the treaty was concluded later required the negotiation of a supplementary fix-up Paix des Braves Agreement.

In 1982, Canada and its provinces amended the country's Constitution, adding Section 35, which states:

(1) The existing Aboriginal and treaty rights of the Aboriginal peoples of Canada are hereby recognized and affirmed.

(2) In this Act, "Aboriginal peoples of Canada" includes the Indian, Inuit and Métis peoples of Canada.[15]

Neither Indigenous leaders nor territorial legislators had a voice or a vote in the constitutional conferences that crafted Section 35. Both were on the margins of the process. Nonetheless, with the later addition of Section 35, Canada's Constitution became the first to recognize Aboriginal rights. On my own hook, as a Yukon MLA, I went to London to lobby British MPs about the repatriation of the Canadian constitution, but to no effect.

In 1984, the Inuvialuit – fishers and hunters of the Western Arctic – also concluded a treaty with Canada. This deal took five years to negotiate, at a time when energy giants were drilling on 476,000 square kilometres of the Beaufort Sea. Through this treaty, the Inuvialuit secured fee-simple title, or collective ownership, to 91,000 square kilometres of land, including mineral and oil and gas rights on a portion of their lands. The Inuvialuit also received federal compensation of C$45 million.[16] The Inuvialuit Agreement may be the best written of all the northern treaties, because, from beginning to end, it had the same two negotiators.

The addition of Section 35 to Canada's Constitution opened a new chapter with the negotiation of modern northern treaties in Yukon and the NWT. Some non-Aboriginal residents of Northern communities – such as Dan Lang, a young conservative legislator – loudly opposed Yukon Aboriginal land claims. Lang helped found a group called the Northern Land Research Society, and on October 20, 1975, a *Toronto Star* story headlined "Indian claims stir Yukon racism" described Lang as speaking for a growing white resentment: "I would hate to split the Yukon but I'm sure we could get 8,000 people behind us if we worked at it ... The animosity that's growing here is unbelievable. I'll tell you this. If you're going to give land away where I've always hunted, the only way you'll get me off it is carry me off."[17]

Anticipating Aboriginal self-government debates to come, Ken McKinnon, another Yukon Conservative quoted in the article, spoke of fears that "the Indians will set up 'a state within a state' if the government does not respond to their needs."[18] These statements didn't tell the whole story. For example, the *Star* failed to mention that both the conservatives quoted in the story were married to Indigenous women. And whenever northerners read news reports conflating debates about land claims in the Far North with Afro-American voting rights struggles in the US Deep South, they cringed. The North has always been a more complicated landscape than the cartoon caricatures presented in the Toronto and Montreal media.

As British parliamentarians like to say, Lang was *not* my enemy, he was my *opponent,* and I quote him only to illustrate our policy differences. To my mind, the *Star* had too easily tagged Lang with the "racist" label. As a working politician, I had to try a little harder to understand those of my constituents who agreed with him. If someone's family had emigrated from Britain, or anywhere in Europe with a feudal past, their ancestors might have come to Canada to escape the oppression of landowner aristocrats, who wasted their days hunting and fishing or drinking and gambling while their underlings slaved to keep their masters in the lap of luxury. For the working-class descendants of those families in Canada, the nightmare fear might be that government would suddenly elevate the Indigenous underclass in their neighbourhood into a landowning, hunting, and fishing aristocracy. Union leaders who supported land claims negotiations might argue that the negotiations offered a path from poverty to equality, but in the beginning, theirs was a minority view.

When I moved from Dawson City to Whitehorse in November 1970, Yukon politics seemed to be all about Conservatives and Liberals fighting for control of the Whitehorse Chamber of Commerce. But the 1970s was a decade of change. As noted earlier, in 1972 the NDP candidate Wally Firth campaigned against the Mackenzie Valley Pipeline to win the NWT's seat in Parliament. In 1973 the Yukon Native Brotherhood presented its land claim to Prime Minister Pierre Trudeau. The United

Steelworkers union locals at mines in Clinton Creek, Elsa, Faro, Pine Point, Whitehorse Copper, and Yellowknife campaigned on workplace health and safety issues. The Yukon Conservation Society became active in pipeline debates. And Sue Ellenton made a local hit of her song "Yukon Women," the lyrics for which include the following lines:

> *Rough, loose, raw and rugged,*
> *Yukon women are we.*
> *We wear plaid jackets*
> *and build our own cabins,*
> *and we all vote NDP,*
> *independently.*[19]

In a sense, the land claims debate pitted the 1970s against the 1950s: the Civil Rights era of optimism versus Cold War pessimism. The opponents of Aboriginal rights and title remained vocal. Dan Lang, an extremely popular territorial legislator, continued to lead his side of the debate – a debate that went on for so long that at certain points he and I seemed to be arguing in a fact-free zone. In the Yukon Legislative Assembly in May 1991, Lang referenced the 1990 Supreme Court of Canada decision on Aboriginal fishing rights and pointedly told me, "I did not ask for Judge Sparrow's decision. I asked what the Government of the Yukon Territory's position was regarding the negotiations of the land claims." Momentarily, I was lost for words, because the "judge" in Lang's question was the Supreme Court of Canada, "Sparrow" was the name of the appellant, and the "decision" was final.

Like Lang, some Yukoners viewed the post-1973 treaty process as divisive and disruptive of the established order of settler privilege. Others recognized that the negotiations built bridges across tribal and ethnic divides. The northern negotiations on Aboriginal rights and title also re-established links among various First Nations chiefs. In Alaska, the Alaska Federation of Natives brought together Iñupiaq, Yu'pik, Dene, Aleut, Tlingit, and Haida leaders, many of whom might have known one another at residential school. In the neighbouring Canadian territory, the Yukon Native Brotherhood (later the Council for Yukon Indians, and then the Council for Yukon First Nations) refused to let the federal government's Indian Act divide their community; instead they chose to unite First Nations (Status Indians) and their "non-Status Indian" cousins in a common front.

Multi-year negotiations in northern communities required active consultation with non-Indigenous citizens. At the outset of northern treaty talks with tribal chiefs, federal negotiators discovered that settler populations had their own demands. That made all the difference. Indigenous leaders and settler legislators began to meet across treaty tables and listen to each other. These conversations changed the character of both the treaties and the affected communities. The long-term benefits of these interactions were that settlers and Indigenous leaders started to work together, as they still do, on the treaties' co-management and land-use planning boards.

In the late 1970s, I attended a day-long meeting of environmental groups concerned about oil drilling in the calving grounds of the Porcupine Caribou Herd. At lunchtime, I slipped out to speak to a USWA miners' union conference on occupational health and work environment issues. Afterwards, I reflected on the fact that two groups concerned about environmental issues were meeting two blocks apart in the same northern town but neither knew the other existed. At that moment, I realized that part of my job as a legislator was connecting experts, such as those attending the caribou conference, to people with serious research needs, such as Yukon's copper, gold, lead, silver, and zinc miners. Although making such connections always seems more difficult in colonized communities, in the Yukon the NDP briefly united a progressive coalition of First Nation politicians, labour leaders, and women's movement and environmental activists to achieve enough of a legislative majority to finalize treaty negotiations.

In practical terms, this coalition of rural Yukon chiefs, miners' union members, and urban progressives delivered twice as much land for First Nations as the Yukon Tories had proposed in 1984, in addition to third-order Aboriginal self-government agreements that a right-wing administration would have fiercely resisted. Negotiators representing Arctic Indigenous peoples involved in concurrent treaty negotiations during the 1990s, from both Dene (Gwich'in, Sahtu, Tlicho, Yukon) and Inuit (Inuvialuit, Labrador, Nunavik, Nunavut) communities, compare notes and work together even today in an Aboriginal land claims coalition to lobby Ottawa on implementation issues.

The feds provided both good moments and bad. A good one was when the Honourable Bill McKnight arrived in Whitehorse to personally conclude an agreement-in-principle in the middle of the 1989 federal election campaign. But it was a bad day when Knight's successor, Tom Siddon, decided to allocate Yukon lands to Gwich'in in the NWT without so much as a courtesy phone call to me as Yukon premier. His peremptory action earned Siddon a unanimous motion of censure in the Yukon Legislature and almost derailed Yukon land claims negotiations. It is reasonable to ask: Had I been the federal minister, how might I have handled this situation? As it happened, a Yukon Kaska First Nation, the Ross River Dena, had a historic claim to land across the border in the NWT.[20] A wise minister might have dealt with both transboundary issues at the same time.

For fourteen years in the Yukon Legislative Assembly, NDP legislators argued with Lang and other conservatives that land claims and self-government treaties would serve the broad public interest and that, therefore, the territorial government should represent *all* Yukoners in negotiations. At the outset, Lang's allies argued that Yukon government negotiators should represent *only* non-Aboriginal or settler interests at treaty tables. We won that one. Still, even with Yukon's successful land claims treaties, assimilationist thinkers continued to echo the sentiments of Vancouver-born US Republican Senator S.I. Hayakawa, who famously said of America's land, "We stole it fair and square."[21]

Indian Title

Modern treaty-making required governments to abandon a particular view of Aboriginal or "Indian" title. That shift in thinking made possible landmark northern treaties, starting with Alaska, Quebec, and Yukon. For decades, British, American, and Canadian courts had employed the term "Indian title" to describe informal ownership of land occupied continuously and exclusively by Aboriginal people over centuries. Towards the end of the twentieth century, in the North American Arctic, Indigenous leaders, federal negotiators, and settler legislators negotiated land claims agreements involving thousands of square kilometres of titled land, quantities unimaginable in nineteenth-century treaties. These same agreements provided significant self-government powers for the Indigenous landowners. Wise developers began to acknowledge Aboriginal title, among them Humble Oil and the Atlantic Richfield Company after they discovered the United States' largest oil field at Prudhoe Bay, Alaska; the province of Quebec while it planned massive hydroelectric projects on the James Bay watershed; and gas producers when they proposed a pipeline across the Yukon. Canada gives Section 35 constitutional protection to modern treaties negotiated between Aboriginal groups, Ottawa, and the province or territory.

Only national governments can make treaties, but provincial, territorial, and state governments can help or hinder negotiations. Federal representatives from both the United States and Canada came north repeatedly hoping to negotiate the surrender of Aboriginal or Indian title to the lands in question. Remembering clearly the broken promises of the nineteenth-century treaties and having a greater appreciation of the value of their lands, Indigenous Northerners had no intention of selling their birthright on the cheap. No quick and dirty deals were on offer this time around.

Some Arctic and Subarctic treaty negotiations took twenty years to complete, something I soundly criticize in my book *Reconciliation: First Nations Treaty Making in British Columbia*. If two days is too short, two decades of talk is far more time than is necessary to conclude a treaty. As a liberal nation that prizes constructive engagement, Canada seems far more committed to negotiation than to settlements.

Sitting on a panel with Thomas Berger at the Canadian Environmental Grantmakers' Network conference in May 2011, however, I heard that the eminent jurist airs a different view. Berger argued that the northern parties in question – chiefs, feds, and legislators – *needed* twenty years to build a relationship. If that were relationship advice, I countered, few of us would ever get married or have children, and our society might soon become a gerontocracy.

The Yukon Treaty

The Yukon Treaty was the first Canadian treaty to be completed without the pressure of a pending megaproject. As noted, the numbered treaties of the nineteenth century had cleared the way for railways and prairie settlement. The 1975 James Bay treaty facilitated a massive hydro project, and the 1984 Inuvialuit treaty enabled oil exploration in the Beaufort Sea. As an alternative to the megaproject driver, the federal government established artificial deadlines like the one that finalized Yukon's Umbrella Final Agreement on March 31, 1990.

As agreed, the three parties stopped the clock at midnight on March 31. Early the following morning I met with Doug McArthur, a former economics professor, education minister, and public servant from Saskatchewan, at that point the Yukon deputy minister responsible for land claims negotiations, and Barry Stuart, a former chief territorial court judge, who was our chief negotiator. I was dismayed to learn that without adult supervision, three lawyers had been left alone in a hotel room to draft the agreement's development assessment chapter. That chapter had two parents – the Yukon 2000 process and the Yukon land claims negotiations, which ran on parallel tracks from 1985 to 1986 and influenced each other significantly.

The Yukon cabinet had issued extremely clear instructions for this chapter. Our ministers wanted something structurally appropriate for Yukon's small population, as well as a single process to incorporate the myriad federal systems. We also wanted a single board with the ability to recruit whatever technical support it required, the power to provide guarantees of community input, and the authority to expeditiously render go or no-go decisions. When Barry Stuart told us how many pages there were in the draft chapter the lawyers had prepared, I was horrified. "I hope we haven't got some kind of Rube Goldberg machine," I told him.

"Don't worry, premier," Stuart replied, "these things never work anyway."

To which McArthur added, "And what's more, we're now going to lock it into the Canadian Constitution under Section 35."

Years later, I ran into Bill Klassen, a former Yukon Deputy Minister of Renewable Resources, and asked him what he was doing those days. "As a consultant for the territory, I'm trying make the Yukon treaty's Development Assessment chapter work," he replied.

Inevitably, the Yukon First Nation agreements that made up the treaty reflected hard bargaining over practical matters. The federal and territorial governments negotiated the umbrella treaty largely in Yukon communities rather than in Ottawa hotels. Both First Nation chiefs and their "non-Status Indian" partners were at the negotiation table. Their joint presence demonstrated the ongoing resistance of these two Indigenous groups to the legislated dividing line between their communities set out by the Indian Act.

The twentieth-century treaties Canada negotiated with the First Nations, the Inuit, and the Métis of the Arctic and Subarctic in the years following the 1971 Alaskan settlement represented great advances in the land and resource rights of Indigenous peoples.[22] In striking contrast to nineteenth-century treaties, which consigned Canadian First Nations to "reserves" (and American Indians to "reservations") on marginal land and left them in almost permanent poverty, the twentieth-century versions recognized the collective ownership of tribal lands according to Indigenous custom, even though the government recorded First Nation treaty lands in the territorial land registry as required in the British legal tradition. Notably, Canada's federal Reform Party opposed collective title, preferring private settlements, as had some nineteenth-century American politicians, who favoured individual Indians receiving government cheques as the means to buy out their rights. No Indigenous nation bought this idea, however.

The new northern treaties also dwarfed their nineteenth-century predecessors in scale. For example, in the 1992 Yukon Treaty, 7,000 Athabaskans (Dene) and Tlingit secured title to 41,590 square kilometres of land, with subsurface resource rights to two-thirds of that total. That is more land than is contained in *all* of the Indian reserves in southern Canada, which are home to half a million First Nation citizens.[23] The Yukon Treaty also guaranteed subsistence or traditional food harvesting, participation in wildlife and natural resource management, and economic and employment opportunities, in addition to compensation of $243 million.[24]

Because the community-based negotiations took almost twenty years and included active consultation with non-Indigenous citizens, the resulting agreements contain sensible measures for sharing power over lands and resources between the Indigenous minority and the settler majority. Besides recognizing Aboriginal title to tens of thousands of square kilometres of resource-rich land, the agreements re-establish Indigenous governance of those lands. They honour the principles of sustainability and stewardship, and they include wildlife co-management boards that favour conservation and subsistence harvesting over recreational and commercial fishing and hunting. In this way, the principle of sustainability is embedded in these northern treaties, which makes them the only part of Canada's constitutional order where that is the case. Because these boards involve the sharing of power between Indigenous northerners and settlers, they operate as instruments of regional rather than national government and remain accountable to local communities.

In 1992, Yukon's NDP government tabled a bill in the territorial legislature to enact land claims and self-government treaties. With Yukon territory negotiators, principally Barry Stuart and Chris Knight, I held dozens of public meetings to explain the land claims and self-government agreements. Some meetings were quiet; others were loud. Several school gyms were packed, and a few church basements were half-empty. At these forums, citizens posed many difficult questions:

Would tax-exempt First Nation companies compete with non-Indigenous businesses? *No, the agreements phased out the exemption.*

What if a First Nation judge treated a speeding settler unfairly with a huge fine or jail time? *A motorist convicted for speeding across First Nation lands could always appeal his or her sentence to a higher court.*

How could a First Nation citizen escape from that nation's self-government? This question pointed to a serious misunderstanding of "self-government." I'm not sure that we answered it satisfactorily, but our answer referenced the federal government's past "imprisonment" of Indians on southern Canadian reserves. *Clearly, the parties to the Yukon self-government agreements intended them to empower and liberate Indigenous citizens, not the opposite.*

The text of the complicated final agreement contained chapters on everything from education, finance, and health to land and language. Unhelpfully, the federal government declined to participate in the public education process until after the territory and First Nations groups had ratified the agreements. To limit the potential for repeats of the nineteenth century's broken promises, the lawyers for the Indigenous parties reviewed the provisions meticulously, dotting every "i" and crossing every "t." As a result, Yukon's final agreement is said to contain more words than the New Testament.

The Yukon NDP lost the next election in 1992. Dan Lang retired from the legislature. The following year, the Conservative governments in Whitehorse and Ottawa enacted the treaty agreements. The Yukon Territorial Legislature unanimously approved the treaty; in the House of Commons only the right-wing Reform Party voted no. By the end of the process, the vast majority of Yukoners, Indigenous and non-Indigenous, were reconciled to the result. The treaty became a Lockean social contract set to create a community of a different character.

All of the northern Indigenous treaties provide tools such as co-management, land-use planning and water boards, and dispute resolution instruments, so that people may use these treaties to better manage their own lands and resource development, and to mitigate climate change. Every treaty counts as a small step in the evolution of Canada's treaty-making policies.[25] Each treaty resembles its immediate predecessor but also adds to the template some element that one of the parties believes has been overlooked in other treaties or removes from it some element was deemed a mistake to include.

The Yukon First Nation final agreements to date include the Champagne and Aishihik First Nations Final Agreement (1995); the First Nation of Nacho Nyak Dun Final Agreement (1995); the Teslin Tlingit Council Final Agreement (1995); the Vuntut Gwitchin First Nation Final Agreement (1995); the Selkirk First Nation Final Agreement (1997); the Tr'ondëk Hwëch'in Final Agreement (1998); the Little Salmon/ Carmacks First Nation Final Agreement (1998); the Ta'an Kwach'an Council Final Agreement (2002); the Kluane First Nation Final Agreement (2004); the Carcross/Tagish First Nation Final Agreement (2005); and the Kwanlin Dun First Nation Final Agreement (2005).

The other existing northern treaties are the Grand Council of the Crees (1975); the Inuvialuit Final Agreement (1984); the Gwich'in Tribal Council (1992); the Sahtu Dene and Métis Comprehensive Land Claims (1993); Nunavut Tunngavik Inc. (1993); the Nisga'a Final Agreement (2000); the Tlicho Agreement (2005); the Labrador Inuit Land Claims Agreement (2005); and the Nunavik Inuit Land Claims Agreement (2008).[26]

None of these treaties would have been possible if Pierre Trudeau, as Canada's prime minister, had not fundamentally changed his mind about Aboriginal rights, Aboriginal title, and Aboriginal treaties after the Supreme Court's *Calder* decision in 1973.

Modern treaties have routinely been negotiated with bands created by the Indian Act, but many Indigenous leaders now question whether these creatures of federal law are legitimate holders of Aboriginal rights and title to lands. In his 2014 *Tsilhqot'in Nation* decision, BC Supreme Court Justice David Vickers wrote:

> b. Proper Rights Holder [1219] Canada agrees with the plaintiff that the proper rights holder is the Tsilhqot'in Nation ... [458] ... They are a culturally homogeneous collective of people, larger than a clan, tribe or band ... [470] I conclude that the proper rights holder, whether for

Aboriginal title or Aboriginal rights, is the community of Tsilhqot'in people. Tsilhqot'in people were the historic community of people sharing language, customs, traditions, historical experience, territory and resources at the time of first contact and at sovereignty assertion.

What this ruling will mean for Indian bands currently at treaty tables is not yet clear.

International Implications

Canada's new northern treaties attracted much attention in the circumpolar world. Greenlanders, who achieved home rule in 1979, followed their Inuit cousins in Alaska and James Bay as they realized their treaty dreams. In 1991, Indigenous Russians attending the founding meeting of the Northern Forum for regional governments at Anchorage swarmed Alaskans and northern Canadians for information about land claims and Aboriginal self-government processes.[27] Based on readings of Canada's Arctic treaties, Norway borrowed northern Canadian co-management ideas for its Finnmark Act of 2005, which transferred power over northern lands and resources to a Municipal/Sámi body, although the law was mainly the product of Sámi activism.[28] A former president of the Sámediggi (Norwegian Sámi Parliament), Sven-Roald Nystø, insisted in 2002 that "when the Sámediggi wants to negotiate with Government authorities over future measures for the Sámi, we won't negotiate ourselves *out* of Norway, but on the contrary, *into* Norway. Into the country's governance, so that we can take more responsibility for our own future and future Sámi."[29] In negotiations with Norway, Finland, and Sweden, Sámi leaders have been developing a Sámi Convention, which could one day become an international treaty with Indigenous signatories.

A handful of the northern Canadian treaties contain clauses related to international obligations for cooperative conservation. For example, the 1993 Yukon Final Agreement calls for Canada to make reasonable efforts to ensure that Yukon First Nation interests are represented when issues involving fish and wildlife management arise in international negotiations. The Labrador Inuit Final Agreement of 2005 includes similar language in relation to aquatic plants, fish habitat, management, and stocks.

No Indigenous American nation yet has a seat in the United Nations General Assembly, but the UN has not been indifferent to developments in Canada and other countries with large Aboriginal populations. The UN Permanent Forum on Indigenous Issues (UNPFII) has a mandate to discuss issues related to the economic and social development, culture, environment, education, health, and human rights of Indigenous peoples. On September 13, 2007, the UN General Assembly adopted the UN Declaration on the Rights of Indigenous Peoples (UNDRIP). UNDRIP's Article 36 addresses the contemporary political realities of the Inuit Circumpolar Council (ICC), the Sámi Council, the Arctic Athabaskans, the Aleut International Association, and the Gwich'in Council International:

> Indigenous peoples, in particular those divided by international borders, have the right to maintain and develop contacts, relations and cooperation, including activities for spiritual, cultural, political, economic and social purposes, with their own members as well as other peoples across the borders. States, in consultation and co-operation with Indigenous peoples, shall take effective measures to facilitate the exercise and ensure the implementation of this right.[30]

At a special UN General Assembly meeting of a thousand delegates and heads of state for the first-ever World Conference on Indigenous Peoples, held on September 22 and 23, 2014, Canada was the only state to oppose a vote on UNDRIP. US President Barack Obama supported the declaration, but Canada filed an objection, claiming that the words "free, prior and informed consent" constituted an Aboriginal veto on resource developments. The Conservative government of Prime Minister Stephen Harper comforted itself with a quote from a report written by UN human rights expert James Anaya: "Canada has taken determined action to address ongoing aspects of the history of misdealing and harm inflicted on Aboriginal peoples in the country, a necessary step towards helping to remedy their current disadvantage."[31] But Harper ignored the important words that followed in that report: "The well-being gap between Aboriginal and non-Aboriginal people in Canada has not narrowed over the past several years; treaty and Aboriginal claims remain persistently unresolved; Indigenous women and girls remain vulnerable to abuse; and overall there appear to be high levels of distrust among Indigenous peoples towards the government at both the federal and provincial levels."[32]

At that moment, a country that should have been proud of its northern treaties with Indigenous peoples allowed itself to be embarrassed before the whole world. The Liberal government elected in Canada in 2015 took a new tack. In a 2016 statement at the UN Permanent Forum on Indigenous Peoples, Carolyn Bennett, Canada's new Indigenous and northern affairs minister, confirmed that Canada now fully supported UNDRIP "without qualifications."[33] However, on Bennett's return to Ottawa, bureaucrats quickly reminded the media that UNDRIP implementation might take some time. In its 2016 approvals of the Kinder Morgan and Line 3 pipeline projects, the Liberal government appeared to abandon its commitments to "free, prior and informed consent" for Indigenous peoples and "social license" for all communities – another twist of the Mobius loop.

Disputes

The 1993 treaty with the Inuit of Nunavut gave the Inuit collective ownership of 350,000 square kilometres, making them the largest private landowners in the world.[34] The Nunavut treaty also promised the Inuit – stewards of Arctic lands and waters for millennia – a Marine Council to monitor the Inuit seas. It took almost twenty years from the time of signing the treaty, however, for Canada to meet this latter obligation.[35]

For largely financial reasons, Canada seems to have decided unilaterally not to implement certain clauses in many of the new northern agreements. The Land Claims Agreement Coalition was formed in 2003 to address the federal implementation failures experienced by its members. Those members, whose comprehensive land claims agreements involve more than 40 percent of Canada's lands, waters, and resources, are the Council of Yukon First Nations, representing nine land claims organizations in Yukon; the Grand Council of the Crees (Eeyou Istchee); the Gwich'in Tribal Council; the Inuvialuit Regional Corporation; the Kwanlin Dun First Nation; the Maa-nulth First Nations; the Makivik Corporation; the Naskapi Nation of Kawawachikamach; the Nisga'a Nation; the Nunavut Tunngavik Inc.; the Nunatsiavut Government; the Sahtu Secretariat Inc.; the Tlicho Government; the Tsawwassen First Nation; and the Vuntut Gwitchin First Nation. Many of these groups have serious unresolved disputes with government about how the provisions of their treaties should be implemented.

Most of Canada's modern treaties with northern Indigenous nations include chapters containing standard (off-the-shelf) alternative dispute resolution (ADR) tools, including mediation.[36] Only a minority of Indigenous groups – notably the Inuvialuit, the Nisga'a, and the Inuit of Nunavut – succeeded in bargaining arbitration provisions into their treaties. Canadian law does offer a continuum of options in dispute resolution to Indigenous peoples, including negotiation, mediation and other forms of ADR, adjudication (i.e., informal and non-binding arbitration), informal but binding arbitration, and litigation (i.e., formal and binding court rulings). Any or all of these processes may be employed in both rights-based and interest-based negotiations. In theory, all of these processes allow for fast, effective, and fair conflict resolution. Unfortunately, these tools have often proved ineffective during implementation.

Canadian federal policy forbids Indigenous parties engaged in treaty negotiations to simultaneously litigate contentious issues – a weird anomaly in national public policy. As a consequence, dispute resolution measures are rarely tested *during* negotiations. The result is that Canadian treaty-making sharply limits opportunities for dispute resolution experimentation or self-design. Federal policy prohibits First

Nations from litigating while negotiating; indeed, federal officials have refused to participate in the dispute resolution procedures established in the very treaties they signed. For example, the Inuit tried seventeen times to invoke the arbitration clauses in the Nunavut treaty, but Canada's Department of Finance rejected even legally sanctioned arbitrations.[37]

In May 2008 the Canadian Senate's Standing Committee on Aboriginal Peoples issued "Honouring the Spirit of Modern Treaties: Closing the Loopholes," an interim report arising from a special study on implementing comprehensive land claims agreements in Canada. In their concluding remarks, the senators wrote: "Signatory nations to comprehensive land claims agreements have every right to expect their treaties will be respected and the commitments made therein will be honoured. All Canadians, Aboriginal and non-Aboriginal alike, have the right to expect that when the Government of Canada makes solemn commitments, it will, in good faith, keep its promises."[38]

The report also states that failure to implement these modern treaties disrespects their intent and objectives and is "as destructive of the process of reconciliation as some of the larger and more explosive controversies."[39] The report closes with a quotation from one of the committee's witnesses: "Failure to faithfully implement the provisions of these treaties as negotiated puts Canada at risk of generating new legends of broken treaty promises for our country. This is not a trivial matter."[40]

Do Indigenous peoples have options for confronting this inequity, besides political agitation? The Inuit of Nunavut (NTI) chose in 2006 to go to court with a billion-dollar implementation-failure lawsuit.[41] Canada settled out of court with NTI in 2015. Other treaty groups may follow NTI's lead.

Canada's Supreme Court has ruled that Indigenous treaties are *sui generis*, meaning they no longer have the status of international treaties. This view is fiercely disputed by Indigenous groups that signed treaties during the colonial period, when the treaties undoubtedly would have had international status.[42] It is only over time that settler governments have "domesticated" the agreements.[43] The principle of independent and final adjudication of treaty disputes still has merit, although no such tribunal operates in any Arctic state. In his 1999 report to the United Nations, special rapporteur Miguel Alfonso Martinez recommended that all colonial states create bipartite courts to address treaty implementation issues.[44] But that will not happen in Canada. Having treaty disputes decided by a Supreme Court, all nine of whose judges have been appointed by only *one* of the treaty's parties, seems, on the face of it, to be profoundly unfair. There are other interesting models for this sort of dispute resolution, and it is unfortunate that Canada does not look to them. For example, New Zealand in 1975 established the Treaty of Waitangi Tribunal, a binational and bilingual court to adjudicate disputes. The tribunal is independent, but its judgments are not final: they are reported to New Zealand's cabinet simply as recommendations.[45]

To its credit, Canada's Supreme Court in the 2014 *Tsilhqot'in* case recognized for the first time a nation's Aboriginal title without the negotiation of a treaty. Moreover, as noted, BC Supreme Court Justice Vickers's rulings in this case indicate that Indian "nations," not Indian Act "bands," are the legitimate owners of land and governance rights. That said, the Supreme Court has yet to define Aboriginal self-government rights under Section 35 of the constitution.

Inches of Jurisdiction

When southern Canadians spare a thought for land claims or northern treaties, they tend to think of the concrete aspect of the agreements: actual land. They pay less attention to the more abstract concept of jurisdiction. In British policy, as set out in the Royal Proclamation of 1763, land and jurisdiction go together. To hold vast lands, one must have the power to make rules about their use; otherwise, what would be the point? As it happens, intellectuals in Europe, the United States, and Canada have argued for centuries about whether Indigenous people have the capacity to govern and administer their own lands.

In 1519, Spanish conquistador Hernán Cortés invaded Mexico. After a campaign of atrocities and torture against Indigenous populations, Cortés kidnapped the emperor Montezuma and destroyed Tenochtitlán, capital of the Aztec Confederacy of 11 million people. Ever since, col-onizers have criticized Indigenous governments as weak and ineffective, even though we now know that in 1521, Tenochtitlán was the world's largest city – one governed effectively by Indigenous Americans.[46]

In 1831, in *Cherokee Nation v. Georgia*, the Cherokee asked the US Supreme Court to recognize them as a foreign state, given that they were signatories of international treaties. Chief Justice John Marshall ruled against the Cherokee, stating, "Their relation to the United States re-sembles that of a ward to his guardian."[47] But in a subsequent Cherokee case, *Worcester v. Georgia* (1832), Marshall found in their favour: "The Cherokee nation, then, is a distinct community, occupying its own ter-ritory, with boundaries accurately described, in which the laws of Georgia can have no force." Together, these two statements about federal responsibility for Indians and the absence of any state authority over them form what might be called the Marshall Doctrine, which took effect on both sides of the Canada–US border.

As Canada opened up its western regions with a transcontinental railway, it negotiated a series of numbered treaties. At Fort Carlton in 1876, Cree chiefs met with federal treaty commissioners to negotiate Treaty Six, an event full of international ceremony and solemnity.[48] Yet that same year, Parliament passed the Indian Act, which completed the transformation of Indian nations from allies of Britain and France into wards of the Canadian state.

Ninety-five years later, Senator Henry Jackson, sponsor of the Alaska Native Claims Settlement Act, did not want to see racial "enclaves" es-tablished in Alaska. So Congress outlawed tribal governments and mandated instead the establishment of state-regulated Native corpora-tions, thereby overturning the Marshall Doctrine and severing Alaskan tribal government from Alaskan tribal lands. Under ANCSA, in an echo of the Dawes Act, Alaskan Native villagers received shares in both a regional corporation and a village corporation.[49] But the idea of tribal government in Alaska did not die completely. In his ten-year review of the Alaska lands settlement for the Alaska Federation of Natives (AFN),

Thomas R. Berger recommended the restoration of tribal government as the means to protect their lands.[50] In a contrasting view, Donald Mitchell, author of *Take My Land, Take My Life,* an excellent history of the Alaskan land claim, dismissed Berger as a romantic.[51] For modernizers like Mitchell, ANCSA and corporate Natives represent the future, and tribal governments and "Indian country" are remnants of Alaska's past.

In late 2016, University of Alaska professor Dalee Dorough called my attention to an article titled "Placing Land into Trust in Alaska: Issues and Opportunities" by Geoffrey D. Strommer, Stephen D. Osborne, and Craig A. Jacobson.[52] In analyzing a significant court ruling on Indian land trusts, the authors explain that US federal law allows the interior secretary to acquire lands in trust "for the purpose of providing land for Indians." However, Alaskans had been excluded until a 2013 federal court decision struck down the "Alaska exception," holding that it discriminated against Alaska tribes:

> The opportunity to potentially place land-into-trust in Alaska could be a game changer: a shift in ownership and land tenure that brings enhanced tribal jurisdiction and opportunities for economic development, cultural resource protection, and the exercise of tribal sovereignty ... Several implementation issues and concerns will need to be resolved, and Alaska tribes will want to participate in this resolution process and ensure a fair and efficient land-to-trust policy and procedure in Alaska.[53]

The scale of the 1971 Alaskan land settlement galvanized First Nations, Inuit, and Métis negotiators in Canada, but Congress's insistence on corporate, as opposed to tribal, governance came as a huge disappointment. The structure of Alaska Native corporations differs from that of US business corporations in that, under ANCSA, each shareholder has only one vote. Indigenous Canadians prefer the cultural familiarity of Aboriginal self-government.[54]

Yukon First Nations negotiated Canada's first "third-order" Aboriginal self-government agreements with the government of Canada and the Yukon territorial government. Third-order means that Aboriginal groups are to be recognized as a third tier of government (the other two being Ottawa and the provinces). The Yukon self-government agreements recognize both local and quasi-provincial powers for that territory's First Nations. Douglas McArthur, a professor of public policy at Simon Fraser University, characterized these "unique and innovative" agreements as new templates for the federal government as it undertook self-government negotiations with First Nations, especially in BC and the NWT.[55] The Yukon self-government provisions have the following elements: agreements and First Nation governments replace the Indian Act and band governments; each claims settlement includes self-government chapters, although these are excluded from Section 35 protection; and First Nation governments have the authority of municipalities as well as – and this is *the* important point – many of the powers of provinces and territories.

The 1999 Nisga'a Treaty recognized tribal title to 2,019 square kilometres of land and guaranteed $190 million in capital.[56] Building on the 1992 Yukon model of self-government agreements, the Nisga'a reversed the historical trend of Indigenous disempowerment by negotiating province-like powers into their treaty, with the support of the governing provincial NDP and the federal Liberal government. BC provincial opposition leader Gordon Campbell had denounced the Nisga'a self-government chapter for creating a "race-based" government and asked the BC Supreme Court to declare the treaty unconstitutional. Rejecting Campbell's argument, the Court stated that self-government "rights cannot be extinguished, but they may be defined [given content] in a treaty. The Nisga'a Final Agreement does the latter expressly."[57] In effect, the self-government model developed in the Canadian North was tested and validated in BC's Supreme Court.

Ironically, the leading court case on Aboriginal self-government is named *Campbell*, after the man who lost it. But Campbell did not call it quits. On becoming the Liberal premier of British Columbia, he appealed the decision in the court of public opinion with a province-wide referendum on Aboriginal self-government. Campbell's 2002 referendum proposed that "Aboriginal self-government should have the characteristics of local government, with powers delegated from Canada and British Columbia."[58] Begging to differ, during the referendum debate I publicly suggested that the vital interests of Indigenous British Columbians and Yukoners lay not in municipal works, dirt roads, and dog bylaws, but in the lands and waters around their villages. Through the treaties negotiated between 1973 and 1992, the Yukon First Nations retain a portion of their tribal lands, mineral rights, taxation and land-use planning powers, as well as co-management of fish and game resources. Canadians usually think of these powers as "provincial," which is a problem – especially for provincial cabinets, which are even less willing to share jurisdiction than federal ministers.

Of the minority of British Columbians (35.84 percent) who actually voted on Campbell's proposition, most endorsed it.[59] However, faced with the determination of First Nations and the Yukon precedents, the BC Liberal government could not maintain this position at the negotiating table. Although Campbell backed down on the issue, progress towards the restoration of Indigenous government has been painfully slow. At the current rate, BC will still be negotiating treaties in the twenty-third century.

In 2015, after eighteen years of negotiations, the NWT community of Déline achieved the first community self-government pact. Yet here's an astonishing fact: twenty years after Yukon First Nations negotiated Canada's first tribal self-government agreements with the territorial and federal governments, those SGAs still represent almost half of *all* such agreements in the country. If it takes twenty years to negotiate each treaty, and another couple of decades to implement it, beneficiaries face the prospect of growing old before anything changes. That would surely have a depressing and demoralizing effect on northern Indigenous citizens, and their non-Indigenous counterparts as well.

Self-Government

Twelve hundred years ago a volcano erupted at White River near today's Alaska–Yukon border. The resulting sea of ash covered 250,000 square kilometres.[60] This may have been what forced the area's Dene populations to search for a new homeland in the south, where they formed a new nation – the Navajo. Today, the Navajo Nation (Diné Bikéyah) governs a territory of more than 71,000 square kilometres in Arizona, New Mexico, and Utah, with a growing population of over 250,000, making it the largest First Nation in the United States.[61] On the Canadian side of the Alaska–Yukon border, the White River First Nation today claims fewer than 200 members.[62]

As a matter of right, the Diné would say they own a right to govern themselves. But is the White River First Nation – a tiny Yukon village on the Alaska border – entitled to self-government? Assimilationists like Tom Flanagan would say no; for them, size matters. First Nation lawyer Debra Hanuse strongly disagrees. As a former treaty commissioner and chief of the 'Namgis Nation, Hanuse feels that size should *not* be a factor when it comes to a jurisdictional right. According to Hanuse, "the only time that size matters" is when examining questions of administrative capacity and "the practicalities of who pays for what."[63] Peace and prosperity reign in self-governing First Nations such as the Champagne-Aishiak and the Teslin Tlingit, in contrast to the evident poverty of most Indian Act bands. Self-governing First Nations demonstrate the confidence, optimism, and resilience characteristic of young people in the springtime of their lives. Self-government has been truly transformative. But unfortunately, outside of the North, few people even know these self-government agreements exist.

Despite the 1982 addition of Section 35 to Canada's Constitution, arguments persist about the right of Aboriginal peoples to self-government. With the adoption of Section 35, Canada resolved to append modern treaties to the Constitution, thereby ensuring that the agreement of all parties would be required to alter a treaty's provisions. That promise seems to have been kept. But what might it mean that Canada has failed to negotiate more than a handful of self-government agreements over the last two decades? Perhaps from an irrational fear of the unknown, politicians in Ottawa and the provinces have effectively blocked the pathways to Aboriginal jurisdiction, self-government, or sovereignty. The facts on the ground in Yukon, the NWT, and BC suggest there is little to fear, especially given that Ottawa still has its fingers tightly wound around the federal purse. But if the current impasse continues, Idle No More, or its successors, will be with Canadians for some years yet. Then as now, the opposite of self-government is the colonialism embodied in the *Indian Act*.

In Louise Erdrich's 2012 National Book Award–winning novel *The Round House*, Bazil, a tribal judge and the book's central character, spends his working life trying to reclaim Indigenous jurisdiction in the United States inch by inch.[64] Indigenous law expert John Borrows believes that in some ways, the situation facing American tribes is better than that of their Canadian counterparts. He writes: "Tribal power in the United States flows from a legally recognized, autonomous, and inherent source of sovereignty that existed before the country's creation and survives to the present day. While this authority is subject to the judicially created federal plenary power to regulate Native American affairs and is constrained by legislative restrictions crafted in this light, tribes still possess substantial inherent powers related to their internal governance."[65]

In the northernmost regions of North America, negotiators for Indigenous groups regained much Indigenous jurisdiction along with collective title to thousands of square kilometres of land. Although the pace of jurisdictional progress has been glacial, the exchange and marriage of Indigenous and settler ideas at land claims tables has been a profoundly character-building process for Arctic residents, both Indigenous and settler, making self-government an all-too-rare good news story from the Canadian Arctic. The northern land claims and self-government negotiations have transformed the region's identity, making its people more confident, open-minded, tolerant, and patient.

Land claims and self-government negotiations pitted Indigenous communities against the federal state. At those tables in the Far North, Indigenous leaders began to deal as well with settler politicians, and that has made all the difference. Yet Aboriginal self-government, born in the northern bush, seems to be dying in southern Canada. Some observers now suggest that the "certainty" of northern treaties is an illusion in southern Canada and that governments should seek new forms of on-going reconciliation.

The November 2015 election of Justin Trudeau as prime minister has sharply raised expectations in Canada's Indigenous communities. But achieving real change will take courage, energy, and imagination on the government's part. Unless the federal and provincial governments muster the will to reconcile Crown and Aboriginal title, major economic projects may die on the drawing board. Ottawa telling First Nations they cannot have much federal jurisdiction, while assuring the provinces that Canada will support them in resisting First Nation claims for provincial powers, will not work any more.

4

No Settler Need Apply
The Arctic Council

The uninvited press their noses to the ferns of frosted glass,
peering at the council fire inside.

n 1985, our minority NDP government in Yukon spent its first few months in office wrestling with two crises: the social crisis of collapsed land claims negotiations and the economic crisis that followed the closing of all the territory's operating mines. Working together over several months with investors, banks, and federal ministers David Crombie and Erik Nielsen, we eventually reopened our largest mine, the lead-zinc operation at Faro. Part of this effort involved my travelling to Japan and Korea for meetings with shipping, smelting, and trading companies, with the view to getting our mineral concentrates back into Asian markets.

Rushing by car from head office to head office, I was delighted to see the Yukon flag flying at the front door of every corporate tower. Later, a Mitsui trader confided that, using an encyclopedia image, a seamstress had sewn a single flag the night before my arrival, and whenever I set out for an appointment a company motorcyclist raced ahead of our car to hoist it at the building just before our arrival.

Debates about rotating chairs, permanent participants, and observers at the international forum known as the Arctic Council remind me of that experience. The organization is still a work in progress, and there always seems to be somebody sewing a flag for a new Arctic Council observer and messengers racing to hoist it before the next host in the circumpolar rotation takes the chair. Unfortunately, the Arctic Council, which has opened itself to numerous outsiders, is not yet open to all northerners. That is a major institutional failure and a grave insult to the Arctic's settler majority and to the legislators who represent them.

Origins

As noted earlier, at Murmansk on October 1, 1987, Mikhail Gorbachev outlined six radical proposals for turning the Arctic from a Cold War theatre of conflict into a zone of peace. The Soviet leader's proposals included a nuclear-free zone in Europe; restrictions on naval operations off the shores of northern Europe; joint initiatives on northern resources, including Canadian and Norwegian assistance in developing energy resources in the Soviet Arctic; cooperation on scientific research and recognition of Indigenous interests; an integrated plan to protect the North's natural environment; and the opening of the Northern Sea Route to foreign ships on the condition that they hire Soviet icebreakers for their transit of Russian waters.

Initially, Canada and the United States responded without enthusiasm to Gorbachev's proposals. Even with their lacklustre response, however, two elements – those concerning peace and the environment – attracted considerable interest in Northern European countries as well as among environmentalists, peace activists, and Arctic political leaders in North America.

Small countries can sometimes play a large role on the world stage, and at that moment Finland, a nation of 5 million people, stepped up. As Russia's northern neighbours and former subjects, Finns had long been sensitive to shifts in the Russian mood, and for them, Gorbachev's "zone of peace" speech counted as a strong mood swing. The Soviet Union based its Northern Fleet, including nuclear-powered submarines, at Murmansk, not far from the Finnish–Russian border, and it conducted numerous nuclear tests on Novaya Zemlya, on the Barents Sea. With the Cold War coming to end and Soviet warships rusting nearby, Finnish fears mutated from anxieties about nuclear war to alarm about radionuclide wastes. With good reason, Finland immediately took note of Gorbachev's environmental proposal, and the Finnish Initiative was the result.

The time seemed right to discuss a common action plan for the Arctic environment. One day after Gorbachev's speech, Finland's president Mauno Koivisto suggested that Gorbachev's aims could be met by creating a joint program for environmental and scientific cooperation.[1] Former Finnish prime minister Kalevi Sorsa, with diplomatic and scientific support, pitched the plan to the foreign ministries of the other seven Arctic states. Sorsa wrote to his colleagues about the deteriorating Arctic environment, the growing fragility of Arctic regional ecosystems, and the need for multilateral environmental management.[2]

Predictably, Finland's Nordic neighbours, also relatively small nation-states, responded positively. Finland persuaded the initially skeptical Norway to come on board, and the latter country soon became one of the group's most active members. The united Nordic front, with support from the Soviet Union and a new Liberal government in Canada, brought even the "laggard" United States around to support the initiative.[3]

Over the coming years, the proposed Arctic Sustainable Development Strategy evolved into the Arctic Environmental Protection Strategy (AEPS), whose program and component activities began to take shape. The Norwegian government agreed to lead negotiations to establish an Arctic Monitoring and Assessment Program (AMAP), which eventually became a key element of the AEPS.[4]

In Canada, scientists had recently discovered high levels of persistent organic pollutants (POPs) in the blood of northerners subsisting on country foods. It was clear from the chemical makeup of these pollutants that they had been carried north from southern industrial sources. For the Canadian Inuit, this finding about airborne pollution rang alarm bells. Mary Simon, president of the Inuit Circumpolar Council (ICC), responded quickly to the problem, leading a delegation of ICC executives to Moscow for a face-to-face meeting with Gorbachev. During their conversation, she invited Inuit from the Soviet Union to attend the ICC's 1989 annual general meeting. Gorbachev immediately supported this visit, which would be the first for the Russian Inuit.

The Finnish Initiative began with a consultative meeting in Rovaniemi, Lapland, in September 1989. After two rounds of negotiations, a draft of the AEPS emerged; it would be adopted two years later. The AEPS's objectives were to ensure the health and well-being of Arctic ecosystems; to provide for the protection and enhancement of environmental quality and the sustainable utilization of resources (including by Arctic peoples); to fully accommodate Indigenous perspectives, values, and practices; and to enable countries to fulfil their national and international responsibilities in a sustainable and equitable manner.[5]

During the Cold War, when military considerations dominated, experts, politicians, and reporters viewed the Arctic as composed of the five coastal states ringing the Arctic Ocean: Canada, Denmark, Norway, Russia, and the United States. With this AEPS initiative, the Finns deliberately expanded the circle to include themselves, Sweden, and Iceland, along with three (later six) Indigenous participants. With the end of the Cold War and the dismantling of many East–West boundaries, the eight states came to a greater appreciation of their common interests. With the Inuit occupying the northern regions of four Arctic states, and the Sámi dwelling in the Arctic areas of three Nordic nations plus Russia, the growing political role of Indigenous actors in the Arctic's emerging theatre became obvious, especially at the crossroads of economic highways and environmental pathways.

The eight Arctic states and three northern Indigenous peoples' organizations – the Inuit Circumpolar Council, the Sámi Council, and the Russian Association of Indigenous Peoples of the North, Far East, and Siberia – signed the AEPS. While it first focused on environmental protection, the strategy gradually expanded to related fields, notably sustainable development.

North America had reacted coldly to Gorbachev's peace initiative; however, Canada liked the general idea of collaboration with its Soviet neighbour. One such project, Polar Bridge, involved a binational team skiing from Severnaya Zemlya across the North Pole to Ellesmere Island.[6] Canadian prime minister Brian Mulroney showed serious interest in such projects and, increasingly, in the Arctic in general. On a visit to the Soviet Union in November 1989, Mulroney signed a formal agreement on scientific cooperation.[7] Addressing the Arctic and Antarctic Institute in Leningrad, he spoke about the possibility of Canada and the Soviet Union building on their environmental and scientific cooperation to collaborate on a wider set of economic and social issues. He then posed the big question: "Why not a council of Arctic countries eventually coming into existence to coordinate and promote cooperation among them?"[8]

Mulroney loved international organizations – and, no doubt, the opportunities they provided a harried prime minister to get out of Ottawa while Parliament was sitting. In November 1986 he had flown to Paris for the founding meeting of La Francophonie, which French president François Mitterrand described as the French "equivalent of the British Commonwealth."[9] And in 1989 Mulroney took Canada into the Organization of American States.

(Since the end of the Cold War, East–West links around the circumpolar North have multiplied "like mushrooms after a rain."[10] Political leaders, chiefs, and legislators met in Anchorage in 1991 to form the Northern Forum, an organization of regional governments, including those in Alaska, Yukon, and the NWT. The Circumpolar Education Ministers' Conference, which included Russia, Alaska, the NWT, Quebec, and Yukon had a short, asymmetrical life in the 1980s; in 2001, universities, colleges, and research institutes formed a collaborative network, the University of the Arctic (UArctic), to promote viable communities and sustainable economies. The Circumpolar Agricultural Conference, which initially focused on food production, reinvented itself by combining with the UArctic Inaugural Northern Food Summit to address food security issues. The Summit held its ninth conference on food security in 2016.)

Following Prime Minister Mulroney's proposal, various disputes shaped the run-up to the launch of the Arctic Council. Some of these set Canada against the United States, given that the two states viewed the Arctic quite differently. For the United States, after the Cold War, Alaska and the Arctic were minor issues; for Canada, the Great White North was fundamental to the country's sense of itself.

Although the majority of Alaskans remain undeclared or "Independent" in terms of voter registration, the state generally votes Republican, and in Arctic negotiations during the 1990s, Washington reflected the views of Alaska's two US senators, Ted Stevens and Frank Murkowski.[11] For example, these two Republicans would not agree to include military security questions on Arctic Council agendas. They also insisted on representation for Athabaskan or northern Dene chiefs. Working out the issues between Canada and the United States therefore took some time.

Eventually, on September 19, 1996, representatives of the eight Arctic states met in Canada's capital to approve the Ottawa Declaration, which formally created the Arctic Council. As Foreign Affairs Minister Lloyd Axworthy wrote: "The Arctic Council is a case where eight states (Canada, Russia, Finland, Iceland, Norway, Sweden, Denmark and the United States) and elements of civil society came together relatively quickly to replace a Cold War framework of non-engagement and military competition in the Arctic with one of multipolar co-operation and collaborative agenda-setting."[12] The AEPS was subsumed by the Arctic Council, but its agenda survived:

> The representatives of the Governments of Canada, Denmark, Finland, Iceland, Norway, the Russian Federation, Sweden and the United States of America (hereinafter referred to as the Arctic states) meeting in Ottawa;
>
> Affirm our commitment to the well-being of the inhabitants of the Arctic, including recognition of the special relationship and unique contributions to the Arctic of Indigenous people and their communities;
>
> Affirm our commitment to sustainable development in the Arctic region, including economic and social development, improved health conditions and cultural well-being;

Affirm concurrently our commitment to the protection of the Arctic environment, including the health of Arctic ecosystems, maintenance of biodiversity in the Arctic region and conservation and sustainable use of natural resources.[13]

Because many Arctic issues were acquiring global significance by that time, most of the action as the Arctic Council evolved took place far from the Arctic's towns and villages. But these northern communities were not untouched by events such as climate change and the opening of new shipping routes, both of which would be addressed in the years to come by important Arctic Council publications.

Months before the report's publication, it was known that the 2004 *Arctic Climate Impact Assessment (ACIA)* would predict profound impacts in the Arctic region, especially the shrinking of the polar ice cap and the potential extinction of ice-dependent species, such as walrus and polar bears. The United States tried in 2003 and 2004 to block *ACIA*-related policy recommendations but failed so completely[14] that the *ACIA* eventually became the most widely read policy document in Arctic history, as its author, University of Alaska geography professor Lawson Brigham, told me.

An initiative led by Canada, Finland, and the United States, the Arctic Marine Shipping Assessment (AMSA) process, involved shipping companies, ship designers, shipbuilders, ship classification societies, marine insurers, non-commercial partnerships, and shipping associations in the development of a comprehensive report for the Arctic Council in 2009. The *AMSA Report*, a consensus document approved by the Arctic Council ministers, made seventeen much-studied recommendations regarding which ministers would receive implementation reports at Nuuk in 2011 and Kiruna in 2013. Lawson Brigham, AMSA's principal author, believes that the ongoing monitoring of AMSA's recommendations reflects how important the AMSA document is. Few Arctic Council reports receive that kind of attention. "This monitoring is critical follow-up to AMSA and one of the only real implementation plans of any of the Arctic Council's many major studies," Brigham told me in correspondence.

Until 2011 at Nuuk, when the eight Arctic states adopted the Agreement on Co-operation on Aeronautical and Maritime Search and Rescue
(AAMSAR), the Arctic Council functioned largely as a policy-shaping
body. By negotiating AAMSAR, the eight ministers effectively transformed the Arctic Council into a policy-*making* body, one with new
confidence as well as a permanent secretariat in Tromsø, Norway. It is
important to remember, though, that AAMSAR and the subsequent
Agreement on Oil Spill Prevention and Pollution, while negotiated under
the auspices of the Arctic Council, are not Arctic Council agreements.
The Arctic Council remains a "soft law" body with no legal character.
Its decisions serve as "recommendations" to the member-states, which
are under no formal obligation to implement them.

Permanent Participants

The formation of the Arctic Council was a major victory for the Inuit
Circumpolar Conference and the Sámi Council. Since their beginnings,
these two international Indigenous organizations had promoted the idea
of a peaceful and cooperative circumpolar North – and, more recently,
a sustainable one. For them, winning status as permanent participants
in an international body was a huge breakthrough. As ICC president
Rosemarie Kuptana put it, the Arctic Council affirmed "the right of Inuit
to participate in the management and development of the Arctic and
its resources."[15] Finnish political scientist Monica Tennberg points out
that in Arctic Council negotiations, the permanent participants – the
ICC especially – did better than environmental advocates.[16]

When the UN World Commission on Environment and Development
published *Our Common Future*, commonly known as the Brundtland
Report, in 1987, the balancing of economic and environmental values
quickly captured the public's imagination, especially in the Canadian
North. Shortly afterwards, the Inuit Circumpolar Council incorporated
sustainability into its policies. Northerners so thoroughly embraced
Bruntland's recommendations that all northern Canadian land claims
treaties finalized after 1987 incorporate the values of sustainability.

Former Canadian foreign minister Lloyd Axworthy credited in particular Mary Simon, a remarkable Inuit leader, with the early successes of the Arctic Council, writing that she was the "single most crucial driving force behind the creation of the Council."[17] In 1996, Axworthy had appointed Simon as Canada's chief negotiator in the Arctic Council formation process. She represented Canada as Senior Arctic Official on the Arctic Council and became the country's first Arctic Ambassador. Other Indigenous leaders played important roles, but Simon contributed as an early respondent to Gorbachev's zone-of-peace proposal. She also played a key role in getting Pertti Paasio, the Finnish foreign minister, to invite Finland's Indigenous leaders into the AEPS discussions between 1989 and 1991. These discussions had been instigated, in part, by the Finns' awareness that Northern Sámi populations were vulnerable to the same air- and water-borne toxins as the Inuit in Canada. So it only made sense that both affected communities be involved.

Simon helped draft the ICC's founding document and became its president in 1986. In July 1989, after her petition to Gorbachev, Indigenous representatives from the Soviet Union attended the ICC General Assembly for the first time. At the "Protecting the Arctic Environment" preparatory meeting in Yellowknife in April 1990, Simon attended as an "observer" but inserted herself into the diplomats' discussions to assert that the Inuit needed a voice at the table because they were consuming toxic foods.[18]

At a private breakfast with ministers at Nuuk in 1993, Inuit, Sámi, and Russian Indigenous leaders complained so forcefully about their exclusion from meetings of senior Arctic officials that the ministers decided to bring them to the table. According to Terry Fenge, a long-time adviser to Indigenous organizations, "this was the genesis of Permanent Participant status, first officially referred to in the 1996 Inuvik AEPS declaration." In 1993 the AEPS recognized the pivotal role of Indigenous peoples in "environmental management and development."[19] Eventually, as noted, the AEPS was folded into the Arctic Council.

Normally, senior Arctic officials lead Arctic Council discussions (except at the biennial ministerial meetings). Those discussions include representatives of international Indigenous organizations recognized by the council as permanent participants, who have consultation rights in the council's negotiations and decisions – a unique status in international forums. Currently, the permanent participants are the Aleut International Association (from Russia and the United States); the Arctic Athabaskan Council and the Gwich'in Council International (from Canada and the United States); the Inuit Circumpolar Council (encompassing Canada, Greenland, Russia, and the United States); the Russian Association of Indigenous Peoples of the North (RAIPON); and the Sámi Council (representing Finland, Norway, Russia, and Sweden). Observer states and organizations also attend Council meetings.

The Inuit and Sámi had established international organizations long before the Arctic Council was founded, so they were well prepared for international engagement. The issue of permanent participants caused some disagreement between the Americans and the Canadians, however.[20] As far as the ICC and Canada were concerned, the three Arctic Indigenous permanent participants involved in the AEPS process were enough for the Arctic Council: together, the Inuit (through the ICC), the Sámi Council, and RAIPON represented more than forty different Indigenous nations, all of whom qualified as Arctic inhabitants. However, in part because the Inuit are a minority of Alaska's Indigenous population, the Americans insisted that all of Alaska's Indigenous people be represented. The US government insisted that Alaska's Dene chiefs and Aleut be included. The admission as permanent participants of the Aleut, the Athabaskans, and the Gwich'in would require those groups to form purpose-built organizations; even so, the Americans, partly in response to strong lobbying, wanted them inside the tent.[21] Besides all this, US officials had problems with the term "Indigenous peoples," fearing that it implied recognition of a right to self-determination. Moreover, the Americans also wanted to include, as observers, environmental groups that were opposed to traditional Inuit hunting – yet another source of tension.[22]

Norway's foreign minister Thorvald Stoltenberg expressed far more interest in the environment and disarmament than he did in Indigenous issues, but he did not oppose participation by Indigenous leaders. By 1993, Denmark had agreed to finance an Indigenous Peoples' Secretariat in Copenhagen. Eventually, the Americans and others succeeded at their lobbying for two Athabaskan groups, the Gwich'in Council International and the Arctic Athabaskan Council, to be accepted as permanent participants. The Gwich'in represent the communities of Arctic Village, Chalkyitsik, Fort Yukon, Birtch, Circle, and Venetie in Alaska; Old Crow (Vuntut Gwich'in) in Yukon; and four communities in the NWT: Tsiigehtchic, Aklavik, Inuvik, and Fort McPherson (Teet'lit Zheh). The Arctic Athabaskan Council represents dozens of Dene communities in Alaska, Yukon, and the NWT.

Permanent participants on the Arctic Council serve in much the same way as member-states. Terry Fenge, who sadly passed away in November 2015, often spoke to me of the challenges faced by permanent participants, who have contributed enormously to the council's work but are inadequately funded by the member-states.[23] There have been many initiatives, dating back to a 2004 report during the Icelandic chairmanship, aimed at overcoming this challenge. Indeed, every ministerial declaration of the council has recognized the need to provide more support to permanent participants, and observers applying for membership are assessed based on their "willingness and ability" to provide them with financial support. Despite this, the problem has persisted. The permanent participants came together to work on creating an endowed foundation to be known as the Algu Fund; this was formally established in January 2017. This will be an important tool, in part because, notes Jim Gamble, executive director of the Aleut International Association, the permanent participants do not agree on all issues.[24] Moreover, some see a widening gap between senior Arctic officials and the working groups.[25]

Regional Governments

On September 18, 2015, the Munk–Gordon Arctic Security Program brought twenty-four Arctic scholars and policy-thinkers from around the circumpolar world to the University of Toronto to examine the issue of Arctic regional governments. The Munk–Gordon invitation read:

> At the front lines of the decisions made for the Arctic regions are municipalities, territorial and state governments, and Indigenous organizations and governments. How do these subnational actors and governments from within the Arctic participate in international diplomacy which could result in outcomes that affect them? With no formal role on the Arctic Council, which is often regarded as the main platform for international Arctic diplomacy, how do these regional governments engage in international affairs in the Arctic? What does the future of the Arctic look like, and how will these subnational and regional governments be involved?[26]

When the time came to consider the place of regional governments on the Arctic Council, the decision unfortunately confirmed the worst fears of northern settlers. Terry Fenge, who had attended the 1999 Washington meeting at which the Northern Forum, the organization representing northern regional governments, made an unsuccessful bid for admission, reported on the discussion in a talk presented at the University of Toronto gathering in September 2015:

> When the United States was chairing the Arctic Council from 1998 to 2000, we had a meeting in the large boardroom at the State Department in Washington, D.C., and there was a high-powered delegation from the Northern Forum, which included the governor of Sakha Republic and senior representatives of Alaska. And I remember this very well, because there were representatives of the states and representatives of the Arctic indigenous peoples sitting in the main floor of the boardroom. The Northern Forum delegates were on a podium. And what the Northern Forum delegates did, in a very clumsy and challenging way, was to say that they were more legitimate in terms of the interests of the North than the people who were actually meeting. This was interpreted at the time by the Arctic

indigenous people as an unwarranted challenge and attack on their legitimacy.[27]

Listening to Fenge's talk, I wondered whether I had played a small role in that turn of events. At a pre-1992 Northern Forum event in Alaska hosted by Governor Wally Hickel, I had been approached in my capacity as Yukon premier by Dalee Sambo, then of the International Union for Circumpolar Health, who believed that her organization had a contribution to make to the forum. She told me that Governor Hickel had declined to allow her or the IUCH to participate in the Northern Forum meeting, telling her that he represented all Alaskans, or words to that effect. (Although Hickel had received only 38.8 percent of the popular vote in the previous election for governor, he was technically correct.) Recognizing the concerns of health care providers in relation to Arctic Indigenous peoples, I allowed Sambo to take the floor as part of the Yukon delegation so that she could explain her organization's objectives and express its interest in the forum's work. I felt that at a minimum, inclusiveness was a more constructive approach than exclusion, but Governor Hickel was not pleased, which I regret. Terry Fenge may have been correct that the Northern Forum shot itself in the foot with its presentation, which allowed the permanent participants to oppose the forum's participation on the Arctic Council. But that doesn't let the member-states, especially Canada and the United States, off the hook.

Former Alaska governor and Northern Forum founding president Steve Cowper still has harsh words for federal officials, whom he accuses of southern liberal and statist bias. As he wrote to me in October 2013: "[On November 19, 1999,] when the Northern Forum was rejected as a participant in the Arctic Council, the Forum represented Arctic regional governments from Norway, Sweden, Finland, the Soviet Union (Russia), Canada and the United States, plus Northern regional governments that could be accurately described as sub-Arctic, from Japan, China, and Mongolia. The members themselves provided the funding for the Forum."

Cowper regretted that a more regionally appropriate requirement for admission to the council had not been adopted from the beginning: "Perhaps, as a qualification, the Arctic Council members should have been required to spend a winter in Kaktovik or Pond Inlet or Tiksi, and to eat the Indigenous fare."

As Cowper noted, members of the Northern Forum felt strongly that their members – regional governors and legislators – were far better informed and able to comment on policies proposed by the Arctic Council than were federal appointees from the distant national capitals, who often had little or no knowledge of the areas they purported to represent. "In fairness," Cowper wrote, "the regional governments generally expected little if any meaningful action from the Arctic Council, beyond creating a monopoly on policy recommendations and issuing gooey proclamations that resulted in no meaningful action whatsoever. In this the regional governments were not disappointed."

When South Africa became ungovernable in the 1980s, its leaders started to negotiate with the imprisoned Nelson Mandela. They wanted to know his intentions towards the settler minority. "I told them," Mandela wrote in his autobiography, "that whites were Africans as well and that, in any future dispensation, the majority would need the minority."[28] Regrettably, there was no Mandela in the room when the Arctic Council rejected the application of the Northern Forum.

Settlers represent about half the population of Canada's Far North and the majority in Alaska. Many of them have lived for generations in Alaska, Yukon, and the NWT. In all other Arctic countries – with the exception of the future country, Greenland – the majority of northern citizens are non-Indigenous. At the time of its rejection by the Arctic Council, the Northern Forum had already shown some promise in representing the views of regional, state, and territorial governments, some of which had both Indigenous and settler representatives in their delegations.

The admission of Indigenous permanent participants to the Arctic Council cheered northern Canadians, who had spent decades at land claims tables trying to reconcile Indigenous and non-Indigenous communities. But they were puzzled to discover that for the Arctic nation-states, including Canada, and perhaps also for some Indigenous groups, the Northern Forum's constituency did not count. The decision to exclude non-Indigenous residents from the Arctic Council may not have been intentionally divisive, but in some cases that was the effect. As Fenge noted in a 2013 report, "certainly the Council has made little effort to engage sub-national Arctic governments."[29] However, Fenge told the September 2015 University of Toronto conference that northern regional governments have "a lot of work to do before ... those interests will be welcomed in, I think."[30] This continuing view of northern settlers as unwashed rednecks, I regret to say, reflects a very southern point of view, one shared by urban liberals of *all* political stripes.

Leaving settler representatives out in the cold inevitably caused northern Canadian conservatives to grumble about "Toronto Liberals" and "political correctness." As a Yukon MLA and an exponent of settler privilege, Dan Lang liked to gripe that the only way to get ahead in Canada was to be a French-speaking Native in a wheelchair. Always, that remark was meant to be light-hearted, but the resentment behind it was real. (Of course, Prime Minister Stephen Harper ultimately proved Lang wrong by appointing him to the Canadian Senate.)

Without endorsing Lang's views, it must be said that in welcoming the permanent participants onto the Arctic Council, the eight nation-states were using Indigenous representatives to validate federal governments as Arctic actors – a polite form of identity theft. At the same time, the nation-states were turning their backs on the Arctic's legislators and settler majorities. The Arctic Council will never represent the full population of the Arctic until it undoes this damage.

For several years, the Northern Forum seemed a shadow of its former self. Today, as a Yakutia, Russia-based organization under the leadership of Egor Borisov, the forum includes the Icelandic town of Akureyri and the province of Quebec as members and is regaining relevance in much of the Arctic. Alaska, a founding member of the organization and once a strong supporter, left the forum for a period but has recently agreed to return. It is possible that if the forum disappears, there will be no formal way for sub-national governments to participate on the Arctic Council. If it survives in a viable form, the Arctic Council should certainly revisit its exclusion.

The 1996 Ottawa Declaration that established the Arctic Council left room for a seventh permanent participant, and that, with a rule change, could well be the Northern Forum. If RAIPON can represent all of Russia's Indigenous communities, why can't the Northern Forum or a successor organization, with a rule change, do the same for the Arctic's regional governments or its settler majority?

In 2012, Alaska's Arctic Policy Commission published an open letter protesting that Washington was ignoring the state's top issues and that Alaska's legislators had no voice on the Arctic Council. Putting things more diplomatically, Arctic scholar Heather Exner-Pirot writes that "the Arctic Council has been a triumph in linking national policies and goals with those of Arctic Indigenous peoples – represented by Permanent Participants – in regional governance. But it can claim no such success with regional, sub-national governments."[31] Given that current Arctic Council agendas include items entirely within the jurisdiction of regional, state, and territorial governments, their absence except as observers counts as a design flaw in the council's architecture.

A breakfast meeting on October 18, 2015, during the Arctic Circle conference in Reykjavik reunited several of the September 2015 Toronto conference speakers – Tom Axworthy, Nauja Bianco, Alaska governor Bill Walker's Arctic policy adviser Craig Fleener, Christin Kristoffersen, Sigridur Kristjansdottir, Svein Ludvigsen, Greenland's Inuuteq Holm Olsen, executive director of the Northern Forum Mikhail Pogodaev, Jessica Shadian, and myself – to discuss the formation of something like a Northern Forum 2.0 that might better connect with the Arctic Council and foster cooperation on practical intergovernmental projects between the Arctic regions. Since that meeting, Lapland has rejoined the Northern Forum and Alaskans have been vigorously lobbying Canadian territorial legislators in the NWT and Nunavut to rejoin.

The Inuit and the Sámi have played constructive roles on the Arctic Council. The other permanent participants have told me that they lack the funding to hire expert researchers or to travel to enough of the working group meetings where the "heavy lifting" takes place. Were a regional government organization to be admitted on an equal basis with Indigenous groups, it might form compacts with permanent participants on regional or national issues. Research partnerships between well-funded regional governments and permanent participants with national and international clout could be one sensible solution. I have proposed, for example, that the Yukon government's Statistics Bureau work with the Arctic Athabaskan Council and Yukon chiefs on common issues that need addressing at the Arctic Council level. All parties would benefit from such collaboration, I believe.

Observers

In 2010 the Munk–Gordon Arctic Security Program was established as a partnership between the Munk School of Global Affairs at the University of Toronto and the Toronto-based Gordon Foundation. The program focused on studying and promoting four overarching areas of concern: emergency preparedness in the Arctic; Arctic peoples and security; the Arctic Council; and public opinion in and about the North.[32] The Munk–Gordon Arctic Security Conference in January 2012 discussed the future of the Arctic Council. Some attendees thought that the eight Arctic states should "do their duty" and properly fund the permanent participants.[33] One interesting idea advanced would have had the council charge observers a membership fee; this could underwrite the permanent participants' activities in working groups,[34] at a time when permanent participants felt especially vulnerable following the admission of aggressive and powerful states to the Arctic Council as observers. Unfortunately, the idea attracted no champion.

At Kiruna, Sweden, in May 2013, Canada assumed the chair of the Arctic Council, and for the second time an Inuk Canadian woman took on a leadership role in the organization. Leona Aglukkaq, at the time Nunavut's MP and Canada's health minister (and later environment minister), accepted the gavel from outgoing chair Carl Bildt, a former

Swedish prime minister. Aglukkaq presented a two-page concept paper, "Development for the People of the North," as her theme for Canada's 2013–15 chairmanship. In her first speech as chair, she spoke about business development and never once mentioned climate change.[35] At the same meeting, US secretary of state John Kerry spoke almost exclusively about climate change and its effects on the North.[36] When she was appointed chair of the Arctic Council, Aglukkaq did consult with the three territorial governments about Canada's Arctic policy. Even so, the issue of regional representation on the council was not addressed under her leadership.

For years, controversy had stormed around the applications by various non-Arctic states and the European Union for observer status on the Arctic Council. Ultimately, the following non-Arctic countries were seated as observers: France, Germany, the Netherlands, Poland, Spain, the United Kingdom, China, Italy, Japan, Korea, Singapore, and India. Supporters of these observers argued that their addition strengthened the Arctic's links to the global system.

The EU was not admitted, but it was granted preliminary observer status until the council made its final decision. Aglukkaq's government had opposed the EU's application for observer status for several years, despite – as revealed in a letter to the press – an eloquent appeal in 2013 to Stephen Harper, Canada's then prime minister, from José Manuel Barroso, president of the European Commission.[37] The deferral likely resulted from Canadian and Indigenous objections to the EU ban on the importation of seal products into the European market.

The admission of China as an observer proved far more problematic. At the Nuuk ministerial meeting in 2011, outsiders heard that the Arctic Council had adopted new rules for observer applicants: first, applicants had to respect the sovereignty of the eight Arctic states, and second, they had to respect the rights of the Indigenous peoples of those states.[38] The littoral states were also keen that China commit to the rule of law, especially the UN Convention on the Law of the Sea (UNCLOS). At two Arctic conferences I attended, one at Michigan State University and the other at the University of Lapland, Chinese representatives said they agreed with the first rule but had "no position" on the second. Despite its failure to expressly endorse the rights of Arctic Indigenous peoples, China, which is greatly interested in the Arctic opportunities provided by climate change, was admitted to the Arctic Council. Had the Arctic Council *not* admitted China, China might well have levered itself into Arctic policy debates by underwriting a rival entity such as the Arctic Circle.

The gullible may believe claims by the PRC that it has made statements in support of Indigenous rights, but consider the relevant passages from a speech by Vice Foreign Minister Zhang Ming at the China Country Session of the Third Arctic Circle Assembly in Reykjavik on October 17, 2015: "With respect to the indigenous community in the Arctic region, China respects their traditions and culture and takes seriously their concerns and needs ... Third, [we] respect the inherent rights of Arctic countries and the indigenous people."[39]

Note that this statement does *not* say that China respects the "inherent rights of indigenous peoples." It indicates merely that China respects "indigenous people" and "their traditions and culture." I have sat at Indigenous rights negotiation tables for more than thirty years, and no serious negotiator would accept these mealy-mouthed utterances as an endorsement of Indigenous or minority rights without the insertion of the word "both" between "of" and "Arctic countries" or the addition of the words "inherent rights of" immediately before the words "indigenous people." In any event, it would be naive to suggest that China, which imprisons and tortures democratic rights activists, will behave any better abroad than it does at home. If you doubt me, just ask the rights lawyer Pu Zhiqiang or the artist Ai Weiwei.

When questioned by pollsters, northern Canadians and Alaskans both objected strongly to China's admission.[40] The Inuit especially have long been concerned that the admission of powerful non-Arctic states as observers would marginalize Indigenous voices on the Arctic Council. Discussing this issue with me on Anna Maria Tremonti's CBC radio show *The Current* in 2012 – prior to the admission of those nations as Arctic Council observers – Mary Simon remained adamantly opposed to China's admission. Once a powerful nation had been admitted, Iqal-uit mayor Madeleine Redfern asked, could it ever be kicked off the council for breaking the rules? Given widespread doubts about whether China would accept the Arctic Council's rules, Redfern's question, posed at the 2012 Munk–Gordon Arctic Security Conference, was a timely one. No one at the Toronto conference believed that China would ever be expelled.

China's equivocation on Indigenous rights stands in sharp contrast to Singapore's message in its application for observer status. Singapore has engaged since its admission with Arctic Indigenous communities and permanent participants. Its Special Envoy, Ambassador Kemal Siddique, has visited the Indigenous peoples of Alaska, Nunavut, and Greenland and the Sámi communities in the Lapland region of Finland in an effort to identify the needs of the Arctic Council's permanent participants and of Arctic Indigenous communities, the better to work with them.[41]

Decisions to admit observers to the council are made at private min-isterial meetings. "As the Arctic becomes increasingly significant in international politics, to have a Chinese voice vetoed or absent would be very difficult," suggests historian John English. "There was an accept-ance, with a small amount of reluctance, to bring China in."[42]

One possible benefit of admitting China and other non-Arctic states to the Arctic Council is that those countries may now contribute to de-liberations on Arctic haze air pollution and on black carbon, a pollutant produced by the partial combustion of fossil fuels that accelerates cli-mate change through the spread of black soot on ice and snow. But black carbon surely did not decide the China question for Canada. It is quite possible that China's aggressive investment agenda was better aligned with Canada's energy development priorities than with the work of the Arctic Council. "Given the fact that China is poised to overtake the United States as the world's largest economic entity within this decade, Xi [Jinping, secretary general of the Chinese Communist Party] is gun-ning for 'a new kind of great power relationship' with the superpower," writes journalist Willy Lam. "The fast-rising quasi-superpower is using its economic and military muscle aggressively to boost its say in the global order."[43]

There may be good arguments for inviting China onto the Arctic Council as an observer, but no one from the US or Canadian governments has publicly articulated them, or broached how rejecting China might affect the credibility of the Arctic Council as a regional organization. The two governments having failed to communicate publicly on the subject, it fell to Lawson Brigham to make the case for granting China observer status. As Brigham told me, "we want China to be in the flow of information (also Japan, Korea, and others) so they have a feel for what decisions are being made in the AC. We also want China and the other non-Arctic state observers to support Arctic initiatives at various international organizations such as the IMO, WMO, International Hydrographic Organization, etc."

University of Akureyri law professor Rachael Lorna Johnstone thinks that, because observers play only a minor role in Arctic Council decision-making, concerns regarding China's admission may be overblown:

> As I understand the new rules, there are no longer "permanent Observers," but only "Observers," and they are *all* subject to periodic reassessment. There has been something of a resurgence of interest – and funding – from the established Observers as they realized this. Not only do Observers now have to "earn" their admission, they have to keep on earning it ... [Furthermore], they can take part in working groups (and indeed, are expected to contribute) but they are well down the pecking order below the Indigenous Peoples' organizations at the Arctic Council table. Member states and Permanent Participants discuss; Observers observe and are not permitted to contribute actively to the debate.[44]

Russia at first opposed China's admission but altered its position on observers after an Arctic Council rule change that made it clear that only the Arctic eight had votes and that observerships would be reviewed every four years.[45]

Arctic expert Oran Young, for his part, advocates *strengthening* the observers' role on the Arctic Council:

> In my judgment, much of the problem stems from the fact that the notion of an observer suggests a purely passive role in contrast to the active roles of the Arctic states and the Permanent Participants. In reality, however, there are many issues where there is a need for observers to act as partners (e.g. the Arctic Migratory Bird Initiative), to accept responsibility for addressing environmental threats originating elsewhere but affecting the Arctic (e.g. the impacts of persistent organic pollutants), or to become active exponents of the interests of Arctic actors in broader arenas (e.g. the COPs [Conferences of the Parties] of the UNFCCC [United Nations Framework Convention on Climate Change]).[46]

Could the China decision be bad news for the permanent participants on the Arctic Council and for their goals of environmental stewardship? An ongoing concern for permanent participants, whose interests have been largely social and environmental, might be that the new Asian observers seem primarily interested in economic questions: of resources and of shipping and transportation.

Finnish scholars Juha Kapyla and Harri Mikkola have contrasted the possible motivations of some observer-states with those of traditional Arctic states, such as Russia, which have significant economic and security interests already established in the region: "China, the US and the EU have also expressed their Arctic interests more explicitly. They are keen to tap into the economic potential and have a say in the way the region becomes accessed, exploited and governed."[47] In 2013, in an opinion piece in the *Globe and Mail*, UBC professor Michael Byers observed that "the globalization and economization of the Arctic will most likely downplay environmentalism and reduce the relative influence of the Indigenous people and small Arctic states in Arctic affairs. Arctic governance is also likely to turn more complex and complicated as the economic and political stakes are raised."[48] Now that the Arctic

Council has admitted observers from distant corners of the planet, truly northern voices may be muffled. More observers will be attending the Arctic Council and engaging with working groups. If permanent participants continue to be underfunded and regional governments banished, the council may lose its northern character.

Some might claim that the Arctic Economic Council (AEC), an independent organization of business leaders from the circumpolar region created in 2014 by the Arctic Council, will substitute for the absent "settler voice" on the council. But that will not fly: the new body is more likely to seat multinational corporations than regional governments or village entrepreneurs.[49] Others say that the AEC reflects a settler agenda that is turning its back on the Arctic Council's foundations as an entity concerned with research, the Arctic environment, and Indigenous peoples. In 2015, Terry Fenge, a perennial observer of Arctic Council proceedings, rued that the council and the AEC have overlapping mandates that could result in institutional competition, with unknown consequences for circumpolar cooperation.[50] In a *Globe and Mail* opinion piece on March 4, 2015, Lloyd Axworthy and Mary Simon identified this overlap, commenting that the AEC had a mandate to foster "sustainable development, including economic growth, environmental protection and social development [further enhanced recently as] responsible resource development."[51] They note, and I concur, that this is a primary purpose of the Arctic Council, and has been for almost twenty years.

Oran Young makes another point:

There is a structural imbalance embedded in the organization of the [Arctic] council arising from the fact that environmental protection is properly treated as an element of sustainable development rather than a parallel concern. The facts that most of the council's Working Group deal with matters of environmental protection and that the Sustainable Development Working Group lacks a coherent program and a well-defined constituency reinforce this imbalance. What is needed is a reconfiguration of the council to identify sustainable development as its overarching theme or mandate and to recognize environmental protection as a critical element of sustainable development ... One way forward in this connection would be to treat the Arctic Economic Council as the mechanism for addressing the economic pillar of sustainable development. This would highlight the need to devise similar mechanisms to address critical issues of cultural vitality and health, education, and welfare.[52]

Whether the issue is structural imbalance or an architectural flaw, these observations support a modest restructuring for the Arctic Council, which is now twenty years old and may be ready for some serious self-examination.

On the Arctic Council, eight national governments have created an Arctic of states and Indigenous organizations and attached to it a legion of international observers who are mostly outsiders. Thanks in large part to Indigenous rights campaigns and land claims settlements, federal states have learned the lesson that Indigenous peoples must be included, but at the same time they have consciously excluded the North's settler majority. This is liberalism gone sideways.

Nowadays, it is regional and Indigenous governments that are doing the heavy lifting of Arctic governance. It is these organizations that are maintaining the airports and roads, educating the children, delivering health care to the elderly, and doing the tough stuff of practical policy making – the daily business of governing the Arctic. National capitals have rudely divided the Arctic by bringing Indigenous leaders to the table while leaving the settlers outside.

COMMUNITY

5

What You Eat and Where You Live
Poverty in the North

In the old days, the hunter used to live not in a house
but out of it, on the land, where the food was.

The young men of Northway lined the dusty roadside and loaded their rifles as Nelnah Bessie John's cortege trundled down the rocky road. Bessie was her Christian name, Nelnah her Tanana name. When the pickup bearing the pine coffin came into sight, the honour guard pointed their rifles skyward and fired a long volley over the treetops. Crow Clan women mourners wailed as the coffin arrived at the driveway of the Pentecostal Church. The family had wanted a "viewing" of the body in the church, but a complication arose: a pall-bearer who was off digging the grave had taken the key to the coffin.

As an "honorary pallbearer" for my friend and former mother-in-law, my job was to stand by doing nothing. A few minutes after the coffin arrived at the church, the Crow Clan women began to smile and laugh as they greeted distant cousins arriving for this memorial – Bessie's second funeral – and, more importantly, for the potlatch to follow. The potlatch is a West Coast tradition; Dene communities over the mountains in the NWT do not follow this practice.

The Pentecostal pastor gave a eulogy for Bessie that made no mention of her late-in-life career as an Indigenous language teacher in Yukon schools or her role as a leader in her family and community, and I wondered whether the pastor knew her at all. The official mourning for her had begun with a Catholic service across the border in Yukon. Both churches wanted to be part of this farewell to respected elder Bessie

John, but the potlatch involving hundreds of celebrants and a mountain of food was the main event – the Tanana tribal homecoming that Nelnah would surely not have wanted to miss.

By the time we entered the community hall, dozens of elders were seated on the wooden benches along the room's four walls. One wall displayed pictures from Nelnah's life. In the kitchen, busy Crow Clan women prepared the first of a dozen meals that tradition required they provide for the Wolf Clan attendees. Northern Dene babies are born into one of two clans, Crow and Wolf, and children inherit clan membership from their mothers. Since Nelnah was Crow, so were her daughter and her daughter's children. Nelnah's daughter Lu is the mother of my children – Tahmoh, and twins Sarah and Stephanie. While they may be "city Indians" from Whitehorse, Sarah and Stephanie, whose Tanana tribal names are Lahlil (Butterfly) and Yahsan (Blue Sky), stepped without hesitation into their Crow Clan roles as kitchen helpers, vegetable choppers, and food servers, alongside their Alaskan aunts and Yukon cousins. My son Tahmoh had been out hunting for food. As always, I was impressed with the way my three kids could slip so easily into the life of this community.

This is interior or bush Alaska, and these are the tribal lands of the Tanana Dene, whose territory straddles the Canada–US border along the Alaska Highway. I'm not a total stranger here. The old people all know me or know of me. As the former spouse of a Tanana woman and a former Yukon legislator, they could easily have greeted me as just another transient settler. Instead, they have embraced me as the father of the three handsome young people who will soon participate tentatively with their mother in the potlatch dances.

The dances begin after supper, when the singer firmly strikes his moose-hide drum once. Then he begins to sing, a long, keening chant. The other old men gather in a circle in the centre of the hall and join in the singing. The women form an outer circle and, with scarves in their hands, add their voices. The lead singer is elderly, but black hair flows out from under his baseball cap and around his shirt collar. From memory, he sings dozens of traditional songs. Visitors from other villages join in and add their own songs. Soon everybody is dancing. By the end, nearly a thousand people have gathered to sing, dance, celebrate, and eat. The local Alaskan and Yukon politicians have come by to pay their respects. People share lots of gossip and some hard news.

A relative tells me that my son Tahmoh is ill. Before my arrival with his sisters, he had got soaking wet dragging the moose shot for his grandmother's potlatch feast out of the bush. He has come down with a bad cold, the elders say, but they all comment on his strength. "He's like two strong Indians," chuckles one old man. After I have heard this story five times, and checked its accuracy with Tahmoh, I wonder about its significance. Does it somehow confirm that, in the community's eyes, he has inherited his grandmother's strength? And what obligations might that load upon his shoulders?

The food comes and comes: bowls of moose stew, plates of salmon, baskets of bannock, giant urns of tea. Crow Clan servers go round the room offering the elders on the wall benches low-bush cranberry jam to go with their bannock. This feast is a celebration of one life, but also of a life lived together and of the foods gathered from tribal lands and waters around the village.

This bush Alaska village is not wealthy. It has no running water, and until a recent post-flood public works project, there was no decent road into the community. The situation confirms something I've noticed before: the poorer the community, the richer the traditional culture. Is that some kind of law, I wonder? Does southern-model prosperity inevitably lead to northern cultural poverty?

In 1884, to advance a policy of assimilation, the Canadian government banned the potlatch, an ancient cultural, social, and economic occasion. Even so, the potlatch survived. In sharp contrast to the individual accumulation that drives southern economies, northern Indigenous communities depend on reciprocity. An affluent Dene may hold a potlatch to distribute his or her wealth to the opposite clan; social standing increases with the generosity of the gifts, not with the personal accumulation of piles of furs or stores of dried fish.

Because Dene children inherit clan membership from their mother, and an incest taboo prohibits marriage within clans, the potlatch celebrants treat me as if I am a member of the Wolf Clan. In this capacity, when Crow Clan leaders distribute gifts on behalf of the deceased at the end of the potlatch, I find myself the owner of a stack of blankets and several rifles. Somehow I'll have to get the rifles back across the US–Canada border at Beaver Creek. As I grab a coffee for the 550 kilometre drive back to Whitehorse, I overhear a non-Native customs officer and a short-order cook make unkind remarks about "these people." These people had harvested a bounty of healthy "country food" from their own hunting grounds, and they had shared it with all comers: mourners, preachers, politicians, and community members, even a racist or two.

For Arctic peoples, there were – and often still are – few food choices. You ate what you could harvest, or you starved. Superficially, this fits the image that southerners customarily hold about the people of the Far North: that the Inuit and the Dene are among the poorest people on the planet. In terms of material wealth, Indigenous people who live off the land *can* experience great deprivation. But as Hugh Brody points out in his great book *Maps and Dreams*, while the Northern Dene may lack material possessions, in their own way they are wealthy.[1] To subsist on a diet of fresh, healthy, protein-rich food is not the same as to be poor, hungry, and homeless in a big city.

For Indigenous families who lived off these lands for centuries, hunger and starvation were constant threats. Great prestige attached to the hunter who could feed not just a family but a community. Wally Firth, the NWT MP, once joked to me that when a hunter came home without bagging any game, his family would eat "fresh air and rabbit tracks" for supper.

Food has repeatedly been used as a weapon against Indigenous people. Some historians contend that the United States encouraged the commercial hunting of buffalo in order to diminish the food supply of the Plains tribes.[2] A similar history played out in Canada. "Despite guarantees of food aid in times of famine in Treaty No. 6, Canadian officials used food, or rather denied food, as a means to ethnically cleanse the area between Regina to the Alberta border in readiness for the Canadian Pacific Railway."³ So writes James Daschuk, author of *Clearing the Plains: Disease, Politics of Starvation, and the Loss of Aboriginal Life*.⁴ Sir John A. Macdonald, acting as both prime minister and Indian affairs minister, boasted during the darkest days of the famine in the mid-1800s that the Indigenous population was being kept on "the verge of actual starvation," in an attempt to deflect criticism that he was squandering public funds.⁵

Between 1942 and 1952, researchers used Indian residential school students as unwitting subjects in a number of nutritional studies, including a well-known survey of the Attawapiskat and Rupert's House Cree First Nations in 1947 and 1948. As Ian Mosby reports, "less well known were two separate long-term studies that went so far as to include controlled experiments conducted, apparently without the subjects' informed consent or knowledge, on malnourished Aboriginal populations in Northern Manitoba and, later, in six Indian residential schools."⁶ Nobody would suggest that today's governments are deliberately starving Indigenous northerners, but in the Canadian Arctic, government food policies continue to harm communities.

As governments pushed northern peoples from their camps and villages into towns and then cities, their diets changed from protein-rich country foods to carbohydrate-heavy commercial foods. Forty years ago, when I first wandered through the Co-op and Bay stores in Eastern Arctic hamlets, I was astonished to find shelves stacked with candy, soda pop, sweetened cereals, and other imported junk foods. Nowhere could I see any affordable fruits or vegetables. It was a sickening sight.

From the 1940s to the 1960s, Canadian government policy was to move the Arctic's Indigenous people away from their fishing and hunting grounds and into government towns. Ottawa forced the Inuit, who were plagued by tuberculosis, into permanent settlements in the Eastern Arctic where they would have better access to medical services. In Yukon, schools were located on highways, which brought in Dene families from nearby rivers and lakes. Western Arctic populations endured similar experiences, in that governments wanted them where they could be administered and policed. Forced displacement was a modern version of colonialism. Even if well-intentioned, the federal policy had negative effects. For a start, welfare-dispensing Indian Agents displaced hunters as providers for Indigenous families, which made people feel ashamed and resentful. Hunters and trappers were treated like childish bush people. The new policy also inflated the egos of the salaried federal agents and filled the worst of them with a sick hunger for more power. In 1970, former Indian agent Alan Fry published a novel called *How a People Die* about the dangers of federal dependency.[7]

These changes had serious long-term consequences. People spent less time fishing, hunting, and picking berries. Young people took jobs in the wage economy and developed a taste for store-bought foods. As people's diets shifted from meaty to sugary, their health declined, and for those forced to rely on government welfare payments, sedentary life worsened the epidemiological picture. Towns grew, more shops opened, alcohol became readily available, and health in Indigenous communities continued to deteriorate: alcoholism increased; dental decay and gum disease became widespread; diabetes, heart disease, and obesity rates soared. In 2014, Dr. Matthew Hirschfeld, director of Maternal Child Health Services at the Alaska Native Medical Center, told *Alaska Dispatch News* that a genetic condition had been discovered that prevents some Native Alaskans from metabolizing sugar – a confirmation of the value of traditional diets and of the dangers of processed foods.[8] The relationship between resettlement to improve access to health professionals and the negative health impacts of removing people from their fishing and hunting grounds seems obvious today. Until the 1970s, too many buck-passing northern legislators saw their Indigenous neighbours as solely a federal responsibility. This three-cornered misunderstanding continues in some parts of the North even today.

Food Insecurity

In 1897, just months before the Klondike was overrun with gold-crazed prospectors seeking a bonanza, Dawson City – the riverfront town that had risen just downstream from the confluence of the Klondike and

Yukon Rivers – faced serious food shortages. About 5,000 people lived in Dawson City, and hundreds more on the riverbanks, and most had no provisions. "Salt was worth its weight in gold," writes historian Charles Emmerson. "Conditions had deteriorated to the extent that US President McKinley considered sending a humanitarian relief mission to the Canadian Yukon."[9] Worse, more gold seekers were arriving by the day: "There wasn't enough food in Dawson's warehouses to feed them all through the months ahead. But managers didn't increase their food orders to match the expected demand ... Instead, the merchants raised prices for bacon, beans, flour and other staples, and tried an informal rationing system ... Hundreds stood in line for hours around the commercial companies' warehouses, begging for a chance to buy *anything*."[10]

That winter, Klondikers subsisted on a steady diet of bacon, beans, fish, and corned beef. Humans are adaptable and creative, however, and by the following year Dawson City's residents had discovered that they could grow huge vegetables under the endless hours of summer sunlight in gardens planted on river-bottom soil. Sadly, governments and politicians have short memories. Today's leaders have long forgotten the lessons of Dawson City's first winter, and they seem in danger of repeating the same mistakes in other Arctic and Subarctic locations.

Town life for Indigenous northerners increased birth rates, life expectancy, and overall populations, and as a result, the harvesting pressures on the Arctic lands surrounding larger municipalities also increased. Employment in the wage economy enabled people to shop for groceries, but it also drew them away from more labour-intensive fishing and hunting and diminished their access to country foods. Meanwhile, the prices for store-bought alternatives increased. All of these changes limited Indigenous peoples' access to nutritious foods, something the UN Food and Agriculture Organization (FAO) identifies as a problem of food security – or, as I prefer, food *insecurity*. Over time, food insecurity in the North has come to include the effects of pollutants and climate change.

The United Nations defines food security as existing "when all people at all times have access to sufficient safe, nutritious food to maintain a healthy and active life."[11] The 2007–8 Nunavut Inuit Child Health Survey found that food-insecure homes were often also overcrowded. The same survey the following year reported that 70 percent of Inuit preschoolers didn't know when they would be getting their next meal.[12] While touring Canada in 2012, the UN Special Rapporteur on the Right to Food found "desperate conditions and people who are in extremely dire straits." Canada's health minister at the time, Leona Aglukkaq, called the UN official "ill-informed," but Mary Simon, the president of Inuit Tapiriit Kanatami, the national Inuit organization, affirmed that "there *is* food insecurity in the North."[13] A 2014 report from the Canadian Council of Academics states that Nunavut has the highest food *insecurity* rate of any Indigenous population in any developed country and that one-quarter of Inuit preschoolers are severely food-insecure: 76 percent skip meals and 60 percent have gone a day without eating.

Speaking as site coordinator for Feed My Family, a Facebook group with more than 20,000 online members, Becky Toretti declared in a 2012 interview with the policy journal *Northern Public Affairs* that price is the greatest barrier to food security in the North. In 2011, Ottawa had replaced an older program that granted northerners postage subsidies on food mailed from the south with something called Nutrition North Canada. According to Toretti, the new program's budget was inadequate to meet community needs:

> The price of food is out of reach for too many people. According to the federal government, the price of a basket of food to feed a family of four in Nunavut is $22,724 per year (not including the High Arctic) but the median income is only a couple of thousand more than that ($26,830 per year in 2009) ... The government is trying to encourage people to eat healthy foods, but NNC [Nutrition North Canada] isn't doing enough to lower the cost of healthy food to the point where it's more affordable to eat healthy food than junk food ... One thing that disappoints us is that the NNC program subsidizes retailers, not Northerners. The direct benefit is going to the retailer and we don't know if it's being passed on to the consumer.[14]

For the expense account traveller, Iqaluit's Frobisher Inn lunch menu offers the Nunavut Burger ("certified Black Angus chuck, aged Canadian cheddar, traditional condiments") for $20 and a "Thirty-Dollar Burger" with "local ground caribou, bacon, ancho ketchup, caramelized onions, smoked Gouda." The high prices experienced by local shoppers have triggered calls for store boycotts in Iqaluit, although retailers insist that the prices for healthy food items have dropped and that the consumption of them has increased. When locals in remote Baffin Island communities consider buying bottles of Sunny D for $30-plus, without realizing that it is largely coloured sugar water, what does that say about the effectiveness of Nutrition North's education program?

In response to a House of Commons question on December 1, 2014, about the high price of food in Nunavut, her home constituency, Leona Aglukkaq, environment minister at the time, waved off the question.[15] NDP MP Romeo Saganash had asked whether "people being asked to pay ten times more for milk or scavenge at the dump is indicative of a program that's working." Aglukkaq responded by pointing to Aboriginal affairs minister Bernard Valcourt and went back to reading a newspaper.[16] During the 2015 federal election campaign, the Liberal Party promised to invest a further $40 million over four years in Nutrition North, which would ease the hardship but not solve the problem.

When the Arctic Environmental Protection Strategy and the Arctic Monitoring and Assessment Program were launched in 1991, very little research had been done on pollutants in the Arctic food chain.[17] However, diet, blood, and breast milk data collected between 1985 and 1988 from the Inuit community of Broughton Island on Baffin Island had shown that all the local Inuit foods tested contained PCBs and mercury. Alarm bells rang, David Stone writes in his book *The Changing Arctic Environment*, because the "blood PCBs exceeded Health Canada's 'tolerable' levels in 63 percent of children and in 39 percent of women of childbearing age."[18] Finnish scientists had found similar toxins in Sámi communities. Together with Norway, Finland launched a circumpolar monitoring program.

In May 2001, after years of lobbying by the Inuit Circumpolar Council, 111 nations, including seven Arctic states, endorsed the Stockholm Convention on Persistent Organic Pollutants. The pollutants addressed by that document included pesticides and insecticides. Russia signed on a year later, but implementation has been uncertain. Around the circumpolar North, research on persistent organic pollutants (POPs) has continued. One of the best long-term studies is a Russian project carried out in collaboration with the Arctic Monitoring and Assessment Program's Human Health Expert Group and RAIPON.[19]

Nevertheless, Harriet Kuhnlein of McGill University's School of Dietetics and Human Nutrition, who has analyzed the daily diets of Inuit as well as the air and ocean currents that bring POPs to the Arctic, has found that country food far exceeds store-bought products in nutritional value. One portion of a country food per day (for example, caribou, fish, or whale) is essential for good health, she says, even for pregnant women and young children, the two groups at the greatest risk from POPs. Addressing a common question about how country food can be healthy even though it lacks fruit or vegetables, Kuhnlein says there's plenty of vitamin C in *muktuk* (whale skin and blubber) and seal liver; traditional foods are in fact nutritionally complete.[20] Their health benefits still trump the risks created by POPs and mercury contaminants.

Inuit consumption of country foods has declined in recent years, especially among youth. This may be partly the result of fears about food contamination. It may also be because hunting skills are not being passed down from the older generation to the next. Before the 1950s, Canadian Inuit lived nomadically, relying on the availability and proximity of harvest species for subsistence. "Their grocery store is out there on the land," writes Wade Davis, a member of *The Globe and Mail's* "Arctic Circle" Panel. "To live they must kill the things they most love. Blood on ice in the Arctic is not a sign of death, but an affirmation of life. Death is the disappearance of the ice."[21] Inuit still have direct access to the land, but they are also highly vulnerable to fluctuations in wildlife. Consumption of both country-harvested foods and store-bought products is greatly affected today by the pressures of climate change and globalization.

Arctic Indigenous communities speak with pride about their "stewardship" of the land, which they contrast with the exploitative behaviour of southerners, who come north to make a fast buck extracting resources, often leaving nothing but an environmental mess behind. Conservation played a large role in the negotiation of northern land claims treaties in the late twentieth century. All sides were aware, for example, that in the Yukon Act (the territory's constitution), one section governed settler hunting and fishing, and another protected the right of the Dene and Tlingit populations to hunt and fish for food. Treaty negotiators for both the First Nations and the territory eventually recognized that these two competing systems of wildlife management undermined conservation efforts. The land claims agreement therefore merged the two systems. It made conservation the first priority of the new co-management regime, under which equal numbers of Indigenous and settler representatives now sit on regional boards to establish harvesting levels for caribou, moose, mountain goats, Dahl sheep, and salmon.

As treaty commitments, these arrangements were supposed to last forever. But less than twenty years after they were signed, climate change has altered the landscape. White-tailed deer have crossed the BC–Yukon border for the first time, and cougar are following them. Inuvialuit fishers along the Firth River, a well-known Arctic char stream, are catching Pacific salmon in their nets. Laurence C. Smith, in *The World in 2050*, reports incidences of interspecies breeding between grizzly and polar bears.[22] These wildlife migrations are affecting food security in the Far North, and none of the northern land claims agreements anticipated them.

The Alaska Department of Fish and Game website reports that subsistence hunting and fishing provide about 375 pounds of food per person per year for rural residents, but only 22 pounds for individuals in urban areas.[23] Leroy Adams, the housing coordinator for Kivalina on the northwest coast of Alaska, said in 2014 that one bowhead whale would feed the village of 382 people for a year: "One good thing about Kivalina is the sharing of the food."[24] A health assessment of Kivalina conducted by the Alaska Native Tribal Health Consortium (ANTHC) found that the ice there in years past had been as much as twelve feet thick and provided a stable surface for travel and hunting, but that in recent years the ice had been thinning. Today, the ice is sometimes too thin for hunting in those places where the whales pass on their journey to the rich feeding grounds farther north. According to Adams, it takes more gasoline, and it's more dangerous, to hunt the whales in small boats far from shore. "The migration pattern is about 60 to 90 miles out," he says, and adds that villagers haven't landed a bowhead whale in ten or twelve years, but won't be giving up.[25]

By any measure, Alaska is a wealthy state, yet food insecurity has become an issue there, especially in rural areas. In 2006, 10.8 percent of adults and 15.2 percent of children in Alaska (80,000 individuals) suffered from food insecurity, meaning they were at times uncertain of having or acquiring enough food for all household members because of insufficient money or other resources.[26] By 2013, this number had risen to 14.2 percent, or 104,750 Alaskans.[27] One Alaska study concludes: "There are many possible faces of food insecurity; whether quality of life suffers as a matter of chronic hunger in sub-Saharan Africa or chronic obesity, diabetes, alcoholism and depression in sub-Arctic Alaska, each represents some failure of a food system."[28]

Solutions

In the Eastern Arctic, people now speak of food security as both a human rights and a public health issue. Community responses to the challenge include infrastructure initiatives such as community food freezers and summer greenhouses, along with changes in public policy. Advocates see both kinds of solutions as necessary – although not fully sufficient – components of a sustainable food system in the Far North.

Community freezers for storing game and fish have been around in the Arctic since the 1970s. In terms of improving food security, they are a sound investment, but they are at best a partial solution to the problem of meeting food needs in mid-winter. Costs of powering and maintaining those freezers will remain problematic until someone develops more energy- and cost-efficient technologies. Before the permafrost began to melt, the traditional cold cellar, dug into the ground, offered a more energy-efficient alternative than an electric freezer. I have a lingering affection for permafrost refrigerators. My family's cabin on the North Fork of the Klondike had a cold storage space under the floor. One day, a bear tore through the screen door. Having left my rifle in town, I pulled open the trapdoor and jumped into the permafrost cooler, and there I hid, freezing in the dark, while the hungry bear trashed the cabin. Sadly, climate change will have since eaten that fridge.

Greenhouses too have long been used in Alaska, Yukon, and the NWT, although experimental ones like the community greenhouse in Iqaluit are relatively recent. In my days as a legislator, travelling the Yukon highways with my vegetarian aide Jim Beebe sometimes provided belly laughs. I remember chuckling as Jim chewed his grilled cheese sandwich lunch beneath the velvet painting of the Last Supper on the wall at the Stewart Crossing lodge. Today, even Anaktuvuk Pass in Alaska's North Slope Borough has a garden project and dreams of opening a produce stand.[29] Greenhouses provide opportunities for Arctic communities to produce fresh fruits and vegetables and even to benefit a little from global warming. Far Northerners have experimented with hydroponic technologies for decades as well; however, the energy costs of producing fresh tomatoes can make them prohibitively expensive. That said, greenhouses are a way for Northerners to maintain their tradition of local food production and to grow medicinal herbs as well.

Alaska, Yukon, and the NWT endure long, cold winters but enjoy short summers of almost endless sunlight, and this growing season is especially attractive for farmers. With more than twenty-two hours of sunlight on the longest days of June, gardens in the Far North can explode like gawky teens, sending out shoots, flowers, and fruits in a compressed and frenzied summer cycle. The early settlers embraced this pattern, mostly because they had to – if a family did not shoot, catch, or grow something local, they simply did not eat. Unfortunately, with the wave of global food marketing and improved transportation, that knowledge has faded.

In Alaska, which currently imports around 95 percent of its food, the state legislators have begun to promote local food production. A *New York Times* story reported in 2014: "At the downtown farmers' market along the banks of the Chena River, a local chef – paid by a state agriculture program, using federal farm grants – handed out samples of scallops on an Alaskan-made chip with minted pea purée on a recent weekday afternoon."[30] Even the state's food stamp program encourages local food consumption.

The Alaskan identity, in particular, the spirit of self-reliance, is the state's secret weapon in encouraging the local food movement. That is what Danny Consenstein, executive director of the Alaska State Farm Service Agency, told the *New York Times*.[31] But Alaska can't produce all the food its population needs, and with high food prices, food must compete with other necessities such as housing, electricity, transportation, and medicine. Food insecurity mostly affects those with little money, and it can become a public health concern affecting people's mental and physical well-being.

Traditional subsistence no longer offers a sustainable path to food security. Nevertheless, the country-food harvest remains an essential component of the Inuit diet and of Inuit cultural life. A barge that was delayed while delivering groceries to the NWT in the summer of 2016 had local residents paying $5 for a can of pop and $25 for a large can of fruit salad. "We're lucky we always have country food," one resident said, while also noting that she missed her cans of fruit.[32]

Stocking country food on northern grocery store shelves might be a good idea, McGill University's Harriet Kuhnlein believes. An economy could even be built around country food, as in Greenland, where commercial hunters earn good money from their harvest. In Canada, Arctic char, polar bear, and narwhal have already been commodified. Some people worry that the sale of wild meat could undermine Inuit food-sharing traditions. If a young hunter takes his extra seal meat to market, might his grandmother go without? But even if everybody in Iqaluit still had the hunting skills to put country food on the dinner table, it's unlikely that the carrying capacity of the land around Nunavut's capital city could supply enough meat to feed 7,000 people on a regular basis. A country-food market might then be part of the solution.

A marketing plan for country food harvested in the North, starting with fish, has been suggested as one strategy to assist Nunavut households whose members struggle with food insecurity. After a northern study tour, the Action Canada Fellows, a leadership program for high achievers, observed that 70 percent of households in Nunavut fall into this category.[33] At a meeting at Simon Fraser University's Wosk Centre for Dialogue in December 2013, the group proposed the marketing idea and recommended that the government of Nunavut, in partnership with Nunavut food processors, create a "Nunavut Brand." They also suggested that the federal government provide local inspectors for country food not intended for export outside of Nunavut.[34]

But it will be decades before the free market can provide the majority of Inuit with enough income to feed, clothe, and accommodate their families. Things may start to improve after resource management devolution in Nunavut, but in the meantime, something basic like a country-food (caribou, seal, char, *muktuk*) school lunch program might help. In 2012, Alaska state legislators funded a $3 million school lunch program that reimburses districts when they buy local products for the state's 131,000 public school students.[35] Alaska may only have one tortilla corn chip manufacturer, but innovators have married corn chips with a local product to provide salmon tamales for schools across the state.

For Inuit communities, food security needs to be understood in the context of the enormous economic and social changes their residents face. In the "mixed economies" of the Eastern Arctic, both wage-earning and subsistence influence every household, and money earned from hourly paid work is often reinvested in tools for subsistence harvest. Beyond northern infrastructure initiatives like freezers and greenhouses, governments need to consider income support programs sufficient to cover the basic costs of food and housing.

The late Terry Fenge, an adviser to both Inuit and Dene politicians, believed that the best hunter support program was the one in northern Quebec, which was negotiated into the James Bay and Northern Quebec Treaty Agreement and the subsequent Paix des Braves Agreement involving Quebec and the Cree. This program subsidizes hunters and trappers to go out on the land instead of staying idle at home.

At the 12th General Assembly of the Inuit Circumpolar Council, held from July 21 to 24, 2014, Inuit from four nations issued the Kitigaaryuit Declaration, which urged the ICC to promote Inuit food security, "including community health and wellness, retention and transmission of Inuit traditional knowledge, use of Inuit management methodologies, improved co-management activities, sustainable utilization of wildlife, contaminants, biological diversity, climate change, and the availability of nutritious foods."[36] A general subsidy would allow people in the North to "make their own choices," argues Nunavut's governmental nutritionist, Allison MacRury: "That's what people do in the rest of Canada."[37] And that's what the North needs. In the meantime, Amazon Prime may offer a cheap food delivery alternative.[38]

Housing

Bad food and sedentary town life have worsened the social pathologies that beset northern communities, especially in the areas of family violence and teen suicide. There's a serious housing problem as well. It has taken decades for Indigenous people to acquire the formal education necessary to take up professional positions in urban centres, and those without such skills have been marginalized in the North's new towns, even if they formerly enjoyed high status as hunters, trappers, or tribal chiefs. This loss of status has affected their physical and mental health. Decades after being wrenched from their former lives, elders testifying before the 2013 Qikiqtani Truth Commission sought "*saimaqtigiiniq*: peace with past opponents."[39] They could still recall the hurt and psychic pain they felt at the sudden rupture in their lives, the forced shift from a rural to an urban existence.

The federal government promised housing, but official Ottawa seemed not to understand that northern Indigenous people live *outside* their houses, on the surrounding land and waters. Arriving one day at my family's North Fork cabin, I discovered that squatters had "borrowed" the cabin's cast iron wood stove for their own poorly insulated shack. I invited them to return it in the spring, which they did. In a southern city, security begins with a locked door. In a northern village, security often means the opposite. For instance, a cluster of tiny cousins might migrate from their grandma's house, where they eat bannock, to their uncle's house, where they drink juice, and then finally to their aunt's place, where they flop down on a couch to watch TV and eventually fall asleep. An African proverb says that it takes a village to raise a child. In the Arctic, it takes family connections and food – not just houses – to create a community.

Along with food, housing remains the most basic of Arctic insecurities. The average price of residential properties in Anchorage, Alaska's biggest city, rose about 13.9 percent between 2011 and 2016. Much of the action in the city's housing market is in the $350,000 to $400,000 range, where persistently low inventory has given sellers the upper hand. Many less expensive properties, including condos built in the 1970s and 1980s, are in similarly short supply.[40]

Over the border in Whitehorse, the Yukon capital, a *Whitehorse Daily Star* report in May 2012 described a "softening" housing market and attributed it to an uncertain world economy and tighter lending.[41] In 1995 the average house price in Whitehorse was $153,067; by December 2015 it had risen to $419,700.[42] Despite a third year of recession in Yukon's economy, residential home sales increased by 7 percent in 2015, and both prices and demand were expected to increase even more as the labour market recovered.[43]

In Yellowknife, the beneficiary city during the NWT's diamond-mining boom, the story was until recently a little different. In 2011 the median sale price of a house was $239,000 – high, but not as high as in Abbotsford, Calgary, or Vancouver – and northern salaries meant a smaller proportion of income was needed to purchase a home.[44]

However, one online commentator noted that, although the Canada Mortgage and Housing Corporation recommended spending no more than one-third of one's income on housing, her rent was more than she earned from two jobs, and a mortgage was virtually impossible.[45] By 2015 the average price of a home in Yellowknife had increased to $417,049.[46]

In these three northern cities, the housing market responds to the laws of supply and demand. In much of the North, however, the housing market as such hardly exists. In years past, most of the housing in Indigenous villages – inadequate as it was – was built by government agencies. That was no less true in government centres like Iqaluit and Inuvik. Similarly, in towns dominated by mining, oil and gas, or other resources, such as Ekati, Faro, Pine Point, and Prudhoe Bay, the employer provided housing, sometimes with government assistance. Over time, however, housing in such places got "privatized," notably in communities like Faro, where many residents chose to stay after the mine closed.

Efforts to impose market regimes on housing have not always worked well. There is a legend about Alaska Native housing that has been repeated over the years. Before the 1971 ANCSA claims settlement, many Native villages employed a carpenter who could build houses to order. If a grandmother told the carpenter she needed a large porch and an additional bedroom for her many grandchildren, he simply built the house that way. After ANCSA, this carpenter was forced to reinvent himself as a "housing corporation." In no time, there were dozens of bankrupt Native housing corporations in the state. True or not, the story highlights a popular northern belief that, given sufficient resources, practical people will take care of a community's housing needs, with lawmakers, bureaucrats, and banks playing supporting, not leading, roles.

A single mother sleeping with her baby next to an ATM is one of many images that *Nunatsiaq News* provided in its 2006 cover story, "Life on Iqaluit's Mean Streets."[47] Many of the article's statistics came from a federal report titled "Homelessness in the Territorial North," a plight that has come to epitomize the failure of housing policy in Nunavut since 1999.[48]

At land claims negotiating tables in the 1980s, the Inuit tried to take over responsibility for social housing from the federal government. The government refused go along with this. Then in 1993, Ottawa cut its federal housing program to zero. In 2003, John Lamb, the CEO of Nunavut Tunngavik Inc., the Inuit political organization, gave a speech in Iqaliut on housing, during which he reminded his audience of these efforts, saying that housing needs were largely an Inuit problem, yet they were excluded from some federal programs.

By 2004 the government of Nunavut and Nunavut Tunngavik had proposed a Nunavut Ten-Year Inuit Housing Action Plan. That plan deplored the 1993 termination of federal social housing programs, especially given that the decision had failed to consider the lack of alternatives for residents of Nunavut.[49] Ottawa admitted that "the conditions in far too many Aboriginal communities can only be described as shameful."[50] In Nuuk, Greenland's capital, visitors can see Eastern Bloc-style apartment buildings that some bureaucrat has charmingly named, like bingo calls, E-10, B-12, and so on. Apart from the occasional polar bear hide or caribou skin draped over balcony rails, these blocks could be located anywhere. I doubt that Iqaluit needs anything resembling these units, but at least in Nuuk they are an option.

Nunavut's ten-year plan discusses the environmental and socio-economic factors shaping Nunavut's difficult housing situation: the extreme cold dictates construction requirements beyond national standards with regard to matters such as insulation and building envelope; Nunavut depends entirely on imported oil for heating and electricity generation; no accessible lumber exists for construction, nor is there any wood for heating; an extremely small population base occupies a vast area of land; the isolation faced by Nunavut's twenty-five communities makes road transportation of goods and materials nearly impossible; new housing supply depends on the public sector; and almost all public housing tenants are Inuit.

The cost of the ten-year housing plan was estimated at $1.9 billion. Few communities have qualified construction tradespeople to complete the proposed work, although some do have general contracting firms. The Nunavut Housing Corporation estimates construction costs at $330 per square foot, compared to $103.45 in southern Canada. That means each new public housing unit would cost between $400,000 and $550,000 to build and $26,000 annually to maintain. In Nunavut, more than 3,000 such units are needed.[51] To further complicate implementation of this plan, Nunavut has fewer existing housing alternatives than almost any other Canadian jurisdiction.

Despite the injection of federal cash, more than ten years after the adoption of Nunavut's Ten-Year Plan, most commentators gave the Nunavut government a failing grade.[52] "Since the Territory's creation, it has been plagued by chronic overcrowding, grinding poverty and a dilemma that leaves residents unemployed even as jobs demanding a higher level of training remain unfilled," wrote one consultant. "For the most part, these problems aren't getting better."[53] In 2016 it was reported that 52 percent of Nunavummiut were living in social housing, many of them paying the minimum rent of $60 per month.[54] Of those tenants, 38 percent were living in overcrowded conditions, and that figure was as high as 72 percent in some communities.[55]

Nunavut premier Eva Aariak told the *Globe and Mail* in 2009, "It's not going to be easy, let me tell you. We have to consider our own resources that are available to us financially, and human capacity issues, as well." She added that little progress could be made without a further infusion of federal money.[56] Terry Audla, the president of the Nunavut Housing Corporation, echoed this sentiment in his presentation to the Standing Senate Committee on Aboriginal Affairs in March 2016, during which he requested "consistent, predictable and adequate funding for new housing, along with increased support for operational costs."[57] When questioned about the ten-year plan, he admitted that it had never been fully implemented, but he felt that its policies and recommendations were still relevant.[58]

Nunavut is already a federal dependent, receiving $1 billion in transfers – more than $42,055 per capita – in the 2017–18 budget.[59] "This puts Nunavut in the awkward position of asking for badly needed government support even as it tries to lessen its reliance on Ottawa," Premier Aariak has pointed out, adding that territorial legislators have been waiting to start devolution discussions with a hesitant federal government. She adds that devolution could give Nunavut "that much more power to look after our own affairs."[60] To solve problems through its own means, Nunavut needs tax revenues. To get revenues, the territory needs an expanding private sector and a tax base. And to achieve that, Nunavut needs devolution of public lands and resource management. Income insecurity for the Nunavummiut is of a piece with their food and housing insecurity problems.

As everyone knows, Indigenous craftspeople designed the dome-shaped snow house or igloo, and First Nations fashioned the cone-shaped tipi. Cones and domes were forms that followed function and were built with local materials and local labour. Settlers, however, preferred box-shaped houses. In the Arctic, the boxes the government provided for Indigenous people were often poorly built, hard to heat, and expensive to repair. Across Aboriginal Canada, poorly constructed homes have compounded housing shortages – a nasty legacy of Canada building shoddy "INAC shacks" for Indigenous peoples.

Celebrity renovator Mike Holmes, star of HGTV's home renovation show *Holmes on Homes*, posted a scathing article on his blog in 2011 titled "Stop Building Junk on Reserves." First Nations housing is in dire need of an overhaul, Holmes noted. Shacks and slop pails equal an infrastructure crisis on Native reserves. Holmes later said in an interview: "When I heard years ago the problems they were having, to me it was like, 'Oh, okay, this [solution] is easy. Why isn't anyone else doing it?' We need to stop building crap. It's as simple as that."[61]

In 2010, Holmes partnered with the Assembly of First Nations on an energy-efficient, environmentally friendly homes project on the White-fish Lake First Nation west of Sudbury, Ontario. The project aimed to develop trade skills for people living on reserves. For Holmes, the ideal First Nations home would be about 1,100 square feet and built of wood, as well as materials that are not susceptible to burning or moulding:

> Let's look at the building technology ... It's using all the products that make sense, nothing but mould-free, nothing but zero VOCs [volatile organic compounds]. This is not hard ... The smartest thing we can do is to teach the First Nations how to do it. It takes refinement over the years, and it's really important to build on the knowledge of people who have experience in the North, not to make the same mistakes over and over again.[62]

The initiative culminated in a set of the First Nations Sustainable Development Standards released in 2013. The document covers building codes, sample housing designs, and labour, financial management, and contracting standards, as well as training needs and community planning.[63] In 2014 a four-unit complex, the first built to the new standard, was unveiled on Whitefish Lake First Nation.[64]

Alaska has successfully tackled some northern building concerns. Every homeowner fears a plumbing "freeze-up," but the Barrow (Utqiaġvik) housing authority has designed super-insulated homes that suffer no such problem.[65] Other Alaska innovators have moved beyond the box, literally. Nunavut may soon follow Alaska's example in cutting out the cold corners of the box house, as the designers of the Quinhagak House have done. Might Nunavummiut begin a search for the kind of stone that could be cemented into higher-density housing, creating structures that are easy to build and heat and that will last?

With food prices high and energy and housing costs even higher, it seems obvious that poverty is the larger problem in the Arctic. Is food and housing security there a problem mainly of costs, technology, and training, or of income? How one defines the problem largely determines the range of policy options. In the EKOS poll conducted among Canadians in 2010 for the Munk–Gordon Arctic Security Program, 90 percent of northerners and 83 percent of southerners agreed that

Canadians should be able to experience the same quality of life throughout the country. Also, 81 percent of northerners and 71 percent of southerners agreed that the best way to protect Canada's interest in the Arctic would be for people to live there.[66] Tackling food prices, housing shortages, low levels of educational attainment, and drug and alcohol abuse in the North could well enhance Canada's Arctic sovereignty.[67]

As the East–West conflict waned, intensified, and then came to an abrupt end in 1992, new conceptions of security emerged. Emphasis shifted from military security to human security, which privileges individuals above the state. This idea was first introduced to Canadian political arenas in 1997, when Liberal foreign minister Lloyd Axworthy defined human security as follows: "Sustainable human security means providing basic needs in both economic and political ways; it means ensuring quality of life and equity; it means protection of fundamental human rights ... In other words, that security should be measured in terms of ultimate outcome for individuals and peoples, rather than in terms of the number of arms control agreements signed."[68]

Food and housing security are now widely recognized as components of human security. However, Arctic scholar Franklyn Griffiths thinks that the concept of human security itself may be a misconception. "Human security emerged as a liberal-democratic response to Conservative statist security practice," he explains.[69] That is why the Conservatives under Prime Minister Stephen Harper hated the idea. Griffiths concedes that large populations may be reference points for security discussions, but he finds it hard to imagine how individuals can respond effectively to large-scale threats or serious wants.[70] He prefers communities to be the reference point for security and poverty debates in the Arctic. If Nunavut were a country, it would be among the poorest in the world.

The lone man with a gun in Wild West movies may be an icon of American culture, but this sort of hero is out of place in the Arctic. In Jack London's "To Build a Fire," a lone man dies, defeated by ice and cold, for want of a match. "The Mad Trapper" is a tragic story about an unnamed man the state would not leave alone. The Arctic needs high-functioning communities as its next-generation heroes. Northern communities require chiefs, legislators, and feds to consider a newer conception of human security, one that considers food, housing, education, and health while recognizing Indigenous communitarianism. As Griffiths puts it, "security is held in common or not at all."[71] And the hunger for community is real.

Here we face two perspectives on human development. The southern view, Griffiths tells us, "starts with the individual and asks how individuals are faring in terms of any number of criteria like life expectancy, education, material well-being, and so forth." An alternative view, he says – one that I would call a northern Indigenous approach – "starts with the community or the social group and views human development through the lens of community viability."[72] Adhering to state-centred security theories developed during the Cold War, Conservative elites in Canada's southern-based national capitals have taken paternalistic or top-down approaches to Arctic security. As Griffiths notes, Liberals like the human security idea, which focuses on individual well-being, avoiding a top-down or bottom-up orientation altogether. Northern social democrats may prefer bottom-up approaches.

Social democrats argue that Arctic economic, social, and environmental security begins with communities – all individuals depend on those around them. Conservatives who care about Arctic sovereignty and liberals who value human security both must recognize that the absence of a large military presence for Canada in the North means they need northerners, especially Nunavummiut. Nunavummiut communities play essential roles in securing the sovereignty of Canada's Arctic; as the territory's most impoverished citizens, the people living in these communities deserve income supports and the investments necessary to achieve Canadian standards of housing and nutrition.

As things now stand, food scarcity and overcrowded housing have deprived Nunavummiut of the full benefits of Canadian citizenship. Many other northerners struggle with basic food and housing. Building strong northern communities requires healthy food and safe housing – but Ottawa doesn't get that. Neither, apparently, do Washington or Moscow. Food and housing insecurity in the North has inspired some excellent writing on both subjects, but policy-makers would make more progress if they recognized both as a problem of chronic persistent *poverty*. Far too many people in the North remain hungry and homeless. The young mother shivering under a blanket by the ATM cannot wait for spring.

The federal government's forced relocations disrupted traditional ways of life. During land claims negotiations, northern Indigenous leaders took on new roles as hunters of treaties. Fifty years on, poverty continues to plague High Arctic settlements. At this moment, Nunavut's legislators don't have the means to address this problem. Only the feds can do it.

6

Knowing Yourself
Education and Health

The teacher learns by teaching, the learner by doing,
and sickness trains the healer.

For a time in the 1960s my father, John Penikett, was *the* doctor in Dawson City, Yukon. After house calls, he would sometimes drop into the Downtown Hotel bar for a single glass of scotch. Within seconds, half a dozen shot glasses might appear on the bar in front of him. Often they came from patients who happened to be in the saloon – merchants, miners, and trappers who had not yet paid their medical bills. My mother, Sally, a former nurse, disliked this method of payment and longed for the day the territory would join Canada's single-payer system of universal public health insurance.

Canada's public health care system remains a work in progress. The country now has a record number of doctors. Most are handsomely paid, and their salaries continue to climb. In 2015, for example, doctors earned, on average, $339,000.[1] Most doctors work in Canada's cities, though, because of the greater income potential there. In 2014 more than 73,000 doctors worked in urban settings, with only about 6,500, or 8.2 percent, based in rural areas.[2] In other ways, too, quality health care still does not reach everyone who needs it.

Patients today are calling for less paternalism from professionals and more family-centred care. As medicine moves out of hospitals – the kingdom of specialists – and into the community, physicians will need to invest more time in prevention and pay more attention to the socio-economic determinants of health and the root causes of disease.[3] Such ideas are not entirely new in Canada. In fact, the 1990 Yukon Health Act made similar proposals, and its principles are still sound.

In the late 1980s, half of my caucus colleagues in the Yukon Territorial Assembly were former First Nation chiefs and community leaders; the other half had backgrounds in mining unions or mining towns. Both groups had long been expressing concerns about substance abuse, occupational injuries, and mental health needs. By 1988, both Indigenous and non-Indigenous legislators in the government caucus were convinced we needed to update the territory's health legislation. The work of canvassing stakeholder groups about their expectations continued through the general election period that year. Following extensive community consultations after our government's re-election in 1989, we drafted new health legislation. As Yukon's health minister, I tabled the Yukon Health Act in November 1990. The act embraced a broad definition of health and focused on wellness rather than illness. Six principles underpinned the legislation: prevention, integration, partnership and collaboration, accountability, accessibility, and cultural sensitivity. While the Yukon Health Act's ideas were solid, however, its execution in the years that followed was unfortunately weak and halfhearted. It would be generous to award the responsible minister anything more than a C– grade.

Prevention

When the CCF/NDP government of Saskatchewan expanded Canada's universal, public, single-payer hospital insurance system to cover physicians' services in 1962, most of the province's doctors downed their stethoscopes and walked away from their offices. Their strike failed in its purpose, which was to kill the legislation; but it did force the provincial government into an expensive compromise that benefited doctors rather than patients or taxpayers. Former Saskatchewan premier Tommy Douglas, the "father" of Canada's "socialized" medicine, had originally imagined a system with salaried physicians. However, the medical practitioner lobby claimed this would destroy the "sacred doctor–patient relationship" and transform doctors from businesspeople into bureau-crats. Douglas's successor premier, Woodrow Lloyd, buckled under the lobbyists' pressure and allowed doctors to bill the provincial govern-ment for each single procedure or patient visit.

In the ensuing decades, as Saskatchewan's approach took root in the rest of Canada, and as hospital, drug, and technology costs climbed, fee-for-service began to generate increasingly high health care costs. This "single payer" system still enjoys a fairly good reputation; how-ever, it gives individual doctors a free hand to write prescriptions and order tests or expensive procedures without much regard for costs. By the 1990s, health care was gobbling up provincial and territorial budgets. Health care expenditures were consuming 30 to 40 percent of provin-cial operating budgets, but the provinces had only blunt instruments with which to contain them. Even thirty years ago, when publicly funded health care cost far less than it does today, provinces worried that health costs were squeezing other essential expenditures, such as that for education.

Universal access does not automatically mean good health care. Costs are soaring, yet policy-makers have found little improvement in the overall health of Canadians. Persistent overruns in provincial health budgets almost guarantee that health money is spent mainly on hospi-tals, specialists, and various technologies, leaving little or nothing for health promotion or disease prevention. Grandmothers once taught that an ounce of prevention was worth a pound of cure. But how does a health minister fund that ounce when cures eat up every dollar?

Borrowing an idea from Michael Rachlis and Carol Kushner's book *Second Opinion*, the Yukon Health Act created a Health Investment Fund that would reserve the *first* five cents – rather than the final five – of every health dollar for investment in preventing disease, injury, and dysfunction and promoting good health. Without that investment, we saw no chance to reduce the ballooning expenditures of the cura-tive system. By 2000, our government intended to allocate a minimum amount, equivalent to 5 percent of the overall medical budget, for pro-motion and prevention activities. The Health Investment Fund would not pay for existing curative programs. It could, however, pay for a nurse to provide sexual health education in high schools or for programs to dissuade pregnant women from drinking and smoking. Our government hoped that over time, the fund would help build a wellness system in the shadows of the existing treatment system.

Did it work? A 2008 Yukon government report found that the "proportion of territorial spending on health has risen by over 80 percent in the last 30 years in Yukon, significantly faster than the Canadian average growth of 22 percent."[4] In 2015, Yukon health care spending per capita was higher than in any of the provinces, at $10,949, or 18 percent of the budget. In Canada, only the NWT and Nunavut are spending more on health care.[5]

The same report recommended that the Yukon government expand public health campaigns and provide education programs for Yukoners at the greatest risk of disease or injury, including programs for accident prevention, excessive alcohol use, tobacco cessation, and obesity. In essence, this recommendation restates the original purposes of the Health Investment Fund. As such, the current situation raises basic questions about whether the fund's monies were indeed invested for their intended purposes.

Integration

Everywhere in the world, evidence has shown that economically disadvantaged people are more likely to suffer health problems. Yukon statistics support this finding. With that in mind, the 1990 Yukon Health Act proposed that health and social services be integrated wherever it was practical to do so, with unified service delivery. This model recognizes that human problems do not present themselves in neatly compartmentalized envelopes. Under the act, we crafted a Health and Social Services Council as the principal means to integrate services. As established in law, the council would have twelve citizen-members from a range of professional and cultural communities. The deputy ministers of health and justice were to participate as non-voting members.

From the start, the council addressed questions ranging from alcohol and drug abuse to community social service delivery and juvenile justice. That approach seems to be alive and well today. In 2007, for example, the council adopted an innovative proposal for what became the Yukon Community Wellness Court (CWC). The CWC deals with clients whose criminal behaviour is related to alcohol or drug addiction, mental health problems, or fetal alcohol spectrum disorder (FASD). The court's main objective is to reduce recidivism, victimization, and the harmful impacts of crime by influencing offenders' future behaviour. To that end, it provides offenders with therapeutic alternatives tailored to their specific needs and addresses victims' needs through restorative justice approaches. A Yukon legislator once blamed summer tourists for the high rate of alcohol consumption in the territory, but all around the North, alcoholism and substance abuse statistics stand way above national norms. So do those related to violence, trauma, and work-related accidents leading to death. These were and still are painful realities of Arctic life.

Partnerships and Collaboration

Through the Yukon Health Act, our government hoped to advance cooperative partnerships to promote health and integrate services. As we envisioned it, these partnerships would develop among governments, professionals, voluntary organizations, Aboriginal groups, communities, and individuals. The act also empowered communities, if they chose, to manage local social and health services through district boards and community clinics. At the most basic level, communities would be able to advise the government on issues such as whether they wanted to add an alcohol or drug prevention worker rather than an extra probation officer to better serve their constituents.

During the legislative debate over the 1990 Health Act, Conservative legislators complained that draft land claims and self-government treaties in Yukon were already proposing too many community boards and that the cost of creating more such boards in the health and social services field would be burdensome. When the Tories returned to power under the Yukon Party banner in 1992, they decided not to implement the act's community boards and clinics. However, eighteen years after the passage of the Yukon Health Act, a study commissioned by a subsequent conservative Yukon administration observed that across Canada, many examples of such collaborative primary care practices existed. About 300 community health centres across Canada have successfully experimented with integrated health and social service program delivery in clinics staffed by salaried professionals, with physicians and nurses working together in multidisciplinary teams. Governed by community boards, these interdisciplinary clinics embrace the principles of primary health care, by which they mean much more than just primary care. Unfortunately, for a variety of reasons, including a lack of political will, in Yukon progress has been slow. Things are worse in BC, where the province is forcing community clinics back into a fee-for-service model.

Accountability

Good public policy requires objective evaluations of health outcomes, health services, and hospital operations. The Yukon Health Act required a Yukon Health Status Report be tabled in the legislature every three years. The Yukon government subsequently published health status reports in 2003 and 2009. The 2009 report opens with this observation:

> Since the publication of the 2003 Yukon *Health Status Report*, the health of Yukoners has changed in a number of important ways – some predictable, and some unexpected. In the last six years, we have seen an alarming rise in the rates of smoking, obesity and diabetes. Injuries, chronic diseases such as heart disease and stroke, cancer, and the effects of substance abuse continue to take a toll on Yukoners year after year. But as the overall population of the territory has grown and the average age has risen, we have also seen life expectancy increase slightly.[6]

Accessibility

Yukon's Health Insurance Act covers the costs of basic physician and hospital care for all Yukon residents. This is the cornerstone of accessibility. Furthermore, a well-funded medical travel program has improved access for rural residents. This has been complemented by the training of Aboriginal health care workers to maximize the likelihood that Aboriginal citizens – the territory's most significant cultural minority – will take advantage of the services available.

Canada's national health care plan guarantees access to basic hospital and physician services for almost all Canadians. While all income groups tend to use the system to the same extent, poorer Canadians have greater needs due to poorer overall health, and across the country, issues remain regarding waiting lists and substandard services in rural and remote communities. In my Yukon youth, most towns had a resident physician, but villagers usually had to travel to a town or to the city of Whitehorse to see a doctor. During my time in government, there was rarely more than one psychiatrist in the whole territory. Most citizens did have access to a nurse or nurse-practitioner, prescription medicines, and an excellent medical evacuation program.

Despite these shortcomings, the majority of Canadians, including Yukoners, support the existing system because it offers them more options than they would have otherwise.

Cultural Sensitivity

Extensive discussions with Yukon First Nations and health policy experts led our government to include in the Health Act a recognition of traditional Aboriginal healing practices and to commit itself to promoting mutual understanding between practitioners of Aboriginal and mainstream medicine. However, the territory did not in any way plan to define or regulate Aboriginal healing practices. Any disputes arising between traditional healers and hospital staff could be referred to an ethics committee.

The language of the Yukon Health Act affirmed a patient's right – assuming legal competence – to make the final decisions about their own health. A companion law, the 2002 Yukon Hospital Act, enhanced the effectiveness of alternative Aboriginal programs – dietary, health liaison, and language – by implementing Health Act measures as well as other commitments made during Yukon treaty negotiations.

Colonization, which included the transition from a traditional protein-rich diet to a carbohydrate-heavy one, seriously damaged the physical, dental, and mental health of older Aboriginal people. As noted in Chapter 5, this led to increases in heart disease, obesity, and diabetes. This is why, during the legislative debate on the 1990 Health Act, the Yukon government promised that patients in the new regional hospital in Whitehorse would have access to traditional dietary options. The idea was that if patients wanted moose nose, Arctic char, bear root, spruce gum, salmon-egg soup, or low-bush cranberries, those foods would be provided. When implementing the 2002 Yukon Hospital Act, the authorities kept this promise.

Practices at Whitehorse General Hospital offer a vision of effective cultural sensitivity for northerners. A March 2009 review of the First Nation health programs at the facility found that "the program is unique in the country and leads the way in the development of a range of First Nation health programs to support patients and families during their stay and into the discharge process."[7] The hospital is governed by an independent community board of trustees, with some First Nation representatives among them, and a separate funding stream supports the hospital's First Nations program. This program includes a First Nation health liaison worker; a First Nation child life worker; First Nation employment equity and training; interpretation services; access to traditional medicines; and access to a traditional diet and nutritional information from a registered dietician.

According to the review's consultants, the Traditional Diet Program is one of the hospital's great strengths. The consultants did identify one serious weakness: some populations – in particular, high-risk patients with addictions – were underserved.[8] Individuals struggling with substance abuse would benefit from improved services and closer inter-agency collaboration with alcohol and drug services, the report said. But in general, the consultants' analysis of patient survey data supported the finding that First Nations, Inuit, and Métis people accessing the hospital's programs were highly satisfied with the service.

Implementation

Of the six principles in the 1990 Yukon Health Act, only two have thrived in practice: collaboration, embodied in the Health and Social Service Council, and cultural sensitivity, in the form of the Aboriginal Health Program at Whitehorse General Hospital. Gaye Hanson, former deputy minister for Yukon's Health and Social Services Department, thinks the act was not systematically implemented because the minister who wrote it had no implementation plan.[9] On that charge, I confess my guilt and regret my failure. Even the autocratic Emperor Napoleon had to learn the painful lesson that just because you give an order does not mean it will be carried out. Politicians have notoriously short atten-tion spans, and if their officials perceive no commitment to a policy or project, the initiative may wither and die in government filing cabinets.

Former US president Barack Obama fought to implement his health reforms in the face of great opposition. The Yukon Health Act faced little opposition but also attracted little enthusiasm. Only Yukon First Nations, who had a direct stake in the act's outcomes and a sense of ownership in the project through their representation on the Whitehorse hospital board and the Health and Social Services Council, felt any deep com-mitment to the legislation. Chiefs with treaties in hand had the leverage to help implement Health Act reforms linked to their land claims and self-government agreements. Thus, the true credit for the successful implementation of parts of Yukon's Health Act goes to the constituencies that promoted them.

Multiple Dimensions of Health

Yvonne Boyer's 2014 book, *Moving Aboriginal Health Forward: Discarding Canada's Legal Barriers*, links Aboriginal health problems across Canada to alienating laws and programs and the attitudes they foster. These laws and programs, Boyer says, are imposed by educated people who have never lived in poverty, been homeless, or suffered cultural contempt.[10] In particular, Boyer mocks Prime Minister Stephen Harper's 2009 G20 statement: "We also have no history of colonialism. So we have all the things that many people admire about the great powers but none of the things that threaten or bother them."[11] Boyer argues that decades of assimilationist policies have led to poverty, poor housing, ill health, "the medicalization of birthing and the decline of traditional midwifery practice."[12] In the 1950s, during a tuberculosis outbreak, Inuit who were tested and found positive were shipped south. Many of those sent away did not return, which devastated the families left behind.

In my father's day, northern physicians practised in splendid isolation. Since then, medicine in the North has become more complex and technical. A glance at the proceedings of the 15th International Congress on Circumpolar Health in 2012 indicates the range of interests of practitioners and researchers and the remarkable extent to which professionals in the field now cooperate across time zones as well as regional and national boundaries.[13] The congress proceedings addressed – among other things – food security, diabetes, home health care, nutrition, and health education curricula, as well as the health effects of climate change. Sample study topics included food allergies among children in eastern Siberia; the antioxidant level of Alaska's wild berries; and susceptibility to hypoxia and breathing control changes after short-term cold exposures.

The conference's plenary speaker, Dr. Kue Young, asked his audience to imagine looking down on the Arctic from a vantage point above the North Pole, and observed: "You will be surprised that many people, including those who are knowledgeable in global health affairs, have never

seen the world presented like that ... The North today is very much part
of the global economy. It may be remote, but it is no longer isolated."[14]
The North may be poor, but it doesn't have to be – so the participants
agreed. Its prosperity, though, will depend on how the proceeds from
its natural resources are distributed, and this will directly affect health
conditions. Poverty shortens lives; it is, in fact, a killer.

It was reported during the conference that of the four circumpolar
regions, the Nordic countries did best on all health indicators. Next
came Alaska, Yukon, and the NWT, followed by Greenland and Nunavut, with Siberia doing poorly by almost every indicator. The Arctic and
Subarctic situation calls for new strategies. As Young pointed out,
"northern regions can build on many proud achievements. Alaska's
health aides, Canada's primary care nurses, and Russia's *feldschers* and
other mobile medical teams come to mind and should freely borrow
best practices from one another."[15] Multidisciplinary teams make good
sense, but so far, there are too few of them on the ground.

In Nunavut, 25 Indigenous babies are delivered for every thousand
residents; that is the most rapid population growth in Canada, where
the average is 11.[16] The birth rate among Indigenous Alaskans is 90 per
1,000 women, while for non-Indigenous Alaskans, it is 30 per 1,000. In
the Russian Arctic, the infant mortality rate among Indigenous peoples
is twice that of the non-Indigenous population. Although death rates
among Russian Indigenous people have been declining since 1960, adult
deaths from non-natural causes (including accidents, suicide, and murder)
are still higher than those from natural causes. Non-natural causes of
death (including industrial and vehicular accidents and alcohol-related
violence) also lead in Alaska, especially in Indigenous populations.[17]

Tragically, suicide is a severe problem throughout the Arctic region.
After years of denial, Greenland's legislators have finally begun to address a number of the country's serious social problems, including child
sexual abuse and suicide. "Most of all, [Greenlanders] were talking to
one another about what they needed to do to take back control of their
lives," author and Arctic traveller James Raffan writes in *Circling the
Midnight Sun*.[18] Greenland has adopted a national suicide strategy, which

has yet to prove its effectiveness, but the province of Quebec's strategy seems successful. Remote communities in Alaska are now exploring approaches based on healing the deep wounds caused by the collision of Native and Western ways.[19] At 135 per 100,000, compared to 24.5 for Canadian Aboriginal people and 11.8 for Canada's general population, Nunavut's suicide rate is Canada's highest. First Nation citizens take their own lives at more than twice the rate of other Canadians, and Inuit kill themselves at five times the rate of First Nations.[20] Despite the implementation failure, the Yukon Health Act may still have utility in addressing this urgent issue. Canada has no national suicide prevention strategy.

Long guns are widely available in Canada's North, just as they are in Alaska. Canadian law requires that rifles and ammunition be stored separately under lock and key. Epidemiologists have stated that the general availability of firearms probably contributes to high suicide rates among young male northerners. Franklyn Griffiths agrees: "Threats to life are central to a restrictive view of human security. They are to be found in Arctic Canada, principally in the extraordinarily high rate of suicide among young Inuit males in particular."[21]

As suicides rates remain high, the intergenerational transmission of colonial trauma proceeds apace. Statistician Jack Hicks talked about this at a 2015 International Association for Suicide Prevention Symposium, where he discussed "suicide rates by community."[22] Hicks believes that the statistics for the Inuit reflect the past traumas experienced by the Inuit culture, including residential schools and other disruptions. Understanding that this trauma is transmitted from one generation to the next is key to developing prevention strategies.

In a celebrated study published in 1998, Michael J. Chandler and Christopher Lalonde examined the notions of personal and cultural continuity and their relevance for understanding suicide among First Nations youth. "Anyone whose identity is undermined by radical personal and cultural change is put at special risk for suicide for the reason that they lose those future commitments that are necessary to guarantee appropriate care and concern for their own well-being," they wrote.[23]

They correlated First Nations suicide rates with the efforts by each community they studied to retain its cultural identity.[24] In essence, they made the case for Aboriginal self-government as an investment in community health and suicide prevention.

But Natan Obed, president of Inuit Kanatami, dislikes Chandler and Lalonde's approach because it tends to absolve the federal government of any responsibility for the conditions that have led to despair and suicide.[25] In 2016, Inuit Tapiriit Kanatami released its own *National Inuit Suicide Prevention Strategy.*

Education

Like health, education generates heated debate in northern and rural Canada, especially among Aboriginal peoples. The Aboriginal education crisis, however, is a story distinct from the northern health care narrative.

For many years, First Nations and Inuit children were torn from their families and sent to residential schools operated by churches and governments. Indian residential schools will go down in history as a Canadian horror story, but they also operated across the Far North. In the 1930s, Stalin forced the nomadic Nenets and Khanty herders of the Yamal Peninsula onto collective reindeer farms and the children of Siberian nomads into residential schools.

A Yukon government report notes that between 1947 and 1954, "new roads and airplanes increased access to communities, permitting enforcement of school attendance and removal of more Aboriginal children by church and government officials, as denominations compete[d] to fill new schools."[26] The Whitehorse Baptist Indian Mission School opened in 1947, the Lower Post Roman Catholic Indian Residential School in 1951, and the Anglican Carcross Indian Residential School in 1954, along with Coudert Hall, a Catholic Indian Hostel in 1960. In 1967, Richard King published *The School at Mopass*, an exposé of the terrible conditions at the Carcross Residential School, where he taught for one year. King wrote: "All non-Indian adults of the school shared an attribute that was even more outstanding than their deviance from Canadian culture norms: ignorance of Indians. This ignorance was surpassed only by their willingness to offer snap judgments, usually unfavourable, about basic Indian motivations or character."[27] The school closed two years later.[28]

In his memoir *You Will Wear a White Shirt*, former NWT premier and now senator Nick Sibbeston remembers as a five-year-old being ripped from his idyllic village existence for a long boat trip to a residential school at Fort Providence:

> Soon people lined the bank, talking as their children cried. Mothers moved slowly down the hill, the children dragging their feet. As soon as the children were within reach, men grabbed them, carried them up the plank and handed them to the sisters [nuns]. Before long all the children in the barge were crying. Up on the hill dogs barked, mothers wept, covering their faces with their handkerchiefs, and fathers stood silently next to them.[29]

Non-Aboriginal visitors to the North sometimes observe that the Inuit are "shy" or that Dene elders seem "quiet." They might well wonder if this behaviour is one of many residues of the residential school experience.

Nowadays, regional governments operate their own schools. Nevertheless, Aboriginal communities in both the North and the South are struggling with the legacy of federally ordained residential schools. Speaking in the House of Commons in 1883, Canada's first prime minister, Sir John A. Macdonald, defended the residential school system, which was created explicitly to separate Aboriginal children from their parents and communities. "When the school is on the reserve, the child lives with his parents who are savages; he is surrounded by savages and though he may learn to read and write, his habits and training and mode of thought are Indian. He is simply a savage who can read and write."[30] This assimilation policy, practised in the United States and by other colonial empires, as well as in Canada, discouraged and at times even outlawed the use of traditional names, songs, and symbols as well as tribal languages. The seductions of assimilation included the Western trade goods essential to town life and its distractions.[31] In 1970, under "Project Surname," the federal government hired Abe Okpik, who had been assigned disc number "W3-554," to travel the North giving Inuit Western-style surnames to replace the numbers the feds had originally given every Inuk. Lucy Idlout's hit song "E5-770" is about her mother's disc number.

For decades, tens of thousands of Indigenous children in church- and government-run schools suffered beatings, hunger, and sexual abuse. Following the Canadian government's public apology to Aboriginal people in 2008, Canada's Truth and Reconciliation Commission heard from hundreds of residential school survivors and examined millions of incriminating documents. In June 2015 the commission published its six-year-long study of Indian residential schools. Commission chair Justice Murray Sinclair, Manitoba's first Aboriginal Associate Chief Justice, said the commission's findings indicated "cultural genocide," a term that opposition leaders in Parliament endorsed but that Stephen Harper's Conservative government did not.[32] When he talked of reconciliation, Sinclair referred not just to treaties, self-government agreements, and other accommodations, but also to a deeper, more substantial repairing of the relationship between settlers and Indigenous peoples. In a video produced to accompany the report, Justice Sinclair added: "Because it took us so many generations to get to this point, it's going to take at least a few generations to be able to say that we are making progress ... Reconciliation will be about ensuring that everything that we can do today is aimed at [the] high standard of restoring balance to that relationship."[33]

Improving Outcomes for Aboriginal Youth

In the Arctic today and across the country, most Canadians recognize the need to improve educational outcomes for Aboriginal youth, but the public is far from sure about the solutions. Shawn Atleo, National Chief of the Assembly of First Nations from 2009 to 2014, once remarked that Canada's "Aboriginal children are more likely to go to jail than to graduate from high school."[34] Improving education on reserves and in rural communities is essential work. Yet the existing governance structures for reserve schools fail the most basic test of meeting the needs of children, parents, and local governments. The irony is that while national governments and Indigenous communities fight for "control" of the Indigenous school system, in truth there is hardly a system to speak of, and not enough money to fund one. In 2009 I worked with Charles Ungerleider and William Demmert on an unpublished report for Indian and Northern Affairs Canada (now Indigenous and Northern Affairs Canada; INAC) titled *The Possibilities and Limitations of New Governance Arrangements for the Education of First Nations Learners on Reserve.*[35]

Today, with financial support from INAC, most First Nations children in Canada attend provincially or territorially regulated public schools. Over the years, the department has gradually handed over the administration of many reserve schools to First Nations. But by virtue of the Indian Act, INAC remains a very poor excuse for an education department. Its performance has been brutally criticized by Canada's auditor general and by other critics. In 1996, Canada's Royal Commission on Aboriginal Peoples called for Aboriginal governance of Aboriginal education, as well as an increase in the number of Aboriginal teachers. In response to these demands, Ottawa has been devolving management of on-reserve schools to First Nations. While mouthing platitudes about "Indian control," federal ministers have generally delegated very limited powers to First Nations. These arrangements may fund *schools*, but they do not come close to covering the costs of operating an on-reserve *school system*. Appearing before the House of Commons Standing Committee on Aboriginal Affairs in 2007, the Honourable Jim Prentice, then the minister responsible, testified that "the biggest challenge with the education system, I would submit, is not the dollars per se; it is rather the absence of an overall school system."[36] The fact is, establishing and maintaining any new system requires investment. Aboriginal schools need both a new system and the investment necessary to support it.

Finding new ways to govern and administer the education system for on-reserve children is an essential step towards improving outcomes and accountability for on-reserve schools. While structural and administrative change could lead to better management of the reserve education system and, by extension, improve education outcomes, this approach has only limited potential. Democratic societies have promised that student achievement will not be constrained by ethnic or geographic circumstances, but for the vast majority of Aboriginal students, this promise has not been kept.[37] Sections of the Indian Act that enabled the residential schools are long overdue for revision. In the right hands, the revision process could provide a meaningful foundation for new structures that would actively support the education of First Nations children.

Since 1972, the chiefs of the National Indian Brotherhood (now the Assembly of First Nations, or AFN) have argued for "Indian control of Indian education." If a First Nation wished to exercise its "inherent right" to self-government – in Canada, a right in name only, as far as Ottawa has been concerned – the federal government might agree to vacate the field. But without federal financial assistance, funding education would be a huge challenge for all but a few resource-rich First Nations.

In 1976, Trevor Bremner, a teacher at the Haines Junction School, volunteered to organize Southern Tutchone language lessons twice a week for half an hour with elder Marge Jackson. The Yukon Department of Education, under education minister Dan Lang, ordered him to stop. Months later, in a job interview for the vacant principal's position at Haines Junction, the school committee asked candidate Wolf Riedl whether he would continue the language program. Reidl remembers that day well. He later told me, "I replied [that] it only made sense given the number of native families and kids in the school." When asked about the people who didn't want their kids to take Southern Tutchone lessons, Riedl replied that he would offer French as an option. The committee's reply was, "Well, we don't want them learning Frog either!" Regardless, Reidl got the job and expanded the Native language program.

Only about 20 percent of Aboriginal students in Canada attend First Nations schools on reserves.[38] The great majority attend provincially run schools. Simon Fraser University's John Richards and his academic colleagues make the point that Aboriginal students do poorly in these provincial schools compared to non-Aboriginal students, even if they perform generally better there than they do in the reserve schools.[39]

By seeking greater control over schooling, Aboriginal people are asking for no more than what other communities already have – namely, the chance to shape the education that will turn their children into adult citizens. First Nations want two things from an education system: schools to help children, youth, and adults learn the skills they need to participate fully in the economy; and schools to help children develop as citizens of Indigenous nations, with the linguistic and traditional knowledge necessary for cultural continuity.

The existing public education systems generally accomplish neither of these objectives. Most Aboriginal youth do not finish high school, and this leaves them unprepared for further education or for full participation in the mainstream economy. Moreover, Aboriginal languages are disappearing at an alarming rate. Calls for more culturally relevant curricula and pedagogy are being heard with greater and greater frequency and urgency.

Building a new school system will not be a simple task. Too much centralization risks undermining the autonomy and discretion of individual communities. Too much *de*centralization, on the other hand, could produce dozens of uncoordinated experiments, and the resulting "non-system" would confound measurement, accountability, and stewardship while aggravating pre-existing inequities. In seeking new models of governance, education reformers might save time by going straight to the "Goldilocks" zone between the extremes of administrative centralization and devolution.

Whatever path communities choose, Aboriginal jurisdiction over Aboriginal education will be the cornerstone of any new system. That is why any option unacceptable to First Nations, Inuit, and Métis communities should not be seriously considered by education policy decision-makers. Something must change to clear pathways so that Aboriginal students can achieve recognized high school credentials and further education. An effectively structured school system needs to be part of this. The goal is to generate outcomes for Indigenous students on par with those of graduates of provincial high schools. First Nations would then have options to pursue the same post-secondary opportunities as non-Aboriginal students. As always, capacity constrains what is possible. Fortunately, where capacity is lacking, with time and effort school leaders can develop it as long as adequate funding is available.

Possible Governance Models

Designers of new models to govern First Nations schools must be mindful that resources need to match goals. In planning cultural and linguistic programming, for example, reformers will need to involve the community's chiefs and elders when recruiting certified teachers.

A significant challenge for any reform is that at present, there is no system in place to measure outcomes across different locations. As a consequence, governments at all levels, and especially elected legislators, cannot see what works and what doesn't. Coordinating inputs and measuring outcomes will require an administrative framework and mechanisms for accountability – hence, the obvious need for an effective administrative structure.

It will not be easy to devise Aboriginal school systems that allow for autonomy, discretion, and flexibility while at the same time providing comparable quality across First Nation communities. To do all of this while containing costs and maximizing efficiency will be a hard challenge. Note that there are many dimensions of Aboriginality in Canada and many sites for Aboriginal education: on-reserve and off-reserve; territorial, provincial, and federal; Status and non-Status. With that in mind, let us consider the merits of some emergent models and innovations.

1. *Indigenous and Northern Affairs (INAC) centralized management*

The Canadian government could embrace its responsibility for First Nations schools and build a new system under the auspices of an "education department" within INAC. The Indian Act confers on the minister the discretionary power to provide or make agreements with regard to providing education for First Nations children. This kind of centralization could simplify administration and foster consistent practices and standards across delivery sites and schools. But while it might improve the status quo, it is likely to find little support among First Nations or Canadians in general, and it could face significant legal challenges for that reason.

2. *Administrative devolution*

Administrative devolution essentially means decentralizing administrative responsibilities and functions to subordinate levels of government. Many school systems are inherently decentralized, in that daily decisions are made at the level of the school or school board. Developing Aboriginal curriculum and language programming is also inherently decentralized, given that each cultural/language group requires its own approach and each may require experts other than teachers. One hopeful sign, outlined by First Nations language developer Darrick Baxter in a recent TEDx talk, is the sudden proliferation of new technologies that allow individuals to teach themselves traditional languages.[40] There's even an iPhone app called "Chert" that lets users add a keyboard to their iPhone and type or text in all twenty Alaska Native dialects. The Magdanz brothers hope that this Snapchat and Facebook friendly app could help invigorate Indigenous language learning among the young.

There are many potential models of devolution for Aboriginal education, including the following:

(a) First Nations management of on-reserve schooling: At present, First Nations across Canada operate around 500 schools on reserves, serving 120,000 students.[41] Although no firm policy supports INAC's devolution of education management to First Nations, the department has for

decades been negotiating such agreements. These agreements, though, may be as much about offloading programs and responsibilities as they are about strengthening school management. Michael Mendelson, Senior Scholar at the Caledon Institute of Social Policy, argues that while such arrangements are a good start, they are inadequate because they lack features important to First Nations education, such as curriculum development; teacher training; development of principals, supervisors, and other education leaders; testing and quality assurance; legal accountability to students and their families; and the general support structure that makes a modern school work.[42]

Mendelson also finds that federal education funding for Aboriginal students in on-reserve schools does not meet government standards of "equivalent funding to the province[s], let alone [being] adequate to provide for an equivalent quality of education."[43] Simon Fraser University education professor Sean Blenkinsop points out that administrators of on-reserve schools must choose between using the provincial curriculum, taught by teachers with at least a BEd, or finding something more personalized to their unique community identity.

(b) *Indigenous programming possibilities*: Language and culture are inseparable. Philosopher Charles Taylor believes that language both *has* a purpose and *is* purposeful: "It is through story that we find or devise ways of living bearably in time."[44] Children learn language and ways of thinking from their families and communities. Alaska legislator Niilo Koponen once shared with me his view that "if you want to understand the way a people think, study the grammar of their language."

If INAC expands support for Indigenous programs in Aboriginal cultures, history, and languages, this will advance First Nations' control over education. Such support would mirror federal contributions to the creation of French first-language schools under Section 23 of the 1982 Constitution Act. The difference between education being the responsibility of one's family and clan, on the one hand, and formal schooling, on the other, has represented for most Aboriginal people a dramatic cultural shift. First Nations educators are making efforts to connect the two educational traditions by bringing traditional learning into the classroom. As Aboriginal scholars develop more culturally sensitive approaches, Aboriginal traditional knowledge is finding its way into classrooms as a supplement to mainstream pedagogy.

But despite its seeming simplicity, implementing this approach at an equitable and consistent level across First Nations could prove challenging. From the time of the numbered treaties and the first Indian reserves, Canadian authorities have tried to fence in Aboriginal cultures. These fences did *not* make for good neighbours. As a result, few people beyond Aboriginal scholars working within communities are currently trusted to develop appropriate Aboriginal cultural content in school curriculums, classroom materials, and textbooks. Also, still-raw memories of the residential schools have contributed to the estrangement that many Aboriginal children feel from formal schooling, and their parents' experience in residential schools has led to a loss of cultural knowledge and language in younger generations. For these reasons, there may not be enough teachers available who possess traditional knowledge.[45]

North American efforts to improve the school success of Aboriginal children include experiments with bilingual schooling, first-language immersion programs, alternative science programs, and, surprisingly, even new-model Aboriginal boarding schools. A Yellowknife-based group of the Gordon Foundation's Jane Glassco Fellows recommended to the Arctic Athabaskan Council that, as a first step, communities, families, and leaders could commit themselves to using their Dene dialects in daily life.[46] The fellows also proposed that Canada open up the Official Languages Act to recognize Indigenous languages.

In 1993, the largest land claims agreement in history created the Nunavut Territory in the Eastern Arctic. Article 23 of Nunavut's agreement commits the federal and territorial governments to certain public-service employment targets for the Inuit, who are 85 percent of the territory's population. In 2006, because neither government had met these targets, the parties to the land claims agreement asked conciliator Thomas Berger to address the implementation of Article 23. According to Berger's final report, "the only way in which we can fulfil the objective of Article 23 is by adopting specific measures in the near term which will increase Inuit representation in the public service, and for the long term, establishing in Nunavut a comprehensive program of bilingual education in Inuktitut and English."[47] Berger recommended that the Canadian government cover "the lion's share" of the cost.[48]

Inuit legislators, who represent Nunavut's majority, have the political power to make education policy for the territory. In the long run, Inuktitut language retention ought to be possible in the territory. If it is in the national interest to fund English/French bilingual education, it seems reasonable for the federal government to similarly underwrite English/ Inuktitut schooling, Berger suggested.[49] Yet according to Nunavut educator John Bainbridge, "it will require a miracle for GN [the Government of Nunavut] to implement its 'commitment' to bilingual instruction from kindergarten to grade 12 by 2020."[50] Unfortunately, the Government of Nunavut has not been able to train enough Inuktitut speaking teachers. According to John Richards, the implementation of bilingual and other Aboriginal cultural programs in most areas of the country, including Nunavut, is limited by issues of capacity – by the lack of superintendents, teachers, and scholars, and of provincial or territorial schools with the competence to deliver such programs – as well as by resistance by unions to the presence of Aboriginal language instructors in the classroom.[51] In Yukon, that resistance faded somewhat after Yukon College in Whitehorse established a Certified Native Language Instructor program. Subsequently, after failing to *negotiate* a solution, the territorial government *legislated* these instructors into the teachers' union. This example is evidence that successful programs will not appear overnight.

On Canada's borders, the Mohawk, the Blackfoot in Montana, and the Tlingit in Alaska are all experimenting with first-language immersion schools. These American schools have experienced many start-up problems, but once established, their programs become popular. Nizipuhwahsin (Real Speak) Center in northwestern Montana has produced the first young fluent speakers of the Blackfoot language in a generation. Aboriginal first-language programs in Canada are likely too new and too few to be evaluated. In 1970, Gwich'in elder Paul Ben Kassi and I watched a group of preschoolers playing on the banks of the Porcu-pine River. Shaking his head sadly, Kassi told me that just a few years before, kids of that age would have been playing in their own language, but once television arrived in the community, English became their language of play. Television has stayed, of course, and Arctic languages are struggling. There are fewer and fewer Aboriginal language speakers in Canada each year, and the survival of these languages depends on the political will of Aboriginal and government leaders to commit to building institutions that value Aboriginal cultures and learning.

(c) *Indigenous institutions*: The 1996 Report of the Royal Commission on Aboriginal Peoples stated:

> It is critically important for Aboriginal adolescents to be able to live at home while attending secondary school. At age 13, they are not pre-pared for life away from a family and cultural base. Eventually, high school should be available in all Aboriginal communities. Where communities are very small, distance education may help make local high school programs possible.[52]

Like most Royal Commission reports, RCAP gathers dust on library shelves. Prime Minister Harper's 2008 residential school apology sup-posedly sounded the death knell for assimilationist policies; however, the idea of boarding schools for Aboriginal youth did not die completely. That said, a world of difference exists between the church-run residential schools of earlier decades that attempted to extinguish Aboriginal cul-tures and languages and today's Aboriginal-controlled, voluntary board-ing schools in which Aboriginal cultures and languages are nourished.

In parts of the United States with large Indigenous populations, and in rural and isolated communities, educators are taking a long second look at the idea of residential schools. The Mount Edgecumbe High School in Sitka, Alaska, was run by the Bureau of Indian Affairs for sev-eral years beginning in 1947, and a number of its graduates were promin-ent in the Indigenous leadership that negotiated the Alaska Native Claims Settlement in 1971. With the state taking over responsibility for educating all Alaskans and the decision to build a high school in every village, the Bureau of Indian Affairs closed Mount Edgecumbe in the mid-1980s. The quality of education offered to the handful of grade twelve students by the village high schools was uneven, however, and many talented Native students felt short-changed. So Alaska governor Steve Cowper reopened Mount Edgecumbe as a regional institution with programs respectful of rural Alaskan traditions. Today that school is still graduating the next generation of Native leaders in Alaska. Cowper wrote to me in 2009 that students thrive in this environment:

> In 1987 I made the decision to take over Mt. Edgecumbe and make it a state-operated boarding school for rural high school students. Through a visionary Superintendent, we installed one of the most rigorous academic curricula in the US. In order to graduate, students had to learn a foreign language and become reasonably fluent in it. Their choices were Japanese, Chinese, Korean, and I believe also Russian. Advanced math, i.e., integral calculus, was also required, as were physics, chemistry, and other advanced science courses. It turned out that the students who were already bilingual (e.g., Yup'ik, Iñupiaq) picked up a third and sometimes a fourth language with ease. Almost 90 percent of the graduates went on to colleges and universities, and many of the others went into the US Armed Services. Not only that, the athletic teams were outstanding.

Another example of a residential school is the Santa Fe Indian School in New Mexico, a boarding school under Indigenous governance and supported by federal funding. The Santa Fe school directly counters some of the alienating experiences that occurred in the old Canadian residential schools. Dormitory staff hired from the students' home communities function as "family" for high school students in residence, and the architecture of the school buildings reflects Pueblo traditions. Just as important, the school is academically very successful, with 90 percent of its graduates going on to post-secondary education.[53] The Santa Fe

Indian School and Mount Edgecumbe could both be models for regional or tribal council schools in certain parts of northern Canada.

Existing facilities might even be used in some cases, although not without complications. When the Council for Yukon Indians (CYI) took over Coudert Hall, a former Catholic school residence, as their administrative headquarters, some CYI employees were quite conflicted. One employee told me that he wanted to run shouting down the halls, something he'd never been allowed to do as a tiny child. When as a legislator I visited another northern residential school as it was about to close, the hallway walls still displayed framed photographs of tiny Aboriginal children dressed in uniforms, like toy soldiers, and marching to a denominational drum.

After visiting the Pelican Falls First Nations High School, a regional school for kids whose home villages have no high school, Manitoba broadcaster, writer, and MLA Wab Kinew walked to the site of his father's old residential school. In his memoir *The Reason You Walk*, Kinew recorded his mixed feelings: "It was difficult for me to ignore the parallels between Pelican the residential school and Pelican the high school."[54] Today's students still have to leave their families and communities, but on the plus side, they study their ancestral languages and cultures. I agree with Kinew that we have made progress but have much further to go.

Exercising Jurisdiction

As pre-existing political communities at the time of European colonization, First Nations claim an inherent right to self-government. Such claims can lead to land claims, treaty, and self-government negotiations. Jurisdiction provides chiefs and other tribal authorities with the power to make laws and regulations governing their schools; however, devolving jurisdiction over Indigenous schools does not necessarily require treaties or self-government agreements as such. Rather, it entails negotiations among First Nations, Ottawa, and the provincial governments.

How does this work in practice? A First Nation may choose to assert its jurisdiction unilaterally by observing a customary tribal law, by writing new legislation, or simply by exercising its authority. In an informative example, residents of Kahnawake, near Montreal, founded the Kahnawake Survival School to teach Haudenosaunee culture and the Mohawk language. The Kahnawake student council makes decisions by consensus, according to Mohawk governance traditions. As well, the school is "modelled on the traditional Mohawk government, which is based on consensus-building."[55] In running the school, the Mohawk are simply exercising their jurisdiction.

Any First Nation that asserts its jurisdiction is taking risks, including loss of funding and possible legal challenges. The federal government may or may not fund projects like the Kahnawake Survival School. In that case, the federal government did provide funding. However, most modern treaty groups that have invoked the right to self-government continue to endure disputes with INAC over implementation funding. In terms of educational practicalities, it likely makes little difference whether a First Nation bases jurisdiction on "inherent right" or formal delegation to Ottawa.

Jurisdictional Transfer

Another path to Aboriginal groups assuming jurisdiction over their children's education requires the federal government to delegate these responsibilities as part of a treaty negotiation or self-government agreement. In British Columbia today, this process involves tripartite negotiations with the federal and the provincial governments. As noted earlier, since 1995, federal policy has acknowledged self-government as an inherent Aboriginal right under Section 35 of the 1982 Constitution Act.

Federal policy guiding Aboriginal self-government allows for negotiations in three broad areas: (1) matters internal to the group; (2) matters integral to the group's distinctive culture; and (3) matters essential to the group's operation as a government.[56] For First Nations, any reform of education governance would have to entail the concurrent application of provincial law, even where the First Nation asserts complete control of any Aboriginal programming.

For example, the Nisga'a Treaty reads: "Nisga'a Lisims Government may make laws in respect of pre-school to grade 12 education on Nisga'a Lands of Nisga'a citizens, including the teaching of Nisga'a language and culture." These laws include provisions for curriculum, evaluation, and certification of teachers. The same treaty supplements the education sections of the Indian Act with Nisga'a law and its own education authority. In other modern treaty areas – James Bay and Yukon – the Cree, Dene, and Tlingit may also exercise control over education.

Yukon assumed responsibility for the education of its First Nations students in 1951. Part of the Yukon First Nations self-government agreement reached in 1992 addresses education programs and services. The Yukon self-government agreements are instructive in this respect, because although they allow First Nations to set up their own schools with Yukon government funding, no Yukon First Nation has chosen that path yet. The reason may be that, parallel to the self-government negotiations, Yukon Education Minister Piers McDonald piloted through the legislature a new Education Act that trained numerous Aboriginal teachers, brought elders into every school as salaried language instructors, and gave every tribal community control of a local cultural curriculum. The power inherent in having the jurisdiction but, for now, choosing *not* to exercise it has given Yukon chiefs considerable leverage in the education system.

Funding is always an issue. A 200-person band in Yukon or BC might well be able to operate its own elementary school or kindergarten; but it probably does not have the means to operate a high school with enough science or language options to equip candidates for universities, or to develop language and curriculum materials, or to establish a school board with the usual range of responsibilities. A tribal council, linguistic community, or larger regional group might have the requisite capacity for these things, so it could be in everybody's interest for the federal, provincial, and First Nations governments to consider aggregating school management under such an authority. Under this model, INAC would be fully justified in declaring that, while it would underwrite the cost of village schools, it would only support high schools, school board functions, cultural curriculum development, and certification and training of classroom teachers and language instructors if these came under the auspices of education authorities run by tribal councils or regional bodies of First Nations. This kind of structure can only come into being, though, if the feds and provincial legislators help build it *before* First Nations take over jurisdiction of their communities' schools.

Self-government means much more than administrative devolution. First Nations' educational deficits cannot be overcome without large investments in institutions, governance, and curriculum development. The only option otherwise is the long, slow walk of local treaty and self-government negotiations.

Provincial Tools

While it is perfectly understandable that Indigenous leaders from the generations of residential school survivors want to set up their own schools, not all Indigenous learners want the same thing. Universities offering teacher or business programs specifically for Indigenous students may find that many of the intended beneficiaries prefer to register in mainstream programs rather than what some students call "ghetto" alternatives. Also, many Indigenous families apparently prefer the provincial school alternative.

Federal funding and provincial expertise can help facilitate Aboriginal supervision of education institutions; shared governance may therefore be a practical option. Education agreements can be negotiated using a variety of instruments: treaties, self-government agreements, or interim measures. Governments can support these initiatives with legislation enshrining the goal of Aboriginal jurisdiction over education. Structural reforms – such as tribal councils or regional authorities that assume school board functions – might not require treaties or even legislation. Policy-makers everywhere can learn from innovations such as magnet schools, BC's First Nations Education Steering Committee (FNESC), and that province's Independent School Act, which requires First Nations schools to be managed by "education societies." These schools operate in much the same way as non-Aboriginal private schools.

In 2007 the BC legislature passed its First Nations Education Act, having in 2006 adopted the First Nations Jurisdiction over Education in British Columbia Act. Together, these acts have established the principle of "Aboriginal control of Aboriginal education." The 2007 act enables participating First Nations to enter into individual Canada–First Nation Education Jurisdiction Agreements governing education on reserves. Other provinces could negotiate similar tripartite agreements, one of the key benefits of which would be the paving of predictable pathways for students on reserves to achieve the provincial high school diploma that facilitates the transition to post-secondary education. This framework could also create opportunities for a more accurate reflection of Aboriginal educational successes in provincial data.

Understanding the circumstances peculiar to BC and Yukon might facilitate similar developments elsewhere. At present, shared governance approaches may not be possible in all jurisdictions. My impression is that the existence of a coordination and advocacy group within the First Nations Education Steering Committee (FNESC) was a significant contributing factor in BC, for example. Of course, a provincial or territorial government committed to reconciliation and partnership with First Nations always helps.

Shared Governance:
An Emerging Consensus?

While recommending separate First Nations school boards, Michael Mendelson thinks that a workable policy must be based on a consensus among all parties.[57] Funding and capacity issues are a clear worry for many First Nations, which also need to put in place mechanisms to ensure accountability, comparability, and quality among their schools and school areas. At the same time, localized agreements and arrangements will continue to emerge organically in response to local needs.

Desirable System Features

Administration and coordination: Canada has long accommodated the educational interests of linguistic and religious minorities. Since Canada has constitutional obligations to First Nations, this means properly acknowledging that First Nations communities need effective school system governance. The federal government has a duty to fund reserve schools, school boards, and other educational authorities at the regional or linguistic community level. First Nations may wish to locate the administrative authority for schools and education management within tribal governments, which through self-government or devolution agreements would secure federal and sometimes provincial funding. In successful shared governance agreements, every party should have defined or distinct and appropriate roles to play.

First Nations: At a minimum, First Nations need the power to perpetuate their tribal cultures in schools under their governance. Wherever possible, they should have this power in public schools as well. In practice, this means that First Nations, Inuit, and Métis parents would be able to oversee any Aboriginal curriculum taught in Aboriginal schools, on reserves, or to their children in cities, as well as in any provincially regulated educational institution. First Nations parents should also enjoy the same right as non–First Nations parents to elect school boards or similar education authorities. Administrative delegation from INAC is simply not enough.

In the James Bay and Northern Quebec Agreement, the Cree opted for their own school board under provincial jurisdiction. This school board is similar to others, although it has unique powers and a special mandate to ensure that education programs are culturally relevant. On their own, however, very few First Nations have the administrative capacity or the funding to sustain a fully functioning school board. As noted, larger aggregations of First Nations, tribal councils, or linguistic communities or regions might take on this job instead.

Provinces and territories: Provinces and First Nations share an interest in seeing their next generations of Indigenous parents and leaders master the skills necessary to succeed in colleges, universities, and the modern economy and society. Based on the Nisga'a precedent, First Nations and provincial governments must commit themselves to provincial standards or the equivalent, and the provinces must respect the domain of First Nations in matters internal to their communities and cultures. A standard model for a First Nations school board or education authority is not necessary. Yukon chose parent councils over regional school boards, while the Nisga'a preferred a tribal authority.

School boards: To improve First Nations schools, parent involvement and community control are essential. This could be through elected school boards or appointed education authorities. Tribal or regional school boards could assume whatever powers First Nations delegate to them. But such boards cannot function properly without a healthy relationship with provincial educational authorities and without long-term federal investment in educational professionalism.

Federal government: Bill C-33: In 2014, after years of consultation, the Harper government proposed Bill C-33, the First Nations Control of First Nations Education Act. Unfortunately, Bill C-33 does *not* provide "First Nations control" of First Nations education. Rather, it offers a measure of shared governance through a joint council of nine education professionals to be named by the Minister of Aboriginal Affairs.[58] As in George Bush's "No Child Left Behind" legislation, the federal government's stated priority was "educational standards," meaning achieving educational parity with the provinces. Schools failing this test could be placed under administrative control.

It is impossible for underfunded reserve schools to meet provincial standards. If First Nations had supported Harper's legislation, $1.9 billion of federal funding would have rolled out in 2016. AFN National Chief Shawn Atleo supported the bill, but chiefs in opposition wanted to hold out for First Nations control.[59] Ottawa was prepared to devolve some management to education professionals, but funding would follow only if First Nations abandoned their notion of control. In May 2014, Atleo resigned as AFN national chief after many chiefs rejected his recommendation that they support the government's "paternalistic"[60] legislation. Until Ottawa is prepared to cede, release, or surrender control to Indian governments, federal funding will go elsewhere. The Liberal government under Justin Trudeau has put Bill C-33 on hold. The 2016–17 federal budget committed $2.6 billion to Aboriginal education over five years; however, APTN's (Aboriginal Peoples Television Network) Jorge Barrera points out that $1.4 billion of that spending is contingent on the Liberal Party's re-election.[61]

Five Ideas for Structural Change

Making First Nations schools successful will require a clear demonstration of political will at every level. But given the diverse interests and cultures of First Nations in Canada, any top-down approach will prove difficult to implement. The alternative – bottom-up processes involving devolution and self-government negotiations with First Nations, tribal councils, and provincial authorities – could over time build a firmer foundation for meaningful reform. The responsible officials in INAC need to ask this central question: Is it possible to integrate into a single comprehensive federal policy changes that would enlarge accountability to local communities and federal and provincial governments, so as to improve school governance and educational outcomes for Aboriginal students?

Whatever their answer, the following five ideas could usefully guide negotiations towards new First Nation School Governance agreements:

1. Canada commits to investing in First Nations schools, Aboriginal cultural curriculum materials, Aboriginal-language instructors, and aggregated or consolidated First Nation education authorities or school boards.
2. Contributions to new First Nations school governance structures flow from all levels of government – First Nations, provincial, and federal – according to their interests and ability to pay.
3. First Nations control the Aboriginal curriculum in schools with Aboriginal children, administration of schools on reserves, and

jurisdiction in self-government agreements through negotiation and devolution of school board powers.

4. The provinces and territories establish core curriculum, standards, and teacher certifications unless, by agreement, a province has agreed to delegate this power to a tribal council or other competent education authority, or to vacate these fields in a self-government agreement.

5. The provinces and territories and First Nations work together to provide students of schools on reserves or treaty lands with opportunities to obtain provincial high school credentials or certificates with equivalent recognition, so that pathways to further education are clear.

Post-secondary Initiatives

Some promising and innovative practices have emerged in the North at the post-secondary level. In the late 1980s the University of Alaska–Juneau flew professors into Whitehorse on weekends to provide students with instruction for a Master of Public Administration degree. For this MPA program, the Yukon government sponsored locally hired public servants, employees who had often been reluctant to apply for senior government jobs without the credential of an advanced degree. The program gave many of its graduates the confidence to apply for senior positions.

When the territorial government began planning the Ayumdigut Campus of Yukon College in the 1990s, Margaret Commodore Joe and Norma Kassi, two Indigenous women in the NDP caucus, contended that candidates for the degree programs in education, nursing, and social work would likely be bright young women from rural communities who had dropped out of high school to have their first child. Therefore, Joe and Kassi argued that instead of building dormitories with single rooms, the college needed to provide residences for families and a child care centre, as well as an early childhood education program. The cabinet agreed, and years later, as the keynote speaker at a graduation ceremony, I watched dozens of beaming young women from rural Yukon communities march up in caps and gowns to receive their degrees while their families loudly applauded.

The northern territories of Canada have no university; however, the University of the Arctic, a virtual institution, is well used by northern students. David Stone of Canada, Lars-Erik Liljelund of Sweden, and William Heal of the United Kingdom dreamed up UArctic at a 1997 Arctic Monitoring and Assessment Program (AMAP) meeting,[62] and it represents one concrete achievement of the Arctic Council in its early years. UArctic is a network of universities, research organizations, and others committed to research and higher education in the North. In 2013 I chaired an international external ten-year review team for UArctic. The team concluded that it was easier to evaluate UArctic as a "network" of 140 institutions rather than as a "university" as such. UArctic's courses and research networks have found large audiences in the circumpolar world.

Canada's not-so-good news is that, while the numbers of Indigenous university students is climbing, their graduation rates are far below those of non-Indigenous Canadians.[63] Unfortunately, when faced with a crisis, cash-strapped governments tend to do no more than the minimum required. Ottawa, northern legislators, and Indigenous governments must to work together in the fields of education and health. It would be very helpful if they viewed funding in those areas as an investment, not an expenditure.

7

Underfoot
Resources, Renewable and Non-renewable

The miners watch as the boss pockets the shiniest rocks.

Northerners have not benefited much from northern resource developments. In the 1970s, whenever a new mine opened, young Yukoners watched the ore concentrates head south to Tokyo or Seoul. The profits went to London or New York, the taxes to Ottawa, and most of the jobs to young men from Edmonton or Vancouver. All the Yukoners got was a hole in the ground, which they could use as a municipal dump – if Ottawa gave permission. Today, most, but not all, of that has changed.

Ideas alter the character of public discourse and the terms of debate. Although the life experiences of African Americans and northern First Nations people are very different, the ideas of Gandhi, Martin Luther King, and the US civil rights movement inspired the members of the sixties generation who negotiated Canada's territorial land claims settlements.

Likewise, the ideas of Marx, the Fabians, and the Social Gospel movement taught northern mine workers that they had a right to free trade unions, a fair day's pay, and protection from unsafe working conditions. At the same time, second-stage feminism opened up employment opportunities for women. In Yukon, old-time miners used to declare that women in mines were bad luck, and territorial law prohibited female mine workers. But in the 1970s, at Whitehorse Copper Mine, Janeane MacGillivray became the first female underground miner in the territory.[1] Young women who had fought for jobs in mining were surprised soon afterwards to find themselves the favoured candidates for jobs as heavy equipment operators, with mine managers having judged that their touch was gentler with the giant machines.[2]

The Arctic's share of global GDP is roughly four times its share of the world population. In 2010 it contributed 0.6 percent to the global GDP while having only 0.15 percent of the world's population. In fact, the region's GDP rose about 42 percent between 2000 and 2010.[3] Yet northern mine workers, male or female, never know if their jobs will last. Mining is a risky business: a development miner driving the first adit into a rock face always worries about cave-ins, and investors are always ready to shift their money to another corner of the world.

China is one nation, among others, that has put effort over the past few years into digging resources from foreign soil, including the Canadian North and the High Arctic. In 2012 the Chinese company H.D. Mining International (formed by Huiyong Holdings Group and Canadian Dehua International Mines Group) opened a metallurgical coal operation on the Murray River property in Tumbler Ridge, BC. Instead of hiring Canadian miners, the company advertised for Mandarin speakers. The BC government gave the mine a permit, and the Canadian government approved the hiring of 200 Chinese workers. For obvious reasons, this decision outraged unemployed miners in Canada, who believed they should have first dibs on jobs in their own country.[4]

A December 2012 report by the United Steelworkers union – "Who Owns Huiyong Holdings and Other Questions on Planned Chinese-Owned Coal Mines in BC" – investigated the ownership of Huiyong Holdings Group (HHG). According to Steve Hunt, the Steelworkers' director for Western Canada, HHG consists of nothing but an unimpressive suburban address and a modest capitalization of $15 million, even though its H.D. mine at Murray River is described as a $1.4 billion project. For these reasons, the Steelworkers believe that HHG is a shell company and that its subsidiary, H.D. Mining, is a Chinese state enterprise.

Ye Qing, identified as HHG's "chief consultant," is a ranking member of the Chinese Communist Party (CCP), vice-minister of China's Ministry of Coal Industry, and president of the state-owned Shenhua Group, one of the world's largest coal corporations.[5] China's rulers may style themselves as devout communists, but they act like unbridled capital-ists.[6] At the 2015 National People's Congress (NPC), ninety deputies declared individual assets in excess of $150 million. "One, Zong Qinghou, has more than $10-billion," writes the *Globe and Mail's* Charles Burton.[7] According to a 2014 article in *New Statesman,* "the richest 70 members of China's NPC have a larger combined wealth ($89.8 billion in 2011) than that of all 535 members of the US congress, the president and his Cabinet and the nine Supreme Court judges."[8]

That the BC government refused to publish the details of its deal with the Chinese mine owners only heightened the Steelworkers' concern. The union believes that either the Murray River mine should have hired qualified Canadians or the Canadian government should have admitted the Chinese miners as landed immigrants, especially because, according to the company's mining's plans, it would be fourteen years before Murray River recruited a Canadian workforce. As a matter of policy, China has generally insisted on employing its own nationals on foreign projects – something it does not permit foreign companies to do on Chinese soil. Two Canadian unions went to court in 2013 over the issue of importing foreign miners. They lost, but the subsequent political furor spurred Ottawa to revisit the temporary foreign worker program. According to a *Globe and Mail* story on August 10, 2016, the new Liberal government may open the door to more foreign workers.[9]

The Steelworkers pray that the Murray River mine will respect Canadian safety standards. Furthermore, the union has legitimate concerns that the Chinese miners may not know their rights regarding a fair wage and safe working conditions in BC. Given China's appalling mine safety record, its investments in overseas resources are not something to take lightly. In 2006 almost 5,000 Chinese coal miners died in blasts, floods, and other accidents.[10] Because China lacks a free press, free trade unions, and an independent judiciary, Chinese bureaucrats are able to routinely hide scandalous mine disasters.[11]

Scarily, the pattern of Chinese investment in resource development looks similar all over the world. In the 2000s, China traded infrastructure investments in Angola for oil rights in that impoverished African state. The reception was not positive, however, when they chose to import tens of thousands of workers instead of hiring Angolans. Enraged local gangs took out their fury on Chinese companies and expatriates. The mess was compounded when Chinese gangs began running extortion rackets and prostitutes in Angola and other African countries.[12] Responding to the criminality of Chinese state enterprises in the United States, then Attorney General Eric H. Holder, Jr. announced in May 2014 the indictment for espionage of five officers of a unit of the Chinese People's Liberation Army accused of stealing commercial secrets from Westinghouse Electric and the United States Steel Corporation, and for hacking into computers belonging to the United Steelworkers.[13]

Imagine now that a Chinese state mining company wanted to open a new mine in Nunavut. Given the territory's high unemployment rate, the Nunavut government would want to see Inuktitut-speaking workers employed on the property, as well as agreements regarding the impacts and benefits for the community, the latter including training programs and business opportunities. It would also want to collect resource rents from the company. But what if the company insisted on importing Mandarin-speaking miners and operating in isolation from an adjacent Inuit community? The economic and social consequences for the community and the territory itself could be calamitous, but would the Nunavut government have the power to reject the project? Today, as it turns out, if Ottawa supported the Chinese state venture, the Nunavut government could do almost nothing. Under the Nunavut Impact Review Board process, the Nunavut government could make a deposition on the project, but that falls a long way short of the decisive role accorded to other provincial and territorial governments. Article 26 of the Nunavut Land Claims Agreement requires that developers respect local interests when negotiating Inuit Impact and Benefit Agreements

(IBAs).[14] But that's all. Nunavut is the only jurisdiction in Canada with an Indigenous majority; it is also the only province or territory that does not control its own lands and resources. Ottawa maintains the control and keeps the revenues.

Since Nunavut does not (yet) get to make crucial decisions about its own resources, Ottawa would control decisions about any prospective Chinese mine in the territory. Under the Foreign Investment Promotion and Protection Agreement (FIPA) negotiated by the former Conservative government, China could even sue Nunavut if it took steps to insist on jobs for Nunavummiut or to actively protect the territory's environment and its people's culture.

Mining Uncertainties

Mining is an uncertain business. One year after the White Pass and Yukon Route completed its railway from the port of Skagway to the inland city of Whitehorse in 1898, the Klondike Gold Rush – the railway's reason for being – ran out of steam. One NWT diamond mine died because it could not meet its transportation costs.[15] Infrastructure such as railways and roads may arrive in the North, or they may not. And if a road does come, instead of bringing miners to the frontier, it may instead help young northerners quit their villages. Over the decades, the uncertainties of resource extraction have led wary citizens to regard mine owners and operators as gamblers or worse. Mark Twain famously defined a mine as "a hole in the ground with a liar on top."[16]

In my Yukon youth, local sages echoed this skepticism with jokey accusations that certain companies listed on the Vancouver Stock Exchange were mining only their shareholders. Or taxpayers: cleanup costs for the former Giant Mine near Yellowknife, NWT, are approaching $1 billion, all of it government money.[17] The Arctic Circle community of Kiruna, Sweden, is being forced to move 3 kilometres east so that the town does not collapse into the mine workings beneath its streets.[18]

In the nineteenth century, somebody calculated that the geographical centre of Asia lay at the fork of the Greater and Lesser Yenisei Rivers in

Siberia, a remarkable northern location that might even be the birth-place of the Athabaskan (Dene) languages.[19] East of the Yenisei looms Norilsk, a Siberian mining city, former gulag, and monster sulphur di-oxide polluter that advertised in 2016 for immigrant workers.[20]

As a former Yukon legislator, I've been there when mines opened in the North and also when some CEO in a southern city gave the "thumbs down" on a northern mining town. No consultation, no discussion, just a death sentence for the community. Miners born in a place like the silver mining town of Elsa might be given only days to vacate their homes. It is cruel to see, but when the ore runs out or commodity prices drop, a shutdown may be only a matter of time. Sometimes, as happened in Faro after 1982, the company behind the town fades away but the community refuses to die.

"Cost of Faro's toxic bomb to top $450 million," a *Yukon News* headline announced in 2009. Moreover, the article said, government maintenance of the former Yukon mine site would need to continue for 500 years.[21] Since the environmental clean up costs of closed mines can be so huge, one would expect governments to be careful of the terms and conditions when they open. Some are; many are not. And the issues can aggravate. At a 2003 public meeting in Whitehorse that I facilitated, an audience member rose to berate the anti-mining panelists: "Do you people not drive cars, use phones, or wire your houses for electricity? Where do you think that metal comes from?"

For Yukoners yesterday, Nunavummiut today, and northerners every-where who want good jobs *and* environmental safeguards, the age-old questions for any mineral development project remain: Who benefits? And who pays?

Devolution for Nunavut?

Having inhabited the Arctic for thousands of years, the Inuit view Nuna-vut's devolution as the third natural and inevitable step – after the 1993 Nunavut Land Claims Agreement (NCLA) and the 1999 advent of the

Nunavut Territory – in their journey towards autonomy within Canada. Yet despite the NLCA, Ottawa still controls 80 percent of the territory's lands. The injustice of this jurisdictional imbalance could eventually injure the Inuit commitment to Canada, but that seems of little concern to Ottawa, which continues to slow-walk efforts to remedy this situation. When Premier Paul Okalik appointed me as Nunavut's devolution negotiator in 2006, he emphasized that I was a "northerner," somebody who has lived there, seen things happen, and helped build community.

The Inuit of Nunavut are the most northerly residents of North America. But their territory remains the only place in Canada where Canadian citizens cannot elect a sub-national legislature empowered to make fundamental decisions about the land (and, in some parts of Nunavut, the ice) beneath their feet. Since the territory's creation in 1999, the Inuit of Canada's Eastern Arctic have struggled to gain jurisdiction over the Crown (public) lands and resources on their territory through the process called devolution: a series of transfers of province-like powers from the federal government to the northern territories.

In 1987, northern legislators lobbied long and hard against the Meech Lake Accord, because Sections 41(h) and (i) of the proposed constitutional amendment gave the ten existing provinces, for the first time, a veto over the creation of new provinces in Canada's northern territories. After learning we were not welcome at the meeting where Canada's first ministers were hatching the 1987 Meech Lake deal, which would permanently enshrine northerners' status as second-class citizens, NWT government leader Nick Sibbeston and I cooled our heels on the sidewalk outside the East Block of Parliament. Later, at a joint NWT–Yukon cabinet meeting, we decided to sue the federal government over Meech; the case came to be known as *Penikett v. Canada*. We lost, and Prime Minister Brian Mulroney went on to appoint our lawyer to the Supreme Court of Canada. Thereafter, whenever Canada left the territories out of meetings, northern legislators grumbled, "Meeched again!"

In the end, not enough provinces ratified the Meech Lake Accord for it to pass. Somehow, though, the provincial veto seems to have become a rule, if not the law; nowadays nobody believes that provincial status is on the horizon for Yukon, the NWT, or Nunavut. For the foreseeable future, devolution of legislative jurisdiction over lands and resources may be *all* the northern territories can hope to get. Meanwhile, energy developments stalk the horizon, and climate change threatens the Arctic environment, especially Nunavut's coastal communities. These three facts have intersected to create considerable uncertainty. Uniquely, the Inuit traditionally fished, hunted, and lived on sea ice. This history underpins Nunavut's negotiating position. Nunavut's first premier, Paul Okalik, repeatedly stated that devolution negotiations must include such topics as net fiscal benefit, trained staff, and jurisdiction over Nunavut's internal waters.[22] However, he conceded that the issues of "internal waters" and ownership of seabed resources could be deferred to a second stage of negotiation.

Since 85 percent of Nunavummiut are Inuit, Canadians need to see the devolution of Nunavut as part of the struggle for Indigenous jurisdiction. Stephen Cornell, an American expert on Indigenous government, argues that jurisdiction is *the* issue that matters. Federal bureaucracies seem to think otherwise, Cornell says, seeing Aboriginal self-government as a set of administrative activities "while the big decisions still get made elsewhere."[23] Across the continent, Indigenous people want *jurisdiction*, tribal "sovereignty," and law-making powers, but Ottawa and Washington offer them program administration – empty of jurisdictional power – and, too often, program dumping, or the transfer to junior governments of underfunded programs.

Lawyer Adam Goldenberg contends that both in Canadian constitutional law and in evolved understandings of Indigenous rights, the Inuit of Nunavut have a "right to devolution" – that is, jurisdiction over their ancestral lands and resource heritage. It is an entitlement of their Canadian citizenship.[24] The Nunavut Act reversed what had been Canada's colonial policy, which required a settler majority for the creation of a regional government. Now Canada needs to rethink its colonial attitude towards Indigenous resource ownership.

The current belief that there may be a trillion dollars' worth of oil and gas in the High Arctic, which may become extractable as the sea ice melts, means that decisions about northern natural resources could have far-reaching consequences and become subjects of not just local and national but also international disputes. "With a comparatively weak military presence, Canadian sovereignty has been borne out primarily in the form of permanent settlement, and the Inuit have played the part of 'human flagpoles' in federal Arctic policy," Goldenberg argues; therefore, the right to devolution "must run parallel to Canadian assertions of Arctic sovereignty."[25]

"The United States is slowly exploring its offshore potential in the Chukchi and Beaufort Seas, and Greenland," writes Heather Conley.[26] In Russia, Gazprom and Rosneft have intimate and often unsavoury relationships with government officials. In the United States, the oil lobby is a Washington super heavyweight.

Until Prime Minister John A. Macdonald bought them out, the Hudson's Bay Company controlled most of Canada's Northwest. Historian Mary Janigan purports that "since [Manitoba Métis leader] Louis Riel first pushed for resource control [in the late nineteenth century] as the key to his community's destiny, the notion has been deeply embedded in the West's identity and pride."[27] The same can be said for the Far North. Nunavut's central, basic demand is essentially the one that shaped the story of the Canadian West: local autonomy.

Indeed, there are some precedents. Canada's constitution, which divides law-making powers between the provinces and the federal government, provides the backdrop for devolution negotiations. Section 91 of the Constitution lists matters under federal jurisdiction, while Section 92 describes the areas of provincial jurisdiction, including non-renewable natural resources. When Alberta and Saskatchewan joined Confederation in 1905, they came in as "junior partners"; these prairie provinces did not take control of their lands, minerals, and energy resources until Parliament passed the Natural Resources Transfer Acts in 1930.

The Nunavut government and NTI negotiators worked out a Nunavut Lands and Resources Devolution Negotiation Protocol with Paul Mayer, special representative of the federal Minister of Aboriginal Affairs and Northern Development (AANDC), in 2007.[28] The protocol stipulated that the parties negotiate an agreement-in-principle for the devolution of jurisdiction over lands and minerals, including a firm commitment to join second-stage negotiations for an integrated onshore and seabed oil-and-gas management regime. However, Ottawa soon filed and forgot the protocol. The federal government did not engage in any serious negotiations with Nunavut about sharing jurisdiction or resource revenues; a federal negotiator appointed in May 2012 was instructed merely "to engage key stakeholders on their views with respect to devolution to identify the next steps required to advance negotiations and to examine how land and resource management capacity can be improved in Nunavut."[29]

Clearly, the Harper government doubted Nunavut's capacity to manage its current responsibilities, much less administer the territory's lands and resources. In January 2011, Canada's INAC minister told reporters that Nunavut and its population were "not at the stage of readiness" to assume responsibility for managing their lands. Ministry officials continued to question Nunavut's capacity to manage the homeland for which the Inuit have been stewards for thousands of years.[30]

For six years following the 2008 election, in which the Conservatives were re-elected, very little happened at the Nunavut devolution table. Still, in keeping with the Inuit principle of self-reliance, Nunavut continued to seek a devolution agreement so that political and economic development could move forward together and give the people of the region the same power to make decisions as other Canadians.[31] As Adam Goldenberg and I point out in an article published in *Michigan State International Law Review*, the "desire [is] to be *maître chez nous*."[32] Yukon won jurisdiction over its lands and natural resources in 2001, and the NWT followed in 2013–14. The day after NWT announced its 2011 devolution agreement-in-principle, Nunavut's second premier, Eva Aariak, told the media, "it is time for Nunavut to begin our formal negotiations."[33] In 2016, talks began again with representatives of the new Liberal government.

Until the Yukon devolution deal, conventional wisdom held that provinces should control their natural resources but territories should not. Devolution of the authority over natural resources makes the territories more province-like, but without giving them full provincial privileges. Devolution means that the territory's legislators, not Ottawa's ministers and deputy ministers, decide all the important questions about the development of publicly owned lands and resources. Although Yukon still does *not* own federal land, the Yukon devolution agreement allows the territorial government to act as if it does by issuing leases and collecting rents.

From the air-conditioned comfort of their cubicles in Ottawa's office towers, federal officials safely grumble about Indigenous and northern governments. Most of their complaints concern administrative deficits. Leaving aside the different needs of a highly centralized bureaucracy and the decentralized, indigenized operations of governance in remote areas, bureaucratic effectiveness depends on strong institutions and solid professional training. The northern and Indigenous governments are newborn institutions whose final form may take decades to emerge.

Federal mandarins point damning fingers at the dearth of Inuit exploration geologists, mining engineers, and chartered accountants and the lack of administrative and professional expertise in Nunavut government ranks.[34] The territory is only seventeen years old, but in the many decades prior to its birth – when the federal government held absolute authority over the Northern territories – how many Inuit geologists, mining engineers, or chartered accountants did Ottawa train?

None. Not one. Zero.

When Thomas Berger recommended that, to achieve the goals of the Nunavut Land Claims Agreement it had signed, Ottawa needed to invest in Inuktitut-language high schools in the territory, the federal government said no. Yet there are other practical ways to address the need to develop capacity. For example, in Yukon's devolution deal, the territory assumed jurisdiction over oil and gas developments, then contracted back administration to the National Energy Board. This innovation gives the territory time to build administrative capacity while allowing it to exercise jurisdiction in a strategically vital field.

In the context of the Yukon experience, and of both Canadian and international law, Ottawa's concerns about "capacity" in Nunavut are ultimately unpersuasive. Adam Goldenberg proceeds from the undeniable inequality of the status quo to argue that Canadian citizens now have the democratic power to choose provincial or territorial representatives, who make decisions about the management of the lands and resources beneath their feet, in every jurisdiction except Nunavut. This raises basic questions of citizenship equality and Indigenous rights that only devolution can resolve. The lack of interest and effort by the federal government also compromises Canada's claims to Arctic sovereignty, especially as the geostrategic significance of the region grows. For all of the reasons stated, devolution is an essential step that would fill a crucial void in the exercise of Inuit self-government in Nunavut.[35]

In 1962 a Canadian prospector found rich iron ore deposits on the northern tip of Baffin Island. Five decades later, that deposit has become a huge mining project. Significantly, the Nunavut government had no say in the decision about Mary River, a $4 billion mine on its territory, which comes with the most extensive infrastructure to date in northern Canada and massive revenue potential for NCLA beneficiaries and the territory.[36] Instead, territorial legislators received a copy of the press release once final decisions and approvals had taken place after a four-year review. This is in sharp contrast to how a similar resource opportunity was handled by Saskatchewan premier Allan Blakeney in the 1970s. As the premier of a province, he had the authority to approve uranium mine developers' requests to lease public lands in northern Saskatchewan and could make demands – including one that northern and Native peoples receive preference in employment and business contracts. The Mary River project will adhere to an Inuit impact benefits agreement and a lease negotiated with the Qikiqtani Inuit Association (the beneficiary corporation that represents Baffin Island Inuit), but these arrangements flow from the land claims agreement and do not constitute devolution or a transfer of jurisdiction to Nunavut.[37]

In 2016 the Qikiqtani Inuit Association decided to reveal its deal with Baffinland Iron Mines, including an impact and benefit agreement (IBA).[38] Article 5 of the QIA's agreement spelled out the benefits, which included an advance payment of $5 million and another $5 million after Baffinland received its water licence; a 1.19 percent royalty on net iron ore sales; and another $10 million to the QIA after Baffinland began building the mine's infrastructure in the second quarter of 2013. The company is now shipping iron ore to Germany.

Development of the vast oil and gas resources in the High Arctic may be decades away, but when it does arrive, without devolution and a fair share of energy and mineral resource revenues, Nunavut will have little capacity to improve the health, housing, or education of future generations. Canada's Arctic residents have contributed very little to global warming, yet they are already among the earliest victims of climate change. As things now stand, they will pay the highest social and environmental costs while receiving few benefits from the extraction of energy riches from their homelands.

As noted, since Canada needs Nunavut – or at least the Inuit – to secure its Arctic claims, Ottawa has a responsibility to complete an honourable devolution deal on lands, minerals, and seabed resources. With time, Nunavummiut will then be able to solve their own problems. As an interim measure, increased federal transfers would allow the territory to address its serious housing shortages, food insecurity, and grinding poverty.

Commenting on the Arctic's internal colonialism, Oran Young concluded: "From the vantage point of many communities in the Circumpolar North, then, government, big business, and the environmental movement constitute a *de facto* alliance to perpetuate dependence ... All of these groups are made up of distant and alien outsiders with their own interests to pursue and with little regard for the needs of local communities."[39]

Of course, power-sharing, or devolution, would threaten the privileged position of southern social and economic elites. For now, Ottawa stands to benefit from an oil boom, and Nunavut will suffer the environmental impacts. "So, why are we in such a rush to develop if we are not going to benefit from it?" asks Inuit thinker Auju Peter.[40]

Outcomes

Even if Nunavut were to win a devolution deal in time to drive hard bargains with foreign mining giants, the territorial government could find the experience surprisingly divisive.[41] The government of Nunavut's neighbour, Greenland, has recently found itself under strong pressure.[42] Right after coming to power in 2009, Greenland premier Kuupik Kleist forged deals to export resources in the hope of solving the country's social problems. Investors flocked into Nuuk.[43] But in 2013 Kleist's government fell after reports surfaced that London Mining would be importing 2,000 Chinese miners to dig out a huge iron ore deposit at Isua.[44] Greenlanders feared that Kleist was selling out his country's interests to Chinese and other multinationals. Aleqa Hammond, the leader of the coalition government that followed, pledged to increase mineral royalties and to compel foreign mining companies to deal with Greenlandic trade unions. Meanwhile, as commodity prices fell, investors shied away from Greenland. So far, none of the wells drilled off the coast of Greenland have struck oil.

Oil and gas developments, perhaps even more than mines, can benefit but also divide northern communities, and divided communities are too weak to deal with giant corporations. Still, it would be a mistake to think that all corporations are the same. Just as with national governments, some keep their word and some do not. Occasionally, a good news story surfaces. One of these emerged in 2014 and 2015 involving another Chinese enterprise, Selwyn Chihong Mining Ltd.

Selwyn Chihong plans to develop a lead/zinc deposit on the border of the NWT and Yukon. The Selwyn ore body straddles the traditional territories of the Kaska Nation in Yukon and the Sahtu and Dehcho in the NWT. Selwyn Chihong CEO Richard (Shilin) Li has said: "I truly believe that a company can only be successful if it can work well with communities and with all stakeholders. This includes local leaders, government, First Nations, and other local communities, working in a fair, respectful way."[45] Despite low metal prices, Selwyn Chihong Mining has continued to invest in the project. The two territories and three First Nations have high hopes for Richard Li.

Revenues

Greenland took control of its own lands and resource riches from Copenhagen in 2009. On achieving self-government, Greenland gained jurisdiction over onshore mineral deposits – gold, lead, zinc, iron, rare earths, and rubies – as well as offshore oil and gas fields.[46] Denmark's negotiators agreed to reduce Greenland's annual grant by just half of Greenland's resource income and allowed the first 75 million krone (CAD$14.5 million) of Greenland's annual intake to escape the previous 50/50 revenue-sharing arrangement. "Greenland's resource revenues and government expenditures can grow but Denmark's grants will continue to flow," writes Arctic policy consultant Anthony Speca.[47] Months later, the NWT settled for a less attractive package. "Not only did Ottawa push off any question of sharing revenues from the NWT's own considerable offshore oil and gas fields, it also capped the revenues the NWT could freely collect from its onshore resources," Speca wrote to me in 2014. (Now that the NWT has gained control of its resources, this kind of deal won't be happening again.)

Yet the NWT's 2009 revenue-sharing deal with Ottawa was much better than the one that Yukon had negotiated in 2001. Yukon had agreed to a hard mineral revenue cap of $3 million, added to the 20 to 40 percent of minor onshore oil and gas revenues the territory had obtained some time before. Ottawa later offered Yukon the same deal as the NWT, thereby setting the standard for the territorial North.

As Speca observes, Nunavut's poverty in the midst of plenty explains why the territory is determined to get a good fiscal deal from Ottawa.

Despite fairly bursting with most of the treasures it is possible to dig from the earth – gold, silver, copper, zinc, iron, uranium, diamonds, oil, gas, and more – Nunavut depends on federal grants for nearly its entire annual budget.[48] That has not changed. Speca also writes that it is not far-fetched to imagine that a resource-rich Nunavut could have "similar or even greater fiscal potential" than newly oil-rich Newfoundland, which was once the poor child of Canadian confederation.

The 1993 Nunavut Land Claims Agreement gave the Inuit of Nunavut ownership of about 18 percent of the territory's lands and 2 percent of its subsurface mineral rights. Revenues from Inuit-owned lands accrue to NTI (Nunavut Tunngavik Incorporated), not Nunavut. NTI also has a right to 50 percent of the first $2 million of any resource revenues collected from public lands, plus 5 percent of any additional resource revenues. NTI views this share of the territory's natural wealth as Inuit patrimonial property, and explicitly *not* as a source for funding public services. NTI has called on Ottawa to allow Nunavut to keep all resource revenues generated in the territory – a deal that would outdo the devolution agreements not only of Yukon and the NWT but also of Greenland. But such a deal would be hard to negotiate.

In his sagacious essay "The Changing Architecture of Governance in Yukon and the Northwest Territories," published by the Institute for Research on Public Policy (IRPP), Simon Fraser University public policy professor Douglas McArthur suggests that Ottawa's policies are very much about money. McArthur reviewed all of the northern devolution and land claims settlements negotiated over the past fifty years and found that the only constant in Ottawa's policy has been the desire of the federal finance department to protect revenues and to cut or contain Canada's costs. Yet Nunavut needs that revenue, and that is why it wants devolution.

Former Alaska governor Steve Cowper believes that Alaska Natives can show Canadians how it might be done. "Alaska Natives have land, money, and political clout," he says. "Not bad." NANA Regional Corporation Inc., one of thirteen Alaska Native Regional Corporations created under the 1971 Alaska Native Claims Settlement Act, licensed

Red Dog, a large Canadian-owned mine on the coast of the Bering Sea, and received a large share of the profits as well as local employment opportunities. Red Dog, now one of the world's largest zinc producers, has employed hundreds of Inuit, though it has hired few local managers.[49]

Cautionary tales from northern history have shaped the thinking of today's negotiators. At one point, a single diamond mine represented a large portion of the NWT's gross domestic product, but the territory and its citizens got very little out of the deal. "Some have said that it was like keeping us on an allowance," NWT premier Floyd Roland told me in 2013. Prior to devolution, a young entrepreneur in Yellowknife might open an electronic appliance shop and do well selling "toys for the boys" (Wii games, flat-screen TVs, and stereo speakers) to miners at Diavik or Ekati. But what did the territory get for its diamonds? Until devolution in 2009, diamond-mine royalties all went to Ottawa.

NWT legislators plan to take advantage of their new devolution and resource revenue-sharing deal by creating a nest-egg heritage fund. In Canada, such funds have a spotty history. Saskatchewan has tried and failed to establish a rainy-day Futures Fund; Alberta's Heritage Fund has grown very little in recent years. By way of contrast, Norway, with a population of 5 million (compared to more than 4 million in Alberta) began in 1990 to put all its petroleum revenues and interest into a fund. The BBC has reported that this fund could be worth $1 trillion by 2020.[50]

NWT legislators consulted widely about heritage funds, determined to get it right. They learned that it was important to build a broad consensus about the rules surrounding the fund, especially regarding fund withdrawal limits (such as, in the NWT's case, no withdrawals for the first twenty years). Significantly, they also decided on the percentages of resource royalties destined for both debt payments and the heritage fund. MLAs insisted that the government be specific about how "golden egg" funds would be able to dampen the effects of the booms and busts of resource development – effects such as northern ghost towns and altered landscapes. In his 2014–15 budget address, NWT finance minister Michael Miltenberger proposed a modest 5 percent revenue plan for the heritage fund.[51] Public pressure forced the minister to revise the target to an ambitious 25 percent.[52]

Oil and Gas

Commercial oil production in Arctic North America dates back to the first discovery of seepage at Norman Wells, NWT, in 1920. Those who had hoped for a new Klondike were soon disappointed, however, as the flow was too small and the cost of transporting it too great. Not until 1968, when Arco/Humble confirmed its major oil discovery at Prudhoe Bay on Alaska's North Slope, did the North show real promise for the industry. Twenty years later, North Slope production peaked at 2 million barrels a day.[53] Today the North Slope supplies only 3 to 4 percent of American oil and gas, yet the myth persists that Alaskan production can save the United States from dependence on foreign oil.

Boomtown dreams for a Mackenzie Valley gas pipeline faded with the publication in 1977 of Justice Thomas R. Berger's report *Northern Frontier, Northern Homeland*, which recommended that Ottawa settle the land claims of the valley's Indigenous people before building a pipeline.

Yet for geographer Laurence C. Smith, oil and gas is the Arctic's grand prize. In *The World in 2050* he writes: "The Arctic's broad continental shelves are draped in thick sequences of shale-rich sedimentary rock, an ideal geological setting to find oil and gas, especially natural gas. In 2008 and 2009, the US Geological Survey released new assessments concluding that about 30 percent of the world's undiscovered natural gas and 13 percent of its undiscovered oil lies in the Arctic, mostly off-shore in less than 500 meters of water."[54] Smith thinks the Inuit will trade in their harpoons for briefcases, but on that point he is probably wrong. Inuit entrepreneurs will undoubtedly want to continue to fish and hunt, and they will arrange their business affairs accordingly.

Given the abundance of the so far inaccessible treasure, the coming decades will see furious debates between oil-thirsty and oil-averse populations. Oil and gas may be dinosaur industries, but they still have strong political clout. Rob Huebert of the University of Calgary reckons that Nunavut's strategic options come down to two: either "small scale development in a highly decentralized territory or large-scale investments of foreign capital and perhaps foreign workers from China."[55]

However this development proceeds, shipping oil and gas out of the Arctic presents unique challenges. To move product from Alaska's North Slope, for instance, authorities in the 1970s had to choose between a railway, an ice-breaking tanker through the Northwest Passage, and an Alaskan pipeline from Prudhoe Bay south to the port of Valdez.[56] They green-lit the pipeline.

When things go wrong in the Arctic, they can go spectacularly wrong, as industry opponents point out. Canada's response to resource development has taken a "polluter pays" approach rather than a preventive one. In 2013 the federal government announced an increase in the liability limit on environmental and other damage from a blowout or an oil spill, raising the limit from $30–40 million to $1 billion.[57] Colonel (retired) Pierre Leblanc, former commander of Canadian Forces Northern Area (Yukon, the NWT, and Nunavut), wishes that Ottawa had increased it even more. "A limit of $1 billion is totally irresponsible," he told the House of Commons Foreign Affairs committee on April 15, 2008. "The Exxon Valdez clean-up was in excess of $2.2 billion 25 years ago. If we have something of this nature under the ice in the Arctic it will be more expensive due to our lack of ice/oil mix recovery technology and lack of infrastructure." Some think it's time for the US Congress to follow Canada's lead and raise the US spill liability limit.

The energy industry spends millions to advertise its concern for the environment, which, of course, is much cheaper than taking concrete environmental action. As drill ships close in on the Arctic's oil and gas, reporters will recycle stories about the Gulf and *Exxon Valdez* disasters. The US Department of Interior had proposed new drilling standards for the Arctic Ocean – standards inspired by the difficulties that Shell experienced in the 2012 season. After investing billions in offshore Arctic leases and a sophisticated drilling program, Shell abandoned its offshore oil-and-gas drilling program in Alaska's offshore waters in

September 2015. At the Arctic Energy Summit in Fairbanks that same year, Institute of the North executive director Nils Andreassen dramatically called for a minute of silence to mourn the passing of the drill ships. Claiming "a very technically successful exploration program," Shell still wants to salvage its Arctic Ocean drilling rights, but overall the US State Department worries about a shrinking interest in the US Arctic.[58]

Other companies may soon be drilling off Greenland, in Davis Strait near the Canada–Denmark boundary, which could create environmental hazards for coastal Nunavut. Both China and the European Union seek access to Arctic waters. Vladimir Putin's doctoral dissertation at the Saint Petersburg Mining Institute championed resource development in the Arctic, a policy he has pursued as Russia's president.[59] Russia has already positioned itself to exploit seabed resources but has been ambivalent about Western partnerships. BP was disappointed by its Russian experience, and as a result, Putin may decide that Russia will go it alone. Exxon had more success with Putin. To muddy the waters further, in 2013, Russia's Coast Guard landed a helicopter on Greenpeace's ship *Arctic Sunrise* following the ship's protest against the Prirazlomnaya oil rig.[60] The Russian government charged the thirty Greenpeace activists on board with piracy and locked them in Murmansk's pre-trial detention centre.[61]

Maritime Issues

Under the UN Convention on the Law of the Sea (UNCLOS), a coastal state has defined sovereign rights over its continental shelf, including the right to exploit resources such as oil, gas, minerals, clams, and crabs. At the 2008 Arctic Security Conference in Vancouver, H.P. Rajan, then deputy director of the UN's Division for Ocean Affairs and Law of the Sea, asked rhetorically, "Is there a legal regime that is applicable to the Arctic?"[62] His answer was UNCLOS, which applies as much to the Arctic Ocean as it does to any other. The convention entered into force in November 1994, with 157 parties, including all Arctic states except the United States. Under UNCLOS, coastal states are entitled to their territorial seas, a contiguous zone, an exclusive economic zone, and a continental shelf over which they have specific rights and jurisdiction. "Under the 1982 United Nations Convention on the Law of the Sea," Rajan reminded the conference, "the coastal state exercises over the continental shelf sovereign rights for the purpose of exploring and exploiting its natural resources ... The rights of the coastal states in respect of the continental shelf are exclusive; if the coastal state does not explore the continental shelf or exploit its natural resources, no one else may undertake these activities without the express consent of the coastal state."[63]

Under Article 76 of UNCLOS, a coastal state may exercise sovereign rights over an extended continental shelf beyond 200 nautical miles when the contours of the seabed and the character of underlying sediments indicate a "natural prolongation" of the state's land mass.[64] Over the Christmas season in 2013, under the cover of the UNCLOS process, Canadian prime minister Stephen Harper bootlegged a claim to the seabed at the North Pole, just as the Danes and the Russians had already done.[65] (In 2007, oceanographer and politician Artur Chilingarov famously planted a Russian flag in the seabed at the North Pole.) In May 2014, the adjudicator of the UN Commission on the Limits of the Continental Shelf recognized Russia's claim to a 52,000-square-kilometre oil-rich area in the Sea of Okhotsk.[66] At present, most of the Arctic region is under the domain of one of the Arctic states. Indeed, the disagreements remain over maritime rather than territorial boundaries. However, non-Arctic states tend to hold that the seabed of the 2.8 million-square-kilometre Central Arctic Ocean belongs to all humanity.[67]

Some, though not all, of Canada's northern Indigenous treaties contain clauses on the nation-state's international obligations regarding cooperative conservation. The Yukon Final Agreement calls for Canada to make reasonable efforts to ensure that Yukon First Nations' interests are represented when issues of fish and wildlife management arise in international negotiations. The Labrador Inuit Final Agreement includes similar language in relation to aquatic plants, fish habitat, management, and stocks. Agreements with the Sahtu Dene and the Métis affirm that amendments to international treaties should not diminish Indigenous peoples' rights.

Yet to cite just one case, twenty years after signing the Nunavut Land Claims Agreement (NCLA), Canada seemed to have parked provisions for ecosystemic and socio-economic monitoring. As the federal government also ignored until 2015 the Nunavut Marine Council provision of the NCLA, which would have given the Inuit a window on safety regimes for ships navigating the Northwest Passage.

In May 2008, representatives of the five coastal nations bordering the Arctic Ocean – Canada, Denmark, Norway, Russia, and the United States – met in Greenland to draft the Ilulissat Declaration, a document that declared the 1982 UNCLOS principles as the basis for resolving all outstanding Arctic maritime issues. The document's authors may have been attempting to shut down chatter about an Antarctic-style treaty that would forbid militarization and resource development for the Arctic by creating a new regime for interstate cooperation. Iceland, which claims coastal status, was excluded from the Arctic Five, as was Finland, which lost its Arctic coastline in the Second World War.

The "Arctic Five" – as they are known – made no reference to international law on the rights of Indigenous peoples, and despite provisions in modern northern treaties that promise a hearing for Indigenous voices on matters affecting their vital interests, Canada did not invite any Inuit representative to join its delegation to Ilulissat. Nor were any of the Canadian-based Arctic Council permanent participants invited to the follow-up meeting of the Arctic Five at Chelsea, Quebec. This marked a sharp demotion from their permanent participant status and led inevitably to questions about the future of the Arctic Council. Arctic Athabaskan Council leader Bill Erasmus observed: "It makes no sense for us to be included in the Arctic Council but excluded from meetings of the five Arctic Ocean states."[68]

To protest their exclusion from the Ilulissat gathering, the Inuit of Canada, Alaska, Russia, and Greenland issued a Circumpolar Sovereignty Declaration. This document builds on modern treaties and reminds all nation-states that the Arctic is the Inuit homeland. Section

4.2 reads: "The conduct of international relations in the Arctic and the resolution of international disputes in the Arctic are not the sole preserve of the Arctic states or other states, they are also within the purview of the Arctic's Indigenous peoples."[69] If Canadians recognized the legitimacy of the Inuit conception that water and land are inseparable, they might also recognize that UNCLOS in itself is an imperfect instrument. John Ralston Saul has written that the Law of the Sea is remarkably unsuited to the modern situation of the Arctic: "[This idea] is derived from old European ideas of ownership, starting from how far a cannon ball can be shot across water from a coastal fortress. Today's realities are about shared problems and relationships and needs that cross the boundaries of ownership, just as fish do, and pollution, and climates. And so the tribunals and courts might find such an Indigenous and integrated approach refreshing."[70]

Although the Inuit are no longer prepared to passively accept international relations as the exclusive preserve of states, they do not actively seek conflict. Just as cooperation and adaptation have been necessary for Inuit survival in the Arctic, today's Inuit see themselves as partners in the conduct of international relations in the Arctic, and they are appealing for a coordinated response to the climate change challenge and the pursuit of global environmental security.[71]

Renewable Resources

Renewable resource users often confront fierce conflicts with developers of non-renewable resources. Many of the most difficult resource conflicts involve contests like these, with Alaska providing some examples. In a 2013 episode of BBC's *Hardtalk*, Stephen Sackur described a contretemps between the sustainable Bristol Bay salmon fishery (worth billions of dollars annually) and Alaska's Pebble Mine, a copper prospect worth tens of billions that promised to provide jobs for decades.[72] After a three-year study, the Final Bristol Bay Watershed Assessment by the US Environmental Protection Agency (EPA) found that the proposed copper and gold mine threatened sockeye salmon in the Bristol Bay area, which holds one-quarter of the world's sockeye population.[73] The Pebble Mine's owners called the study "rushed" and claimed that the mine would "replace" lost fish habitat. Shortly afterwards, a major investor, Anglo American, pulled out.[74]

In this dispute, as in the long-running conflicts between oil explorers and the Porcupine Caribou Herd of northern Alaska, the NWT, and Yukon, and between mining companies and reindeer herders in Arctic Scandinavia, there seems to be no middle ground apart from the artful use of technology such as GPS and iPads by Finnish Sámi foresters and reindeer herders.[75] Each side has the fixed idea that the other is wrong. One side distrusts the oil industry's environmental record after BP's disastrous spill in the Gulf of Mexico and the *Exxon Valdez* disaster in Alaska; the other questions the motives of those environmentalists who support Native peoples and their renewable resource economies. In 2015, US President Barack Obama tabled a final Comprehensive Conservation Plan for the Arctic National Wildlife Refuge; it extends wilderness protection to the vulnerable coastal plain. Alaska's only congressman, Republican Don Young, responded by calling the president a "wacko."[76]

Images of huge herds of caribou migrating across Arctic landscapes are etched on our brains, but caribou and reindeer numbers are now in sharp decline. "In some cases, the numbers are dramatic – the Baffin Island herd in Nunavut, for instance, dropped from 235,000 animals in 1991 to just 3,000 in 2014. But the reasons for this free fall remain unclear. Caribou numbers do fluctuate naturally, but not generally all in the same direction at the same time."[77] Some blame climate change and industrial development projects but, as yet, there's no agreement on the causes.

Beyond the battles between copper and salmon, caribou and oil, conflicts exist between communities over hunting rights and between states over who has rights to offshore seabed resources. Generally, as noted, the non-Arctic states view the Arctic waters as a "global commons." A less icebound Arctic will inevitably open opportunities for natural resource exploration and exploitation, and a number of non-Arctic states have already expressed their eagerness to exploit these resources. Agreements such as the 1994 Convention on the Conservation and Management of Pollock Resources in the Central Bering Sea (CBSPC) may be hard to land.[78]

In many regions, hunting is yet another ground of contestation. Northern Indigenous peoples proudly insist that they waste nothing. Barry Lopez has described how the Inuit make full use of the caribou: "They made clothing, bedding, and bags from its skin and tools and weapons from its bones and antlers. They used the marrow of its bones for fuel; its blood in glues; its sinews for lashings, bindings, and thread. What they did not eat [immediately] they cached, against the lean months of spring."[79]

In Russia today, there is conflict between the culture and needs of Indigenous peoples (whose special status is written into legislation) and the desires of Russian elites who enjoy hunting. In 2009, the Russian Duma adopted a hunting law that allows the use of vehicles, aircraft, explosives, gases, and other devices to annihilate animals and birds. The law does not ban spring hunting, nor does it ban the killing of rare species, even those under the protection of international law.[80] Why? Because Russian elites crafted the law in their own interest. "Hunting is a favorite business of the highest Russian bureaucracy – governmental, parliamentarians, regional political elites," writes Russian epidemiologist Alexey Dudarev.[81] "The law is directed for the benefit of very rich people who are able to pay for the hunting all over Russia."[82] Under the 2009 law, hunting grounds are allocated by auction, and Indigenous groups on the lands they have occupied for centuries are required to pay big money for the right to hunt, have to participate in tenders, and have to pay for licences.

Despite conflicts like these, University of Lapland anthropologist Florian Stammler argues that Indigenous communities do not have a single perspective on what extractive industrial development in the Arctic means for them. He writes:

Among the Yamal Nenets neighbours in Siberia I was impressed by the following saying about their most intense 30 years' relationship with Gazprom [the Russian energy giant]: "We first thought it's a disaster, but now we got used to it." Further on the Russian Far Eastern Kamchatka Peninsula, our reindeer herding host told us about the relation to the Nickel and Gold industry on their pastures, a message of tolerance and distance at the same time: "We have our own lives, let them have theirs."[83]

The late Finn Lynge, Greenlandic anthropologist and EU parliamentarian, questioned whether subsistence hunters can survive industrial development: "Can Esau find a secure niche in a social setting dominated by Jacob?"[84] Optimists may point to the 1973 agreement by Canada, Denmark, Norway, the Soviet Union, and the United States to protect the polar bear from the predations of trophy hunters from affluent southern cities.[85] Pessimists may decry the "privatization" of Indigenous hunting grounds and – it follows – the food sources of subsistence harvesters in post-Soviet Russia.

Fair Shares

What might constitute a fair shares regime in the Arctic? Despite the obvious tensions between renewable and non-renewable resource users, and between hunters and conservationists, there may be some room for optimism. Charles Emmerson reports extraordinary examples of international cooperation. "Partly to reduce the costs associated with making a claim and partly to avoid the risk that the Commission will tell them to go back and do it again, countries have on occasion pooled their survey resources in the Arctic," he writes. The United States and Canada did so in the summers of 2008 and 2009. Canada and Denmark did so in 2007; that expedition, known as LOMROG (Lomonosov Ridge Off Greenland), hired a Russian icebreaker because it was the only ship that could give the expedition the sustained capacity it needed.[86] To keep the piggy bank beyond the reach of big-spending politicians, Norway invests most of its petroleum revenues offshore.[87] Although this wealthy Nordic country, like Putin's Russia, may be something of a petro-state, it has worked hard to create cooperative fisheries management regimes with its Russian neighbour.[88]

In his 1992 essay on Arctic land-based resource conflicts, Oran Young described a series of possible approaches to resolving conflicts, including market mechanisms, private bargaining, exchanges of transferable rights, litigation, and legislation.[89] "As soon as we move beyond the realm of straightforward utilitarian calculations, there is no simple or obvious way to rank conflicting uses or values," he concluded.[90] Beyond the traditional cost–benefit analyses, and trade-offs between fish and oil, caribou and money, perhaps the only sustainable approach is the kind of "balance" that Norway seems to have achieved in fjords, where the government crafts environmental regulations that allow industrial plants to operate side-by-side with fish farms and orchards. Emmerson notes: "The model of oil and gas development in Norway may not be perfect. But it is far better than the approaches taken in most countries. Some hope that the Norwegian example could provide a template for environmentally sustainable oil and gas development across the Arctic."[91] Others see hope in the kinds of arrangements negotiated at Alaska's Red Dog Mine, between the company and Inuit residents of the Northwest Arctic Borough. Currently, however, the company and the borough are involved in a dispute over taxes.

As explored earlier, in the 1980s and 1990s Indigenous and settler communities in Canada's territories negotiated co-management regimes for renewable resources. These regimes established a hierarchy for resource uses and for users that was subsequently embedded in law by territorial legislators and the federal Parliament. As noted, the regimes ranked the priorities as follows: conservation; subsistence; sport hunting and fishing; and commercial use.

To my knowledge, nobody has yet crafted a credible definition of sustainable mining or oil exploitation, although Anthony Hodge, a former Yukoner and president of the International Council on Mining and Metals from 2008 to 2015, suggests that if you consider the whole cycle of extraction, production, and distribution, sustainability may be feasible: a circle economy idea. [92] If northerners were to borrow the renewable resources co-management model for non-renewable resources, the ranking of resource extraction priorities might look like this: local employment and environment protection; maximum regional economic benefits and minimum negative social impacts; national revenue; and global demand (multinational corporations). As with co-management regimes for fishing and hunting, such a model would require the agreement of all stakeholders, big and small. Given the power differential between global and local players, this would be difficult – though not necessarily impossible – to achieve. Where mine workers have a union, they might be able to negotiate a fair wage and safe working conditions. Indigenous landowners and northern territories with devolution agreements could drive hard bargains. However, when a national government and a multinational miner gang up on local authorities, as the Canadian federal government has already done with pipeline projects, communities in regions such as Nunavut will surely get the shaft, and the resource-use hierarchy above will be reduced to a dream.

In the present day, northerners and northern communities too often find themselves in a weak bargaining position, and many impact benefit agreements are secretly negotiated, although the details should not be impossible for a competent researcher to uncover. At the High North Dialogue conference in Bodø on May 25, 2016, I suggested that a designated university or NGO begin to document Arctic resource deals, wages, resource revenue-sharing, and benefits agreements to build a database of this information. Building on this data bank, it might be possible over time to establish best practices, or an "Arctic Standard."[93] Something of the sort is already in place with the Alaska Native Knowledge Network (ANKN), a group that allows interested parties to "compile and exchange information ... regarding a diverse range of topics relevant to indigenous life, including the subsistence lifestyle."[94]

When the federal state maintains control of northern resources, both Indigenous and settler communities suffer the negative environmental and social impacts while receiving only transient economic benefits. Historically, resource booms and busts have exploited northerners. In the future, as land owners and legal governors, Indigenous leaders and regional legislators are determined to get their fair share of returns from Arctic resource developments.

CONFLICT

8

Arctic Security
Control or Cooperation?

In the southern city, security means locks and keys; in the Arctic,
it may be an open door for cold and hungry travellers.

n June 2006, at Old Crow – the northernmost First Nation community
in Yukon – I chatted with a Canadian senator, who seemed astonished
at the prosperity of this little Arctic village. Busy construction crews
were building houses, four-wheel ATVs trundled about, and people
were offloading freight from a regional airline they partly owned. The
senator was clearly taken aback at a scene, which was so sharply different
from the clichéd image of Indian reserves: abandoned car bodies, "INAC
shacks," sedentary youngsters, and so on.

In 1992 the Vuntut Gwichi'in (People of the lakes) First Nation of
Old Crow reached land claims and self-government agreements with
the federal and Yukon governments. The First Nation took collective
ownership of approximately 7,744 square kilometres of land and received
$148.4 million in a cash transfer, much of which it placed in trust for
future generations. Fourteen years on, the community was reaping the
benefits. North of Old Crow, muskrat flats and tundra stretch all the
way to the Arctic Ocean. A few miles west, in Alaska, the United States
has based more than 20,000 armed forces personnel to protect its security and Arctic sovereignty. During my time as leader of the Yukon government, our territory had a permanent military establishment of two
soldiers: a major and a corporal.

Gesturing towards the new houses, the senator asked me, "But how
does Canada justify such expenditures?"

"Investments," I countered.

"How does the government justify investment on *this* scale?" Since he'd read his briefing notes, the senator meant this as a serious question, despite the evident results of Northern land claims and self-government agreements.

"My guess is that somebody in the Canadian government decided that viable Arctic communities best express our sovereignty," I said, without much forethought.

Nowhere had I seen public policy articulated in exactly that way, but I realized as I spoke that it was largely true. Validation of this came in an 2010 EKOS Survey that found that an overwhelming majority of northern (81 percent) and southern (71 percent) Canadians believed that the "best way to protect Canada's interest in the Arctic is to have Canadians living there."[1] The greatest threat to Canada's Arctic sovereignty, the survey's respondents agreed, came not from foreign warships or bombers but from the social, climatic, and economic challenges that keep those who live in the North from enjoying anything like the usual Canadian standards of education, employment, and health.

Chance or Control?

After skirmishing with the Luftwaffe over France and Belgium in the dreadful first winter of the Second World War, my father John Penikett was the only Hurricane pilot from RAF Squadron 87's B-Wing to return to England alive and uninjured in May 1940. Two days after the RAF sent him to Bomber Command in 1942, the Wellingtons of his Squadron 460 made their first sortie against Emden, Germany. Over the course of the war, British and Commonwealth bombers dropped hundreds of thousands of tons of bombs on cities like Hamburg and Dresden, incinerating tens of thousands of German civilians. Bomber Command itself lost half its number, with more than 55,000 combat deaths.[2] Against the odds, my father lived to see the end of the war, although he could never quite reconcile himself to the mass killing of civilians. His subsequent medical career may have been, in part, an act of atonement.

Did Bomber Command's survivors owe their fate to a combination of bravery, their skills as pilots and navigators, and their thousands of hours of flying experience? That's what the military brass believed at the time. But perhaps it was just luck. "I was a statistician before I became a scientist," writes mathematician and physicist Freeman Dyson. "I did a careful analysis of the correlation between the experience of the crews and their loss rates, subdividing the data into many small packages so as to eliminate effects of weather and geography ... There was no effect of experience on loss rate. So far as I could tell, whether a crew lived or died was purely a matter of chance. Their belief in the life-saving effect of experience was an illusion."[3] My father would have agreed that he was lucky to survive.

In war – the most brutal of competitions – controlling all variables is simply impossible, even with total command of military resources. As discussed in Chapter 2, during the Second World War and throughout the Cold War the Arctic became a militarized region, mainly under the command of superpowers. For realist scholars like the University of Calgary's Rob Huebert, national security debates continue to focus on old ideas about control and competition, and Cold War Arctic interventions reflected that mentality. In times of peace, however, cooperation and coordination are generally the preferred tools for building security and international relations.

For children of the Cold War era, security meant *military* security, or defence. Baby boomers learned from their parents about the *social* security provided by a pension and the *economic* security that came with a steady job. All the while, though, the threat of nuclear war hung over the lives of kids growing up in the postwar years. We might have laughed at the Cold War's absurdities as expressed in movies like *Dr. Strangelove*; even so, the awesome military might of the United States and the Soviet Union facing each other across the frozen Arctic frontiers haunted our sleep. The Cold War is now over, and the Arctic is no longer quite so frozen. Our notions of security have expanded to include the concepts of food, human, and environmental security, with the idea of "homeland security" dominating in a military sense.

Since September 11, 2001, the Department of Homeland Security has become a hugely important branch of the US government. Crossing the border between Canada and the United States used to be an un-remarkable event. Nowadays, national insecurities can make it a trial. Vancouverites on their way to Seattle learn that if the declared purpose of their trip is shopping, the border crossing goes smoothly. Should the traveller even hint that she might earn a few dollars by giving a lecture at a Seattle university, delays may follow. (On occasions like the latter, US policy starts to look more like protectionism than defence). Travel by train from Vancouver to Seattle requires two separate encounters with US authorities – Immigration at the station before boarding, and Customs one hour later at the border. With regard to the Arctic today, one is tempted to ask: Which is more secure – the US Arctic with its nuclear weapons, or the Canadian Arctic without?

Control over Arctic lands, seas, and skies seems next to impossible, so will chance necessarily favour the nation that is most heavily armed?

The Illusion

Arctic mariners know that the ocean obeys only the laws of nature. All the admirals in all the Arctic navies cannot stop the sea ice from melting or the permafrost from thawing or the Arctic shoreline from changing shape. Hunters do not control the weather, nor where animals decide to roam or where fish choose to feed; a co-management board can do much for conservation, but it cannot prevent climate change from driving new species northward. Regardless, conventional thinkers still align, and even equate, security and sovereignty with control. This assumption continues to be reflected in both American and Canadian Arctic policy statements, with the great power privileging security and the middle power emphasizing sovereignty. As Rob Huebert asserts, "defending Canadian Arctic sovereignty is really about the control of the region."[4]

In Heubert's view, melting sea ice will open the Arctic's waters to a range of aggressive new actors that will surely reduce the Canadian government's ability to call the shots. He points out that "popular con-cerns about the implications for Canada, and particularly its control over the Northwest Passage, [grow] apace ... and reveal ... growing political will to improve surveillance and control over this part of Canada."[5]

Events over the past five decades demonstrate Canada's anxiety about both its sovereignty and its lack of control. In response to the unauthor-ized transit of the American oil tanker *Manhattan* through the Northwest Passage in 1969, Pierre Trudeau's government asserted Canadian sover-eignty with the Arctic Waters Pollution Prevention Act of 1970. After the US Coast Guard icebreaker *Polar Sea* sailed the Northwest Passage from Greenland to Alaska in the summer of 1985 without requesting Canadian consent, Brian Mulroney's cabinet promised to build new Polar 8 class icebreakers to defend Canada's Arctic waters. The following year, 1986, Canada redefined its Arctic boundaries by drawing straight baselines around the Arctic Archipelago.[6] Despite these initiatives, Amer-ican and Soviet submarines continued to cruise beneath the Northwest Passage, just as they had done throughout the Cold War. Even today, Michael Byers asserts, Soviet-era charts "show more depth soundings in the Northwest Passage than Canada's most recent charts do."[7] Franklyn Griffiths describes this reality: "No Arctic sovereign is omnipotent in its own space and its immediate surroundings."[8]

McGill University military historian Desmond Morton once sug-gested that during and after the Cold War, Canada traded some of its sovereignty, and thus control, for the security that only America's mil-itary could provide.[9] Today, both security and sovereignty appear to be mutable concepts. For Griffiths, the security discourse revolves around states, alliances, and military competition. Huebert also understands this, commenting that "[the concept of] human security was an attempt to move security away from state-based analysis. This movement was due in part to the recognition that in many instances the state was the cause of insecurity of some or all of its peoples."[10]

Sovereignty has many definitions, but according to Arctic historian Shelagh Grant, only a few of these are relevant in Arctic history.[11] Sover-eignty is an evolving concept in Canada, says constitutionalist John

Whyte, who explained to me that "there is lots of domestic law evidence ... that sovereignty has been reconstructed into a notion of regime multiplicity."

Ernie Regehr, a research fellow at the Institute for Peace and Conflict Studies at the University of Waterloo's Conrad Grebel University College, has written that Arctic security is "ultimately about the safety and well-being of the people of the Arctic."[12] Rosemarie Kuptana offers a particular Inuit view: "Security is about more than arms build-up. Security is about ensuring that Inuit are equal members of the human family and have the economic basis to ensure a reasonable life-style as defined by contemporary Canada."[13] The Arctic's vast distances and tiny populations ought to teach us to be modest about what we seek to control. Nevertheless, states still compete over the Arctic, sometimes fiercely.

True Arctic security will demand sizable investments over time in Arctic communities, both small and large. Being neither a military strategist nor an academic expert, I propose a very different framework for Arctic security, one that is suited for sparsely populated northern landscapes whose inhabitants struggle to fund the civilian (never mind military) infrastructure needed to guarantee Canada's Arctic sovereignty. My framework has four key dimensions: cooperation, coordination, community, and investment

This framework starts with a deep conception of Arctic security, one that encompasses state or military security, human security (food, housing, and income), community security, broader environmental security, and economic security. This broader conception of security depends on broad cooperation among villages, cities, regions, nations, and states. Achieving security on this scale will depend also on effective longitudinal coordination between chiefs or governments of communities, legislators of sub-national entities, federal governments or nation-states, and international bodies like the Arctic Council, the International Maritime Organization, and UNCLOS. Such coordination can be achieved only through two-way communication, not top-down, south-to-north *diktats* from national capitals. It will also require functioning relationships at every level, including with the private and not-for-profit sectors.

Since many Arctic communities are isolated besides being challenged by economic and environmental concerns, as well as education, health, food, housing, and other insecurities, this objective of a secure Arctic community can only be achieved over time, through firm political commitments by chiefs, legislators, and feds, who will have to build a consensus concerning long-term infrastructure investments.

Securing the world's emerging Arctic community might sound like an idealist's dream, but survey research suggests that building towards such a goal would appeal not only to Canadians but to other Arctic residents as well. By itself, the Canadian military could not defeat the army of any major power. Taking a multidimensional approach to securing the Canadian Arctic and the wider Arctic community is more realistic than making empty promises of military expansion, which offers only the illusion of command and control.

Cooperation and Coordination

Throughout the Cold War, the West tried to avoid war by preparing for war with the East – a paradox that at the time seemed to make perfect sense. During those years, national security remained a key responsibility of the state; according to Swedish diplomat and security expert Rolf Ekéus, this "could be achieved only by developing military force (either potential or actual)."[14] But only in the Arctic were two nuclear powers situated so close to each other. Even today, according to Ekéus, we will achieve little on a larger scale without the cooperation of both Russia and the United States, which at the Bering Strait are separated by only a few miles.[15] Canada, while it needs to cooperate with both its Russian and its American neighbours, also needs to cooperate within NORAD, NATO, and other organizations.

The current threats to Arctic security are economic and environmental.[16] They are also more civilian than military.[17] Residues of Cold War conflicts do linger, with the possibility of armed conflict in the Arctic region sometimes fuelled by the overheated rhetoric of nationalist politicians.[18] Cooler heads point to the 2010 resolution of the long-standing boundary dispute between Norway and Russia, ongoing scientific cooperation among Arctic nations, and shared commitments to the rule of law in settling boundary disputes. As Russia's former Arctic Ambassador Anton Vasiliev often used to say, "there are no issues between Arctic states that could call for a military solution."[19]

In a 2012 report, Rob Huebert and colleagues warned that Arctic states would soon need to deal with the renewal of military strength in the Arctic.[20] They proposed that the Arctic Council open discussions on military issues. "Many people believe that states are like people and behave nicely like friends," Huebert said. "I am afraid that I have a somewhat darker view of state behaviour in the international system."[21]

But politicized discussions about national security could undermine the Arctic Council's tradition of informal dialogue and weaken its emphasis on scientific cooperation related to environmental concerns. A third point of view, expressed by Lawson Brigham of the University of Alaska, holds that the council already addresses broadly defined security questions, especially such topics as search-and-rescue (SAR), emergency preparedness, and environmental security.[22] It just doesn't deal with global *military* security.

In 2011 the eight member-states of the Arctic Council established a permanent secretariat and negotiated a multilateral SAR treaty, the first legally binding accord it had ever negotiated.[23] However, writes oceanographer Paul Arthur Berkman, this shift towards being a more formal international body in no way readies the council to take on the immense task of addressing military security.[24]

While remaining in international airspace, Russian aircraft regularly buzz the borders of its neighbours.[25] Such games of "chicken" inevitably provoke alarmist comments in the Canadian media.[26] Because they closely shadow each other, nuclear submarines from different nations do on occasion collide, an especially dangerous event in Arctic waters. Michael Byers notes that two American and six Russian or Soviet subs have been lost in this way.[27] To protect its interests in the region, Russia plans to keep expanding its Northern Fleet. Rolf Tamnes, at the Centre

for Norwegian and European Security, doesn't find this cause for concern. According to Tamnes, Russia's icebreaking and ocean monitoring
capabilities "far outstrip those of any other Arctic country. But the force
projection capability of modern Russia does not approach that of the
Soviet Union."[28]

Lawson Brigham expects to see more cooperation among Arctic states
in maritime enforcement and policing in connection with the developing Arctic fisheries. He does *not* expect to see military confrontation.[29]
For both Tamnes and Brigham, a second Cold War is unlikely.

Rob Huebert contends that it is still far from certain whether the
Arctic will be a zone of peace or conflict. Two foreign ministers, Russia's
Sergei Lavrov and Norway's Jonas Gahr Støre, jointly wrote in 2010 that
they "firmly believe that the Arctic can be used to demonstrate just how
much peace and collective interests can be served through the implementation of the international rule of law."[30] Unfortunately, Russia's
2015 annexation of Crimea has led other foreign ministers to re-examine
Russia's intentions.

In Canada, the Conservatives under Stephen Harper failed to fully
acknowledge Inuit historic occupancy; at the same time, they mounted
aggressive offshore Arctic claims and exaggerated threats to Canada's
sovereignty, such as Russian aircraft approaching our northern borders.[31]
The United States, for its part, has amped up its own security programs
to the point where its government can track almost every citizen's phone
and e-mail traffic. With Bill C-51 (the Anti-Terrorism Act), Canada appeared to be moving in the same direction. Under the new Liberal
government in Ottawa, that law's fate remains unclear.

But for all the missile rattling, very few boundary disputes trouble the
Canadian Arctic. Below, I review some of the more significant ones.

Beaufort Sea Boundary. Since 1976, Canada and the United States
have been disputing the offshore boundary between Alaska and Yukon.
This dispute, driven by differing interpretations of an 1825 French-
language treaty between Russia and Great Britain, involves a 21,436-
square-kilometre wedge in the oil-rich Beaufort Sea.[32] According to

Canada, that treaty suggests that the Beaufort Sea's maritime boundary is an extension of the arrow-straight 141st meridian land border between Yukon and Alaska. The Americans counter that the "equidistance principle" defines the offshore boundary and insists that it must lie at a right angle to the coastline, which tilts towards the Northwest.

At the invitation of Michael Byers, I attended a meeting of experts in Anchorage as they explored an interesting paradox: neither of the positions adopted by these two governments would appear be in either government's best interests. As a CanWest News Service story reported: "What emerged from the meeting was the realization that a large swath of ocean north of Alaska in the central and northern Beaufort would come under Canadian jurisdiction using the controversial American formula for drawing the international boundary."[33] Banks Island, a large offshore presence, makes all the difference. "In simple terms," Byers explains, "the US line appears to favour Canada beyond 200 nautical miles, and vice versa."[34] Ironically, this paradox may offer an opportunity to resolve the dispute, but Canada will need to involve the Inuvialuit, whose 1984 land claims settlement makes them an interested party.

Northwest Passages. The Arctic Marine Shipping Assessment (AMSA) describes five recognized passages through Canada's Arctic Archipelago.[35] For 400 years, the fabled Northwest Passage obsessed European explorers. Norwegian explorer Roald Amundsen made the first transit between 1903 and 1906.[36] The *St. Roch*, under the command of RCMP Sergeant Henry Larsen, made the first eastward transit between 1940 and 1942. Foreign vessels plying the Northern Sea Route across the top of Russia must now employ Russian ice pilots, as well as icebreaker escorts. Given its limited equipment and resources, this is a policy Canada has little capacity to duplicate.[37]

Canadian governments have long asserted that the Northwest Passage is Canadian internal waters. The Nunavut government also insists that these waters are "internal" to Nunavut. Inuit have been using eastern Lancaster Sound for thousands of years. "Copper Inuit occupied and used the sea ice and sea water in the Prince of Wales Strait for seal harvesting in the winter and for fishing, whaling, and bird hunting in the spring," writes Rosemarie Kuptana in her article "The Inuit Sea," and the Inuit retain usufructuary rights in these waters.[38]

Canada has reinforced its claims to the Northwest Passage with promises to acquire patrol boats for the area. Meanwhile, though, the US Arctic Strategy insists that the passage is an international strait through which every nation's vessels have the right of innocent passage. The Northwest Passage is "the highway of the Arctic," contends US Senator Angus King of Maine, founding co-chair of the Senate Arctic Caucus. King also argues that American icebreakers will be needed to maintain shipping routes in the Northwest Passage as global warming makes shipping there more feasible, although vessels will not likely be in service before the 2020s.[39] Not surprisingly, major shipping countries like China and South Korea support the Americans' view. Russia, however, not only agrees with Canada but has also drawn straight baselines around its own Arctic islands.

While increased traffic, related both to shipping and to increased human activity in the region, could boost economic development, national Coast Guards see it more as a matter of preparing for the worst. Corporate interests are fixated mainly on the trillions of dollars' worth of oil and gas reserves that the Arctic is said to hold; Coast Guards worry about what will happen when a ship spills oil or a drilling operation goes horribly wrong.

Michael Byers suggests that once we all get beyond the Ukrainian crisis, Canada and Russia should be able to resolve the Northwest Passage issue with the United States.[40] If the Arctic sea ice continues to melt, it will not be long before ice-strengthened ships are able to sail through the Northwest Passages from east to west in a couple of weeks. At present, neither the Northern Sea Route nor the Northwest Passages are completely reliable supply routes. Eventually, both will offer considerably shorter shipping routes between Asia and Europe than the Panama or Suez Canals.[41]

As allies, Canada and the United States have long agreed to disagree on the issue.[42] Neither the current delimitation disagreement in the Beaufort Sea nor the status of the Northwest Passage in any way endangers relations between the two countries. Signed by the Trudeau and Reagan governments in response to the *Polar Sea* controversy, the 1988 Canada–US Arctic Co-operation Agreement offers a positive example of the "agree to disagree" approach.

Hans Island. Hans Island, an uninhabited 1.3-square-kilometre rock in the waters between Greenland and Nunavut's Ellesmere Island, has generated bemused headlines in both Canada and Denmark. A 1973 maritime boundary dispute between the two countries left the issue unresolved, but by all accounts the problem is well managed.[43] Recently, soldiers from both Canada and Denmark have left flags, notes, and bottles of alcohol for their opposite numbers to find. Given that the waters around the island may hold rich oil and gas reserves, these friendly encounters disguise the potential seriousness of the dispute. In any case, the Inuit in Canada and Greenland may have an Aboriginal land claim to the island. Already, Greenlandic Canadian artist Laakkuluk Williamson-Bathory has declared herself president of the Republic of Hans Island or Tartupaluk ("looks like a kidney").[44]

Some claim that competition comes naturally to human beings and that, except during life-and-death emergencies, cooperation even within families and communities requires hard work. That may be especially true of cooperation between states. Yet as European governments chop defence budgets, cooperation and collaboration have become necessities. The United States has called for increased defence spending in NATO; Europe has responded with greater regional cooperation – with pooling and sharing. Doing more with less anywhere requires cooperation, writes Norwegian defence scholar Andreas Osthagen: "The same trend is taking place in the Arctic, where arenas are developed to promote collaboration across borders. This is perceived to be the most resource efficient way to deal with an increasing number of challenges."[45]

Both Ottawa and Washington recognize the enormity of the changes at work in the Arctic and the desirability of intergovernmental co-operation. In Canada, the Defence Science Advisory Board expressed the situation in this way: "Emergent national policies for comprehensive government action in the Arctic require coordination of effort in new ways and at higher levels of integration between local and national interests, across government departments and amongst governmental and non-governmental stakeholders and interests including but not limited to Indigenous peoples and their organizations."[46] The 2013 US Defense Department Strategy states: "The Department will continue to build cooperative strategic partnerships that promote innovative, affordable security solutions and burden-sharing in the Arctic, and seek to increase opportunities with Arctic partners to enhance regional expertise and cold-weather operational experience."[47]

During the Cold War, neither side could have predicted how the world has evolved since 1989, nor how the Arctic has warmed. The Arctic Coast Guard Forum, created by the eight Arctic states in 2015, is meant to be an instrument for strengthening cooperation on environmental protection, public safety, and search and rescue.[48] Because of Putin's recent actions, questions have been raised as to whether the other Arctic states would allow Russia to fully participate, but the Arctic is one area where cooperation is necessary. As US Admiral Zukunft said of the new forum: "We have an opportunity to ... make [the Arctic] a region that focuses on humanitarian concerns, on environmental concerns, on the way of life of indigenous tribes, and not as a war-fighting domain."[49] Ernie Regehr writes that "the agreement to foster cooperation and coordination among the region's Coast Guards is one part of the response to steadily changing Arctic realities. Increasing maritime traffic, the potential for intensified resource extraction, and hopes for expanded fishing are challenging Arctic states to improve their capabilities in areas such as search and rescue, environmental protection (including oil spill response capacity), aids to navigation, border control, fisheries inspection, policing services, and maritime domain awareness."[50]

Peace activists have long lobbied for an Arctic treaty that would mirror the Antarctic one. They point to Article 1 of the 1959 treaty, which states that "Antarctica shall be used for peaceful purposes only."[51] They hope for a single comprehensive treaty to govern the Arctic. However, numerous treaties and other accords (such as UNCLOS, SAR, and various Indigenous treaties) already cover the circumpolar North. Notwithstanding the lack of American, Canadian, or Russian action on climate change, Franklyn Griffiths sees "stewardship" as a potentially unifying principle of Arctic governance.[52]

Some advocates for a nuclear-weapons-free Arctic have called for a step-by-step approach to "build down" military defences left over from the Cold War. For some old warriors, Russia still represents an ongoing threat. "The Cold War is over, but Russia still takes the Arctic seriously," writes James Holmes, an ex-US naval officer and now blogger who keeps an eye on all things military. "Russian nuclear-powered submarines still sail under the sea ice, where Canada's diesel-powered submarines cannot venture."[53] Former Canadian Ambassador to Moscow Christopher Westdal responds to militarists like Holmes by making three points: one of the best ways to promote Arctic security is to promote constructive security and other relations between Russia and the United States; given its geography, Canada has an obvious national security interest (if not indeed a global security responsibility) to encourage amity between the two nuclear powers; and an essential early step to promote more constructive relations is to correct the Western media's relentless distortions of Russia.[54]

Western-backed protests and loose talk about Ukraine joining NATO are like poking the Russian bear with a sharp stick, yet they continue. Putin might have few friends abroad, but the Crimean incursion and his destabilization of Ukraine's new government have rebuilt his popularity at home.[55]

According to financier George Soros, "Putin turned aggressive out of weakness. He is acting in self-defence."[56] Michael Ignatieff contends that Putin's actions have permanently fractured post–Cold War relations and sealed the bond between the two great authoritarian states, Russia and China. Authoritarian oligarchies can be politically fragile, he says: "They must control everything or soon they will control nothing."[57]

Others see things differently. "Interactions between Russian President Vladimir Putin and US President Donald Trump already reflect a significant change in Russian–US relations," writes Paul Arthur Berkman. In the *Alaska Dispatch News* on December 7, 2016, Berkman affirmed that "the high north is also a region of low tension – contrary to media hype – where all Arctic states have been cooperating around science since the Cold War."[58]

Although Canada's relations with Russia have cooled, agreement on the Northwest Passages and the Northern Sea Route might rewarm the relationship. Should events in eastern Ukraine or the Middle East undo years of constructive engagement and Arctic cooperation[59] – or, heaven forbid, trigger a new Cold War – communities of opinion in the circumpolar region will have to begin again to repair fractured relationships within their own states, and with governments at every level and across the boundaries of race, religion, and language. Even if Rob Huebert is correct about the nasty character of states and the tendency of aggressive nationalist zealots to undermine regional peace and order, wise leaders can rebuild security in all four dimensions of my framework if they start by building out: not down from the state, but up from the community. No longer is the state the only actor that matters.[60]

The Arctic Council has established itself as a safe place for frank but friendly dialogue among its member politicians, public servants, permanent participants, and others. As a result, mutual understandings have emerged, demonstrating the effectiveness of cooperation. The council's permanent participants hope to link villages, nations, and the circumpolar world by integrating local and international agendas. Some efforts towards cooperative agreements in the Arctic region have already succeeded, others not so much.

Ilulissat. The agreement reached by five Arctic states at Ilulissat, Greenland, in May 2008, which I discussed in Chapter 7, would make a fine advertisement for Arctic cooperation were it not for complaints from three states: Finland, Sweden, and Iceland. The five coastal states – Canada, Denmark, Norway, Russia, and the United States – chose to ignore that trio's interests, telling "the rest of the world that their continental shelf activity is related to law of the sea implementation rather than a scramble for resources," as Timo Koivurova from the University of Lapland's Arctic Centre explained to me. They similarly excluded the region's Indigenous peoples from the discussions.[61]

The Ilulissat Declaration relies on a binding international legal instrument, the UN Convention on the Law of the Sea (UNCLOS), which, as noted earlier, was adopted in 1994. As of September 2016, 168 countries had signed on to UNCLOS.[62] The United States is not one of them, though it views the convention's articles as forming part of customary law. "Much of UNCLOS was a codification of existing customary international law," Rob Heubert explains. "But it also introduced new means of ocean governance."[63] The leadership role taken by Russia, as the only non-NATO state involved in this cooperative effort, raised hopes for future joint initiatives, but Putin's Crimean adventure has probably put such prospects on the back burner for now.

Search-and-rescue (SAR). In 2011, EKOS's Arctic public opinion survey *Rethinking the Top of the World* confirmed the perception that, while the environment was the most important issue for them, "northern Canadians ranked the ability to respond to disasters and emergencies second and third on a list of what impacts their lives in Arctic Canada." Over 85 percent of respondents agreed that these issues were important, but only 10 percent thought the level of response readiness was satisfactory. A follow-up survey in 2015 echoed these findings.[64] Together, the surveys highlight the importance of emergency response to northern leaders, chiefs, and legislators, as well as to the federal government. The Arctic Council has reflected this priority to a large extent in its SAR initiative and in the continued work of its Emergency Prevention, Preparedness, and Response Working Group.

In signing the Agreement on Cooperation on Aeronautical and Maritime Search and Rescue (AAMSAR) in May 2011, the eight members of the Arctic Council underscored the value of cooperating in emergencies. The agreement identifies the agencies responsible for responding to SAR incidents in each member-state and recognizes the need to promote information exchange and multilateral training.[65] It also rearticulates the most important legal instruments that protect the Arctic Ocean, including the 1974 Safety of Life at Sea Convention, the 1979 International Convention on Maritime Search and Rescue, and UNCLOS.[66]

Some observers heralded AAMSAR, which allows resources to be pooled and coordinated, as a transformative event. Skeptics claimed that the agreement simply codified existing practice. Historically, maritime law has required that mariners "render assistance to any person found at sea in danger of being lost."[67] The agreement may especially benefit Canada, which governs a huge Arctic territory yet bases very little rescue capacity in the region.[68] Political pressure to address these capacity deficits will surely grow following a 2013 report by Canada's auditor general. "Significant improvements are needed if [the Canadian Forces and Canadian Coast Guard] are to continue to adequately respond and provide the necessary personnel, equipment, and information systems to deliver SAR activities effectively," asserts Wilfred Greaves, an instructor at the Trudeau Centre for Peace, Conflict, and Justice.[69] Given the length of Canada's Arctic coastline, patrolling it is a major challenge. Both the Canadian and the US Coast Guards have forward operating bases in the Arctic, but only during the summer months.[70]

Currently only Iceland, Norway, and Russia are adequately equipped for SAR responsibilities.[71] Norway has invested in a new port, new ships, and all-weather helicopters for Svalbard.[72] By further expanding the world's largest icebreaker fleet as well as its bases along the Northern Sea Route, Russia has reinforced its position. In contrast, Canada, Greenland (Denmark), and the United States have been slow to bolster emergency preparedness on the Arctic coast of North America.[73] In 2013 the Munk–Gordon Arctic Security Program convened three regional emergency preparedness round tables in the northern territories; these were followed by a national round table in Ottawa, which heard reports from these regional discussions. The issues identified were recognizing the resiliency of northern communities; emphasizing local needs and capabilities instead of focusing on visitors to the region; noting the increasing frequency of incidents, with an unmatched ability to respond to this increase; and observing the distinctive approach each territory takes to emergency management.

Alaskans and northern Canadians tend to agree that there is a gap between existing resources for SAR and the region's growing needs. The

US Coast Guard currently has only one active icebreaker, the *Healy*, with medium capacity; the *Polar Star*, an ancient vessel, is in its final stages of refurbishment for active duty.[74] The Coast Guard bases the *Healy* and other equipment in Kodiak during summer months; this still leaves long stretches of Alaskan coastline with little or no SAR capacity.[75] In 2013 the US Coast Guard examined its polar region capacity and recommended the purchase of six new icebreakers and the establishment of "home-porting" by stationing two of those icebreakers on the US Arctic coast.[76]

At the Arctic Circle Forum in Quebec City on December 13, 2016, Mead Treadwell, Alaska's former lieutenant-governor, said that icebreakers supporting scientific research in Antarctica could be dedicated to the Arctic Ocean in the northern winter. He also reminded the forum attendees that UNCLOS Article 234 seems to allow countries to act beyond their offshore jurisdiction if necessary. For a best practice in international shipping cooperation, Treadwell pointed to the regime in place along the St. Lawrence Seaway.

Like Canada, the United States currently has no deep-water port north of the Arctic Circle. This makes home-porting difficult. Richard Beneville, the mayor of Nome, Alaska, is promoting the use of Port Clarence, 120 miles northwest of his municipality, as a facility for servicing the growing number of ships crossing the Bering Sea and the Arctic Ocean.

Canadian Forces Lieutenant-Colonel John St. Dennis notes that while the Canadian Forces may be the first responder for aerial/coastal SAR in the Arctic and elsewhere, their role in emergency response and ground/inland water search-and-rescue is as the responder of last resort.[77] The RCMP is responsible for land-based SAR in Canada; the Canadian Forces play a supporting role for communities and territorial governments when all other resources are tapped out. Through Joint Task Force North in Yellowknife, the Canadian Forces stay in touch with local partners and monitor all threats, including earthquakes, forest fires, and marine vessels, along the Northwest Passage.

Military thinkers recognize that some circumstances are beyond their control and that security begins in Arctic communities, where knowledgeable locals matter.[78] Alaskan Nils Andreassen pointed out to me that while the Alaska Land Claims Settlement extinguished Aboriginal title to the ocean, "customary use" conventions have brought Alaska Natives to the table. The US Coast Guard long ago made room for tribal or co-management representatives on its Arctic Waterways Safety Committee. The Alaska Territorial Guard was formed as far back as 1942 to engage Indigenous people and their skills. Canada organized the Canadian Rangers five years later, for similar purposes.

The Canadian Rangers have no assigned SAR roles, but their training makes them capable of assisting in any emergency event. As concerned community members, they might already be volunteering in a SAR mission before they were formally dispatched. Too much top-down Ottawa-to-Arctic command and control would only slow that response.

Canada established a National Search and Rescue Program in 1986 to serve as a central nervous system for the many federal and territorial departments involved. Some parts of the country have plenty of coverage; others have far less. The Joint Rescue Coordination Centre (JRCC) in Victoria, BC, handles air SAR for Yukon; the JRCC's Trenton, Ontario, centre handles SAR for most of Canada's land mass; JRCC Halifax covers parts of the Eastern Arctic.

On average, twenty aeronautical searches per year require the Victoria centre's involvement. For aeronautical SAR, the coordinators first deploy assets from Victoria; after that, they use northern charter aircraft, which can get to the scene more quickly. In the case of a large-scale emergency, Victoria would implement a Major Air Disaster Plan, which could summon stand-by support from Joint Task Force North, the Canadian Forces, and the US Air Force. Under international SAR agreements, Victoria can also request the use of aircraft on standby in Alaska (or the northeastern United States) without gaining approval from national decision-makers.

Linking resources, responsibility, and training is critical to successful rescues. This means that all SAR participants need to exchange knowledge with their partners. In Yukon, and to some extent in the NWT, ground search-and-rescue (GSAR) remains a greater need than air and sea operations. As noted, the RCMP takes the lead in managing GSAR, with the support of territorial governments, municipalities, and First Nations. A search may cover a wide area, but most rescues are local. The Yukon community of Teslin, for which the local government and its First Nation wrote a joint GSAR plan, offers a fine example of cooperation and coordination. Not all northern communities are as well prepared, but in any community, the residents, no matter how busy they are with other things, will drop everything to help during an emergency. "They pulled together and we are very, very grateful and we're very appreciative of all the support," reflected Norman Yakeleya, NWT legislator for the Sahtu constituency, after a 2012 search effort.[79]

Nonetheless, Canada found itself woefully unprepared for the nearly disastrous grounding of the cruise ship *Clipper Adventurer* in the Coronation Gulf on August 27, 2010. The ship started to take on water after crashing into a shoal, and its 117 passengers strapped on life jackets. Fortunately, the weather was calm and the ship did not shift off the shoal and sink in deep water as feared. Air rescue was eight hours away, however, and the *Amundsen,* the nearest Coast Guard ship, had 500 kilometres – more than one day's sailing – to cover before it could arrive on the scene.[80] Early reports blamed poor navigational charts for not locating the shoal, but it was later revealed that the *Clipper Adventurer* had failed to upload 2007 revisions to the charts. Worse, the ship's captain had deviated from established routes in search of more interesting scenery – an alarmingly common practice; cruise ships in Arctic waters offer their elderly passengers, who pay thousands of dollars for the experience, a chance to see the old Arctic before it's gone.

The *Amundsen* escorted the passengers and crew off the *Clipper Adventurer* two days later and delivered them to Kugluktuk. Former NWT constitutional adviser Bernard Funston reported that no one in Kugluktuk knew the rescued group was on the way until the evening of

August 29, because almost everyone in the community of 1,400 had gone fishing. Such rescues can overwhelm the local populations of Arctic communities and exhaust their resources. Indeed, no small community could have prepared adequately for the unexpected offloading of passengers from the stranded *Clipper Adventurer*.

An emergency event in the Arctic, whether the cause is human or natural, can quickly become even more serious because of remoteness, inclement weather, limited transportation and communication options, and other factors. Indeed, system failures (heat, water, power, transportation, communication, resupply, etc.) and the hazards that lead to those failures (fire, flood, blizzard, extreme cold, high winds, human error, etc.) are what cause the most critical emergencies faced by many Arctic communities, especially in winter.[81] If Arctic communities are to play a role in responding to emergencies, they need to be properly equipped and trained.

Lawson Brigham reminds us that only a small percentage of the Arctic Ocean is charted. Canada, for example, may have charts for less than 10 percent of its Arctic waters.[82] A partial solution might be to invite ships with hydrographic instruments to share their data with governments. For now, the top of the world is still covered in ice for most of the year. "Cruise ships off the West Coast of Greenland have *no* safety net," Brigham points out. "No large commercial cargo ship or passenger vessel should be outside the Polar Code and operate in polar waters."[83] The summer of 2016 saw the 820-foot, 68,000-ton luxury cruise ship *Crystal Serenity* make a month-long transit of the Northwest Passage from Alaska to New York City.[84]

Navigating Arctic waters requires rare skills; that is nothing new. "The navigation of the Polar Seas, which is peculiar, requires in a particular manner, an extensive knowledge of the nature, properties and usual motions of the ice," wrote Captain William Scoresby in 1820. "And it can only be performed to the best advantage by those who have long experience with working a ship in icy conditions."[85] Some luck is useful, too. Canada certainly got lucky when large numbers of lives were not lost in the *Clipper Adventurer* incident. But even Coast Guard vessels can run aground, and if that were to happen, Canada would be in real trouble. For northern Canadians the *Clipper Adventurer* incident proved the need for a mandatory International Maritime Organization Polar Code.

Transport Canada adopted the Arctic Ice Regime Shipping System (AIRSS) in 2003 to strengthen the regulations on ships transiting icy waters. Ships transiting waters covered under AIRSS are required to report information to Northern Canada Vessel Traffic Services (NORDREG). This real-time information allows the Canadian Coast Guard to independently assess whether a ship is complying with the regulations governing which ships can navigate through what sorts of ice. Also, the aggregated vessel reports allow other mariners in the area to determine conditions at some distance from their current positions.[86] Coast Guard officers at the Marine Communications and Traffic Services office in Iqaluit direct shipping across Canadian Arctic waters from Alaska to Greenland.[87]

On December 31, 2012, an ice-strengthened conical drill barge grounded off the stormbound northern coast of Alaska. Owned by Royal Dutch Shell and named *Kulluk*, the vessel was carrying thousands of gallons of fuel.[88] The grounding rang warning bells for Americans about the need for tighter regulation of offshore oil exploration.[89] For others, the warning came in 2013 from the first-ever sailing of a cargo-carrying freighter, the 75,000-tonne *Nordic Orion*, through the Northwest Passage, which shortened the journey from Vancouver, Canada, to Pori, Finland, by a thousand nautical miles and four days' sailing. The *Nordic Orion*'s Danish owners worked with Canadian officials to successfully complete its historic transit.[90] Other shippers, however, may not respect Canada's Arctic Waters Pollution Prevention Act from 1970 or other federal rules.

For a time, rumours circulated that the cruise ship industry was seeking an exemption to the Polar Code. Perhaps this is what led the International Maritime Organization (IMO), a UN agency based in London, England, to produce a lowest-common-denominator Polar Code in 2014. During the code's drafting stages, worries persisted that the IMO would pay insufficient heed to the training of ice navigators.[91]

As eventually adopted by the IMO, the Polar Code put some of these fears to rest by setting a number of mandatory shipping rules for ship design, navigation, crew training and education, search and rescue activities, and the discharge of oil, chemicals, sewage, and garbage.[92] But the code's environmental provisions are weak.

In 2014, thick ice prevented any commercial transit of Canada's Arctic coastline. Debates about regulations as an essential precondition for extracting Arctic energy resources and shipping them through the Northwest Passage are ongoing. The Lloyd's Market group of insurance underwriters have already warned that northern shippers face extreme risks and that the rate at which maritime traffic is increasing in Arctic waters may be "outstripping policy makers' ability to create a legislative framework in the high north."[93]

Arctic Marine Shipping Assessment (AMSA). As noted earlier, at the 2009 Arctic Council ministerial meeting in Tromsø, Norway, Arctic ministers approved the Arctic Marine Shipping Assessment (AMSA), a study essential to policy-making for Arctic maritime matters. A product of the labour of 200 experts in the Protection of the Arctic Marine Environment (PAME) working group established four years earlier, this study followed the Arctic Climate Impact Assessment and the Arctic Marine Strategic Plan, both released in 2004. "Overall, AMSA is a message from the Arctic states to the world that contains an environmental security framework and strategy to address the many complex challenges of protecting Arctic people and the environment in an era of expanding use in the Arctic Ocean," Lawson Brigham explains.[94] Resource development will come with high commodity prices and will further integrate the Arctic into the world economy. New mines, oil fields, and roads will require safe marine transportation infrastructure.

Thorough and accurate charting will be a critical part of all this. As noted earlier, navigational charting in northern Canada has been far less thorough than in the country's southern regions. And where charts do exist, they are often incomplete or lack adequate detail for full navigation of the Northwest Passage, Hudson Bay, and other Arctic waters. The same is true of navigational charts of the Alaskan Arctic: they may be in better shape than Canada's, but they are incomplete and not nearly as thorough as those of waters farther south. As a result of their submarine transits, both Russia and the United States have superior charts of Canada's Northwest Passage – obviously a source of embarrassment for the Canadian government.[95] In Canada, the Canadian Hydrographic Service (CHS) is responsible for producing and updating nautical charts. In the United States, this task falls to the National Oceanic and Atmospheric Administration (NOAA). These organizations are improving charting in the Arctic by working together.

Cooperation is necessary during the response *and* non-crisis phases of an emergency. Truly international cooperation cannot be achieved until actors at all levels of government make Arctic emergency preparedness both a policy and a fiscal priority. Contributions from the private sector at the community level and internationally will also play an essential role.

Securing Arctic peace will also require multi-party coordination at all levels, from community to region to nation, as well as long-term infrastructure investment plans, such as those the most successful private operators make. In the polar regions, coordination and communication between the private and the public sectors is just as critical. Sometimes, as in the following example, it can be a matter of life and death.

In 2001, Dr. Ronald Shemenski, the only physician among fifty researchers working at the Amundsen Scott–South Pole Research Station, suffered a gall bladder attack that led to a diagnosis of pancreatitis, a potentially life-threatening condition. Though flights to the South Pole station are normally halted from late February until November because of the extreme winter cold and darkness, rescuers worried that Shemenski's condition could worsen in the coming months, when an airlift out of the South Pole would be virtually impossible. To retrieve the fifty-nine-year-old doctor, an eight-seat, twin-engine plane fitted with skis for landing gear flew from the Rothera Research Station on the Antarctic Peninsula.

At the time, my brother Steve Penikett was general manager of Kenn Borek Air Ltd., the Canadian airline company leading the Twin Otter evacuation. "The wind's blowing like hell," Steve told the media. "We're getting reduced visibility and blowing snow. If the winds calm down and there's less cloud cover, we'll get better visibility."[96] According to aviation experts, the successful rescue effort was the first time a plane had attempted a landing at the South Pole during polar winter, when temperatures are in the range of –75 degrees Fahrenheit (–59 degrees Celsius) or –143 degrees Fahrenheit (–97 degrees Celsius) with wind chill, and where the skies are nearly pitch-black for twenty hours of the day.[97]

As Adam Galinsky and Maurice Schweitzer indicate in their book *Friend and Foe*, an event such as Shemenski's dramatic rescue was possible only because of close collaboration and cooperation among parties at all levels. "The costs of hierarchy can exceed its benefits in tasks ... that go beyond instinct and physical coordination, and instead require intellectual integration. Why? Because to make the best complex decisions, we need to tap ideas from all rungs in the hierarchical ladder and learn from everybody who has relevant knowledge to share."[98]

Operation Nanook, an annual military exercise held at different locations in Canada each year, exemplifies the kind of coordinated effort that could be undertaken more often. Nanook tests the capabilities that various federal, territorial, and municipal governments in Canada, as well as some international partners, might bring to emergency scenarios.[99] For Operation Nanook 2012, held in Yellowknife, thirty airmen from the 920th rescue wing of the US Air Force at Patrick Air Force Base, Florida, travelled to Canada to participate in the operation, alongside the 435th Transport and Rescue Squadron based out of Winnipeg, Manitoba, and the 440th Transport Squadron from Yellowknife, NWT.[100] Also, the US Coast Guard Cutter *Juniper* travelled 3,700 kilometres from Newport, Rhode Island, to participate.[101] In commenting on the operation, Rob Huebert noted at the time that "Canadian Arctic policy needs to go even beyond this [level of cooperation] ... Territorial governments must also be included, as well as the various Northern Aboriginal peoples and their organizations."[102] Two years later, in 2014, Nanook focused on an emergency response in Nunavut, where the Government of Nunavut Emergency Measures Organization took responsibility for the command and control of resources. The 2016 Nanook exercise, which involved an August earthquake near Haines Junction, attracted a wide and deep intergovernmental response.

Canadians – young Canadians especially – seek cooperation rather than confrontation with Canada's Arctic neighbours. They care deeply about climate change and the environment. They want to develop northern resources in responsible ways. They want competing claims among Arctic nations to be resolved peacefully. To a large extent, they have bought into Gorbachev's vision of the Arctic as a "zone of peace." They also recognize that the reconciliation between Indigenous and non-Indigenous northerners begun over the past forty years has been the greatest contribution that Canada, the territorial governments, and Indigenous communities could make to peace and security in the Arctic.

Community and Investment

At Yellowknife in 2007, the three territorial premiers announced a plan to address their regional security concerns. Their report, "A Northern Vision: A Stronger North and a Better Canada," concludes that sustainable communities with (at the very least) well-supported education, reasonable living costs, and adequate infrastructure are at the heart of sovereignty.[103] It also widens the concept of security, calling for tighter shipping regulations to "balance commerce with environmental protection." The same report calls for more collaboration between the federal government and its territorial counterparts and for an increase in the capacity of the Arctic through the building of a permanent Arctic military base and a deep-water port, increased support for the Canadian Rangers, and refurbished icebreakers for the Canadian Coast Guard.[104] According to the northern premiers, "Canada's sovereignty is based on Northerners' use and occupancy of lands and waters through the centuries and is enhanced by 'strong and healthy communities.'"[105]

For the three northern premiers and other territorial legislators, adapting to climate change means maximizing benefits and minimizing negative impacts through research, information-sharing, cleaner energy sources, and modifications to infrastructure, so that the Arctic can withstand environmental and socio-economic changes. In circumpolar forums, these three premiers have emphasized that "Northern issues must be addressed by Northern voices," and they promise in their report to "support increased efforts by Canada to strengthen bilateral relations with our Arctic neighbours to help ensure that our circumpolar interests remain a priority area for multilateral co-operation."

In his background paper for the 2014 Munk–Gordon Arctic Security Program's National Roundtable on Arctic Emergency Preparedness, Bernard Funston discussed the concept of "safe communities." According to the World Health Organization, a healthy community is "one that is safe with affordable housing and accessible transportation systems, work for all who want to work, a healthy and safe environment with a sustainable ecosystem, and offers access to health care services which focus on prevention and staying healthy."[106] Also, community means more than individual villages. As Franklyn Griffiths puts it:

> I suggest we take the referent object for life and quality of life in the Arctic to be neither the state, nor the individual, nor civil society, but the *community*, typically the remote small Indigenous community which is embedded in the natural environment. Characterizing the referent object, the term "community" also sums up the many and varied purposes of collective action for the good in Arctic conditions. It connotes order without law. This is order that's based on shared norms or standards of behaviour that govern human relations and, especially in an Arctic setting, human relations with the world of nature.[107]

Wise words. In this regard, if Old Crow and the Vuntut Gwich'in community show what Canadian government investment can achieve, Inuvik is an example of what disinvestment can do. Canada gave birth to Inuvik as a new regional centre for the surrounding Dene and Inuvialuit communities, but according to the local people I spoke to in

March 2015, the removal of military personnel in 1985 began the decline of the community.

The United States, Alaska, Canada, and the northern territories all have their own wish lists for northern civilian, military, and infrastructure investments. All of the interested parties plead for long-term plans and commitment, multi-use facilities, and inter-agency cooperation. US Senator Angus King, founding co-chair of the Senate's Arctic Caucus, for example, wants to add money to the US Coast Guard budget for the construction of icebreakers. King lists the number of icebreakers – public and private – in operation in 2015 as approximately 80: Russia 40; Finland 7; Sweden 6; Canada 6; United States 5 (two fully functional Coast Guard icebreakers under Coast Guard command, one of them in the Antarctic Ocean, and three other US icebreakers owned privately); Denmark 4; Estonia 2; and Norway, Germany, China, Japan, Australia, Chile, Latvia, South Korea, South Africa, and Argentina 1 each.[108] It is useful to remember that, in the whole world, there are only fifty *large* icebreakers.

An icebreaker costs nearly $1 billion to build. At that price tag, each new ship proposed will take some patient politicking, potentially allowing industry to surge ahead. UK science journalist Alun Anderson comments: "In the United States, it takes an estimated ten to fifteen years to win the budget for a new icebreaker and then design and build it. In a Korean yard, a new commercial icebreaking oil tanker can be ready in three months."[109]

Canada revised its plan for an Arctic naval docking and refuelling facility at Nanisivik in 2013 after the cost of the proposed development mushroomed from $100 million to $258 million.[110] With federal funding, Iqaluit has been promised a deep-sea port by 2021. Time will test that promise. Canadians have long been accustomed to loud announcements of defence procurements followed by quiet excuses for their non-implementation. Peace and conflict studies scholar Ernie Regehr states that Canadian politicians routinely "invoke temporary Northern visions to curry temporary Southern favour."[111]

In 1985 the Conservative government of Prime Minister Brian

Mulroney promised to build the *Polar 8*, the most powerful icebreaker in the world, along with a fleet of nuclear-powered submarines and six other icebreakers.[112] The delivery date for the Polar 8 was to have been 2017 but is now 2022.[113] The Canadian Coast Guard apparently needs $720 million to buy a replacement for the icebreaker *Louis St. Laurent*, built in 1968. The rest of the Coast Guard's outdated fleet, nearly forty years old, is a decade overdue for replacement.[114] Even at the top of their game, these vessels would still be hours or days away from most Arctic emergencies.[115]

The Canadian Arctic/Offshore Patrol Ship (AOPS) project will deliver six ice-capable ships, designated as the Harry DeWolf Class. The first such vessel will be delivered in 2018, the government says. Some critics have complained that these Arctic offshore patrol ships may be too slow, too expensive, and too light for icebreaking.[116]

The Canadian air force has its own wish list of replacements, one that includes eighteen outdated Aurora maritime patrol aircraft, five Globemaster transports, and seventeen Hercules. It also hopes that authorities will lengthen four of its Arctic military runways and build a new fixed-wing SAR aircraft. The new fixed-wing SAR planes promised by the federal Liberal government in 2003 have yet to appear.[117] In December 2016, however, the new Liberal government announced that it had chosen a supplier – Airbus – and that sixteen new C-295W aircraft modified for search-and-rescue missions were on order for a cost of $2.4 billion.[118] Some wish lists include new F-35 fighter jets, the most expensive of that breed ever, to replace Canada's aging CF-18 fleet. Prime Minister Justin Trudeau has not smiled on this idea, but Lockheed Martin, their US manufacturer, is still pushing.

At Anchorage, the US 176th Wing (National Guard) relies on four HC-130s, Hercules aircraft specifically modified for aerial refuelling and combat SAR missions.[119] Another rescue squadron, based at the Eielson Air Force Base in Fairbanks, has HH-60G Pave Hawk rescue helicopters to support SAR missions.[120] The US Department of Defense has identified no need to expand its current aerial SAR assets in Alaska.[121]

If Ottawa listened to northern Canadians, it would invest in improved multi-use infrastructure serving communities, industry, and the military. Instead of a dock at the northern end of Baffin Island, Arctic residents want to see a deep-water port of the kind that would be useful for a large population centre, as well as an icebreaker based on the coast. Given that the only permanent Coast Guard station in the Canadian Arctic is in Hay River, NWT, 700 kilometres by sea from the Arctic Ocean, northern-based aircraft could be used for search and rescue.[122] It is unrealistic to expect northerners to rush out to rescue passengers from a downed 747, Rob Huebert once told me; and, as my bush pilot brother used to say, flying is not dangerous, but crashing is. That said, northern-based aircraft could respond quickly to search requests. Meanwhile, if Arctic communities are to keep playing first-responder roles in emergencies, their residents will need to be properly equipped and trained. Other items on northerners' long list of urgent infrastructure needs include updated communications, the proposed Polar Weather and Communications (PWC) satellite, removal of rain gauges from airports, and weather and avalanche monitoring and warning systems.

Happily, Canada's Department of National Defence Science Advisory Board (DSAB) seems very much in tune with northerners.[123] The April 2012 DSAB Report 1001, "Defining a Comprehensive Approach to the Canadian Arctic Theatre of Operations," begins with this observation: "A common characteristic affecting virtually all undertakings in the North is the paucity of infrastructure. It is therefore in this area that ... the interest of all involved parties can be advanced through a process of cooperation and collaboration in the development of shared infrastructure." The report goes on to note that "a collaborative approach between mining companies and DND, on infrastructure financing/development, could also be of value in the long term to local Inuit communities." It recommends further that "in addressing these requirements ... DND adopt a 'northern first' policy for procurement for Arctic Operations support services," and it suggests that "consultation with potentially affected communities be among the first orders of business when contemplating potential Arctic activities and operations."[124]

A "North First" Perspective

A report issued in the fall of 2014 by Julie Gelfand, Canada's Commissioner for the Environment and Sustainable Development, included a section titled "Marine Navigation in the Canadian Arctic"[125] that revealed that federal departments – Transport Canada, Environment Canada, and Fisheries and Oceans Canada (including the Canadian Coast Guard and the Canadian Hydrographic Service) – are currently not up to the task of supporting safe marine navigation in Canadian Arctic waters. Gelfand's report also indicated that unlike those of the United States, Denmark, Norway, Finland, and Sweden, Canada's northern strategy had failed to focus on the components of Arctic marine safety: charting and hydrography, navigation aids, ice and weather information, vessel detection, ship design and construction standards, and, critically, icebreaking. No department had a coordinated strategy, which meant that no one at the federal level recognized the importance of marine transportation to the Arctic economy and the security of Arctic communities. Nor did the federal government seem to realize that it lacked the capacity to handle oil spills, shipwrecks, and environmental damage as traffic through the Northwest Passage increased.

The Nunavut Research Institute has announced grants of $2 million for marine safety projects, which is a start.[126] Public consultations on a new defence policy conducted in 2016 were meant to engage Canadians with regard to the principal challenges to Canada's security, the capacity of the Canadian Armed Forces to address threats and challenges, and the resources needed to do so.[127] However, the results of that consultation have not yet been released.

A long-term "North First" investment in Arctic infrastructure will require a multi-party, multi-level commitment to spending on both defence equipment and infrastructure. All levels of government and industry will need to support that plan. Canada spends plenty of money in the Arctic, but it lacks a capital infrastructure plan. A Canadian government serious about Arctic security will consult widely, construct such a plan, and stick to it. This approach will require a prime minister or defence minister who is open-minded enough to involve counterparts from opposition parties in talks, as well as to consult with Indigenous and territorial governments. Table proposals, I suggest, talk them up, be open about the costs, and give every interested stakeholder a say. In the national interest, create in Parliament an all-party plan, then carry it through.

From individual hamlets to the larger community of Arctic states, building security in the circumpolar North will mean making strategic investments in a diverse range of social goods – safe housing; access to education and healthy, affordable food; energy development that benefits northerners while also protecting the northern environment; and transportation systems that connect villages, towns, regions, and nations – as well as carrying out diplomacy and good governance so as to link everything from international authorities to parliaments to regional capitals to local mayors. Timely investments of energy and imagination have created the northern land claims settlements, the idea of sustainable development, and the Arctic Council. Essentially, this was the vision of Gorbachev, Koivisto, Mulroney, and Bruntland, but also of Thomas Berger and Mary Simon. It was echoed by the three territorial premiers in 2007, and it seemed completely possible to me during that Old Crow conversation with my Canadian senator friend in the summer of 2006.

States, including Canada, need to stop thinking about the Great White North as an empty space or a potential battleground and start viewing it as an emerging "community of communities," to use Joe Clark's description of Canada. The "North First" approach of the Defence Science Advisory Board makes a lot of sense, especially if, together, the federal parties in Parliament, after consulting with Indigenous communities and territorial governments, could be persuaded to adopt a long-term plan to build multi-purpose infrastructure, ports, and runways and to base icebreakers and rescue aircraft in the North. On the cornerstone of community, Canada could build Arctic security using the tools of cooperation, coordination, and long-term investment.

9

Hungry Ghost
Climate Change

A hungry ghost haunts the hunting grounds, upsetting houses,
and raising strange storms.

ecent headlines tell the story. "Captain Cook's detailed 1778 records confirm global warming today in the Arctic." "North Pole
forecast to warm 50 degrees above normal Thursday." "Ice growth
slowing in the polar regions." "Reindeer Shrink as Climate Change in
Arctic Puts Their Food on Ice." "Polar bear numbers seen declining
a third from Arctic sea ice melt." "Change in the Arctic this year was
unlike any ever seen, scientists say." "Scientists are frantically copying
US climate data, fearing it might vanish under Trump." On December
13–14, 2016, Honolulu hosted a symposium on Climate Displacement,
Migration, and Relocation. Unfortunately, too many powerful people
simply avert their eyes.

Arctic life has always relied on ice. Ice binds so many life forms in the
North. Polar bears depend on sea ice to provide platforms for hunting
seals and stopping-off points as they swim from one area to the next.
Several species of seal give birth and nurse their pups on the ice. In his
1986 book *Arctic Dreams*, Barry Lopez wrote about the chain of life that
ice supports:

> To stand at the edge of this four-foot-thick ice platform ... is to find
> yourself in a rich biological crease. Species of alga grow on the bottom
> of the sea ice, turning it golden brown with a patchwork of life. These
> tiny diatoms feed zooplankton moving through the upper layers of

water in vast clouds – underwater galaxies of copepods, amphipods, and mysids. These in turn feed the streaming schools of cod. The cod feed the birds. And the narwhals. And also the fox.[1]

Due to the abnormal weather events, warming water, and melting polar ice cap caused by climate change, all of this is now at risk. As the treeline creeps northward, millions of birds that nest and feed on the tundra will be in jeopardy. Caribou and their domesticated reindeer cousins face huge habitat losses as the tundra shrinks. In turn, Dene and Inuit country food supplies will contract, with devastating impacts on Indigenous community cultures.

As Arctic residents, the Inuit have a vital interest in combatting climate change. Sheila Watt-Cloutier, who became international chair of the Inuit Circumpolar Council in 2002, has been a tireless campaigner on the issue. By attacking the issue on many fronts, Watt-Cloutier caught the world's attention, sounding the alarm on global warming.

At their second ministerial meeting, the Arctic Council ministers commissioned a report that led to the publication in 2005 of the 1,042-page Arctic Climate Impact Assessment (ACIA) Report.[2] (The ACIA report was preceded in 2004 by a summary report titled "Impacts of a Warming Arctic.") Three groups put the ACIA report together: the Arctic Monitoring and Assessment Program, the Conservation of Arctic Flora and Fauna Working Group, and the International Arctic Science Committee. Among the immediate regional impacts of climate change, the report predicted shrinkage of the earth-cooling polar ice cap, coastal erosion, and permafrost thawing.[3] (Permafrost is ground that became frozen during a colder period and that has remained that way through the heat of at least two summers – sometimes thousands of summers.) During the development of ACIA, Watt-Cloutier led the permanent participant group representing Indigenous hunters and trappers. Her advocacy lent more meaning to projections regarding the possible extinction of marine life in the Arctic and the destruction of the Inuit hunting and food-sharing culture.

In summary, here are some of the report's harsh findings.

Environmental Change

The Arctic climate is quickly warming, and this will lead to rising river flows, rising sea levels, diminishing lake, river, and summer sea ice, melting glaciers (especially the Greenland Ice Sheet), and changing ocean salinity. As Arctic vegetation zones shift, wetlands will change, fires will increase, and insects such as the mountain pine beetle will destroy boreal forests.

Wildlife species are affected as ranges change. Northerly shifts in some species will put Arctic marine and land species at risk.

Coastal communities will face greater exposure to winter storms, erosion of shorelines, and the undermining of buildings.[4]

Social and Economic Change

Reduced sea ice will increase marine transport and access to resources.

Melting permafrost will unsettle buildings and infrastructure.

Indigenous communities will experience major economic impacts as hunting cultures respond to the changes in wildlife habitats and increased food insecurity.

Northern freshwater fisheries will decline, but marine fisheries, agriculture, and forestry will be enhanced.[5]

Higher ultraviolet radiation levels will affect all Arctic beings.[6]

Since both scientists and Indigenous experts drawing on traditional knowledge (TK) contributed to ACIA, the resulting assessment was credible to both northerners and southerners. "ACIA['s] hybridity of expertise marks a major milestone because it's only since the 1980s that terms like TK, 'traditional ecological knowledge' (TEK), or 'indigenous knowledge' (IK) have been widely used, and then often only in indigenous, academic, or policy arenas," writes Candis Callison in *How Climate Change Comes to Matter*.[7]

As a former television reporter and a member of the Tahltan Nation (a Dene community whose traditional territory lies near the border of British Columbia and Yukon), Callison responds sensitively both to perceptions about media coverage of climate change and to Indigenous northern perspectives.[8] Her book flowed out of her MIT doctoral research about communications on climate change, during which she interviewed people in the Alaskan Inuit community of Kotzebue in July 2007. In Kotzebue, she encountered not "climate change," the abstraction of the airwaves, but a hard, on-the-ground reality that threatened communities.

Because traditional knowledge captures the observations of hunters, trappers, and others in the community as well as those of anthropologists, biologists, and geologists, some commentators think of it as concrete rather than abstract science.[9] Callison considers TK a separate knowledge system, one that she defines as "qualitative, intuitive, holistic, moral, spiritual, empirical, lived, oral, systematic, detailed, and diachronic as opposed to the specialized, quantitative, rational, synchronic, systematic, detailed, objective qualities usually associated with science."[10] Traditional knowledge, based on experience and observations of a wide area over many decades, may seem a world away from the day-to-day data collecting of scientists. Nevertheless, it is a legitimate form of knowledge. As Julie Cruikshank writes in *Do Glaciers Listen? Local Knowledge, Colonial Encounters, and Social Imagination*, "elders talk about the same issues that concern scientists."[11] Scientists look for physical relationships, while people from oral traditions examine moral and spiritual relationships as well. For a group visiting Kluane National Park in May 2016, guide Craig McKinnon summarized it this way: "Traditional knowledge is qualitative, not quantitative."[12]

Indigenous communities possess a deep knowledge of their traditional territories and hunting grounds. Telling stories with a moral centre transmits this knowledge to each subsequent generation and, sometimes, to policy-makers in the present day. First Nations, Inuit, and Métis all have lessons to share about the ecology and management of the lands, forests, tundra, ice, and waters of their particular landscapes. Most scientists do not work or live in Arctic communities; mainly they are summer visitors with no stake in the community. As Callison puts it, "[scientists] are interlopers that may make a contribution to the life of a community, but their goals, norms, and practices differ significantly from residents."[13] Nevertheless, the Arctic's Indigenous peoples and southern scientists have learned over the past few decades how to interact with each other.

Long before the terms "global warming" and "climate change" entered popular discourse, the Inuit were noticing significant changes in the character of sea ice and other features of their environment.[14] While Callison was conducting her research, Caleb Pungowiyi, a Kotzebue elder, took her out on the tundra, where they saw fields of invading cotton grass, markings of newly arriving moose, melting permafrost, and moss that was displacing the lichen on which the caribou feed. Given that these animals are a staple of the Inuit diet, such changes have significant repercussions.[15] Pungowiyi said that for the big picture, the Inuit might look to science, but "they depend on their own observations for ground truthing that scientific instruments miss," Callison records.[16]

Callison learned from former Inuit Circumpolar Council (ICC) chair Patricia Cochran that Alaskan villagers are familiar with climate change but use specific terminology: they talk about worsening winter storms, premature sea-ice break-ups, and rapid coastal erosion – the observable local effects of climate change. In other words, for them climate change is an issue of survival. Rather than something on the TV news, or a data set collected by scientists, climate change has imposed in real ways on the Inuit way of life.

With her focus on the communication aspect of climate change, Callison observed that people everywhere tend to discuss events in light of their own experiences and evolving political opinions. This seems true of Greenlandic, Canadian, and American approaches to climate change, all of which have shifted as much as the sea ice in recent years. At the time of her research, Callison found that issues related to global warming were already being widely and publicly debated in Alaska; the ACIA had held hearings in the very region she was studying.[17] The year after Callison conducted her interviews, nearby Kivalina sued several major oil companies for damages and for the cost of relocating their village, as greenhouse gases (GHGs) and rising sea levels had caused the community to sink. This quixotic lawsuit made headlines around the world, but Alaskan journalists could not resist reporting that it was the federal government that had located the community on this shrinking gravel bar in the first place. The experience weighed on small communities, and ICC chair Patricia Cochran, an Alaskan, begged visiting reporters to give Shishmaref, another threatened village, a break from the media spotlight.[18] President Obama's 2016 budget requested $400 million to relocate vulnerable villages in Alaska.[19]

International Human Rights

As the ICC's international chair, Sheila Watt-Cloutier quickly earned a reputation as an Indigenous environmentalist. Given that the people she represented held the United States primarily accountable for generating the GHGs that were destroying their way of life, it is perhaps not surprising that US officials on the Arctic Council did not immediately endorse her efforts in the ACIA or other arenas.

In September 2004, Watt-Cloutier appeared before the US Senate Committee on Commerce, Science, and Transportation. Warning of unaccountable suffering for the world if growing CO_2 emissions poisoned the atmosphere, Watt-Cloutier told the senators that defending the Arctic's peoples and their cultures represented the front line in the struggle to turn back global warming. She so impressed Republican Senator John McCain that he took a trip to Alaska to see for himself.[20]

The Kyoto Protocol took effect in 2005. In December of that year, Watt-Cloutier presented a human rights petition to the Inter-American Commission on Human Rights. In it, she and sixty-two other Inuit individuals named the United States as a violator of the Inuit "right to be cold." Their definitive statement on climate change was intended to address "the havoc it was bringing to Inuit communities in the Arctic."[21] The petition stated, in part, that "the impacts of climate change, caused by acts and omissions by the United States, violate the Inuit's fundamental human rights protected by the [1948] American Declaration of the Rights and Duties of Man and other international instruments.

These include their rights to the benefits of culture, to property, to the preservation of health, life, physical integrity, security, and a means of subsistence, and to residence, movement, and inviolability of the home."[22]

Scientists and Indigenous people had reached the same conclusion, Watt-Cloutier insisted, citing the ACIA findings. In the 2005 *New York Times* series "The Big Melt," Watt-Cloutier put it candidly: "As long as it's ice, nobody cares except us, because we hunt and fish and travel on that ice. However, the minute it starts to thaw and becomes water, then the whole world is interested."[23] Remarkably, she described the petition "as a gift from our hunters and our elders to the world. It is an act of generosity in fact from an ancient culture that is deeply, deeply tied to the natural environment and still very much in tune. And, it is a gift from us to an urban industrial modern culture that has largely lost its sense of place in position to the natural world."[24]

Despite the global importance of the petition, in 2006 the Inter-American Commission ruled the petition inadmissible because Watt-Cloutier and the ICC couldn't establish that the Inuit were "victims."[25] Lawyers continue to debate the wisdom of the commission's ruling. The Inuit petition remains the only international human rights petition against global warming, University of Lapland professor of international law Timo Koivurova reminded me, since the Kivalina lawsuit was a national case.

In 2007, Watt-Cloutier was nominated for the Nobel Prize for Peace for her efforts to raise awareness of the effects of man-made climate change. She did not win; instead, the prize went that year to the Intergovernmental Panel on Climate Change (IPCC) and former US vice-president Al Gore, who in 2006 had produced the climate "slide show," *An Inconvenient Truth*. The media covered these events thoroughly. Even so, maintaining public awareness about climate change has proven to be a hard task.

The goals of the ACIA report were to synthesize research on evolving climate conditions and to support the IPCC, which the UN had established in 1988 with a mandate to consider "environmental, human health, social, cultural, and economic impacts and consequences, including policy recommendations."[26] Subsequent IPCC reports have reinforced the ACIA's analysis.[27] Since its founding, the IPCC had occasionally summarized published journal articles related to climate concerns, but it did not seriously examine Arctic data until 2007.

The IPCC's 2007 report drew from sophisticated scientific studies of ice cores, tree rings, and whalers' log-books to determine that the Arctic summer sea ice had shrunk to its lowest level in 2,000 years, turning much of the Arctic ice to water. Consequent flooding could prove calamitous, the report said; rising sea levels could inundate some of the world's great cities and uproot a billion people.[28] The report noted that scientists were stating with confidence that the Northern hemisphere's snow cover had decreased since the 1950s and that permafrost temperatures had increased since the early 1980s.[29]

The IPCC's Fifth Assessment Report, released in September 2013, again addressed the effects of climate change on the Arctic specifically: "Over the last two decades, the Greenland and Antarctic ice sheets have been losing mass, glaciers have continued to shrink almost worldwide, and Arctic sea ice and Northern Hemisphere spring snow cover have continued to decrease in extent. It is *very likely* that the Arctic sea ice cover will continue to shrink and thin and that Northern Hemisphere spring snow cover will decrease during the 21st century." [30]

Alarmingly, the report noted, Greenland's darkening ice sheet was losing its reflective quality as it absorbed more and more solar rays, speeding up the pace of melting.

In the Far North, climate change is taking effect twice as quickly as in more southern regions. A key contributor to this is the steady loss of ice and snow. Climate scientists refer to the "albedo effect" to explain why Arctic warming has been so rapid: as the white ice and snow melt, darker land and waters trap more solar energy; this in turn raises atmospheric temperatures. North winds carry airborne toxins from southern industrial plants into the Arctic, including the Arctic food chains. Mercury from burning coal finds its way into the flesh of seals, walruses, and whales and thus into the diets of Inuit children, mothers, and elders.[31] Southern soot blackens and also heats Arctic snows.

What the Inuit had already observed on the ice and on the land, IPCC scientists reinforced in their 2013 report. The IPCC's fifth assessment reaffirmed that human activity was the largest contributor to our changing climate.[32] *New York Times* reporter Justin Gillis summed up some of the report's findings, noting that lack of action by political leaders over the past several decades has left the planet facing increasingly rapid GHG emissions.[33] With "an intensive push" over the next fifteen years to sufficiently control emissions, the IPCC report says, we may be able to just barely keep global warming in check. The good news, the IPCC affirms, is that aggressive agendas are becoming more affordable. Renewable energy costs have fallen, and tougher building codes and tighter emission standards will help.

There have been some genuine efforts at mitigation since the 2007 report. Many political leaders, including in China and the United States, have approved serious climate programs. President Obama welcomed the IPCC's fifth report, for it provided him with tools to pressure both China and the recalcitrant Republican Congress. The report "found that the emissions problem is still outrunning the determination to tackle it, with atmospheric carbon dioxide levels rising almost twice as fast in the first decade of this century as they did in the last decades of the 20th century."[34] But in the face of relentless opposition from an oil-fuelled Republican Congress, Obama had only regulatory and rhetorical tools at his command. And on the day that Trump took office, the climate change page on the White House website was deleted.

Reporters have published stories about bumper potato crops in Greenland, and there may be other benefits of climate change – for some people. ACIA chair Robert Correll, who worked with Watt-Cloutier, framed the climate change issue in these terms: "If you're Indigenous people living along the coastal margin, reduction of sea ice is a powerfully difficult thing to absorb. If you're in the oil-and-gas industry, it opens up pathways that were only dreams some decades ago."[35] The Arctic is rich in oil and gas, and Canada, Greenland, Norway, Russia, and the United States all have issued exploration licenses. As noted earlier, the Asian economic giants are planning investments in ice-strengthened ships, and Russia has opened the Northern Sea Route along its Arctic coast to assist in shipping its Arctic resources to world markets. Russian leaders speak of "sustainable development," but the concept has not been embedded in Russian law.

"Right now it is the fashion to see the Inuit people of the Arctic as helpless victims of climate change," writes UK science journalist Alun Anderson. "It is certainly true that the sea ice is vanishing, weather patterns changing, whales and seals moving to new locations and traditional hunting lore growing less useful. International Polar Year researchers list many tough challenges. But 'victims' they are not."[36]

By 2030 or earlier, the Arctic could see ice-free summers. "Climate change is actually doing what our worst fears dictated," says Jennifer Francis, a sea ice expert at Rutgers University. But for countries that border the Arctic, she argues, the melt offers big benefits: "New shipping lanes between Europe and the Pacific are opening up. Vast amounts of oil and natural gas that were once locked beneath the ice can now be exploited."[37] But exploiting those resources will increase the climate peril.

Arctic Security and Political Will

Some northern experts, including Rob Heubert and his colleagues, are raising security concerns related to a rapidly warming Arctic. Their 2012 report, "Climate Change and International Security: The Arctic as Bellwether," embraces the scientific consensus and points out that many Arctic states have begun to re-examine their military capacity to operate in the Arctic region.[38] Some states have already started to rebuild their military forces; most others are drawing up plans to do so.[39]

However, scholars like Thomas Homer-Dixon of the Balsillie School of International Affairs in Waterloo, Ontario, challenge the notion that climate change is a security question. "These state-centric concerns divert policy attention from far more critical issues, including the larger climate consequences of Arctic ice loss," Homer-Dixon argues. Any economic benefits of exploiting and shipping High Arctic oil through the Northwest Passage will pale in comparison to the global consequences of a melting polar ice cap, he believes. "Policymakers need to focus on what is really important, not what fits their 20th century worldview."[40]

As noted earlier, geographer Laurence C. Smith thinks that the mid-northern hinterlands of countries like Canada may realize economic benefits as Subarctic lands open up for agriculture and Arctic coastal waters become transportation routes. But at the same time, Alaska, Canada, and Russia are likely to lose more and more valuable forest lands to forest fires. Moreover, the southern regions of all northern states may need to deal with a flood of climate change refugees.

The science may be complicated, but most scientists now believe that humans have caused the world's climate to warm, increasing the occurrence of heat waves and droughts, violent storms, and coastal flooding. The annual global temperature increases may sound slight, but as the *New York Times* asserts, "the heat accumulating in the Earth because of human emissions is roughly equal to the heat that would be released by 400,000 Hiroshima atomic bombs exploding across the planet every day."[41]

Despite the growing public concern for the planet, Arctic climate change petitioners have had to struggle, often and everywhere, against powerful political and economic forces. The energy giant ExxonMobil has spent hundreds of millions of dollars lobbying against climate action. In 2001 its top lobbyist sent President George W. Bush, who had just been sworn in, a note demanding that the White House get rid of the scientist who chaired the UN Intergovernmental Panel on Climate Change (IPCC). ExxonMobil's man also demanded that other scientists be dumped in favour of known climate skeptics. Hearing this, EPA administrator Christine Todd Whiteman allegedly said, "We just gave away the environment."[42]

In June 2001, President Bush declared the Kyoto Accord "fatally flawed" and suggested that more research was needed. White House advisers persuaded Bush to use the term "climate change" in his public statements rather than the more ominous "global warming." Despite this rebranding, the issue would not go away, and in 2004, the Bush administration, devoted servants of the energy giants, laboured mightily to delay the publication of the ACIA report.[43] Three days before the US presidential vote, the *New York Times* published leaked excerpts from that report; two days after Bush returned to the White House, a *Washington Post* headline roared, "US Wants No Warming Proposal: Administration Aims to Prevent Arctic Council Suggestions."[44] Later that month, at the November 24, 2004, Reykjavik ministerial meeting, the ACIA report finally saw the light of day.

In a pair of articles for the *New York Review of Books*, David Kaiser and Lee Wasserman explain that ExxonMobil's bosses knew that human consumption of fossil fuels was warming the planet but continued to fund causes denying human-generated climate change. They cite *Los Angeles Times* stories about the contradictions between the company's internal research and its public posturing:

> As Ken Croasdale, a senior ice researcher at Imperial Oil (in which Exxon owns a majority share), told an engineering conference in 1991, concentrations of greenhouse gases in the atmosphere were increasing "due to the burning of fossil fuels. Nobody disputes this fact." Accordingly, any major developments with a life span of say 30–40 years will need to assess the impacts of potential global warming. This is particularly true of Arctic and offshore projects in Canada, where warming will clearly affect sea ice, icebergs, permafrost and sea levels.

Croasdale based these projections on the same climate models that Exxon's leaders would spend the next fifteen years publicly disparaging. Yet following his warnings that rising seas would threaten buildings on the coast, that bigger waves would threaten offshore drilling platforms, and that thawing permafrost would threaten pipelines, Exxon began reinforcing its own Arctic infrastructure. Similarly, as Steve Coll wrote in *Private Empire: ExxonMobil and American Power*, the company's "investments in the skeptics of the scientific consensus coincided with what at least a few of ExxonMobil's own managers regarded as a hypo-critical drive inside the corporation to explore whether climate change might offer new opportunities for oil exploration and profit." When Rex Tillerson – Donald Trump's choice for Secretary of State – became ExxonMobil's CEO in 2006, he declared: "We know the climate is changing, the average temperature of the earth is rising, and greenhouse gas emissions are increasing."[45] Yet Tillerson refused to admit that fossil fuel consumption might be a cause. ExxonMobil has said it supports a carbon tax, yet it finances the campaigns of congressional opponents of such a tax. Although a majority of Americans support government action to curb global warming, the Republican majority in Congress is still in denial. So too is President Trump.

Alaska is the United States' most energy-rich state and also faces that nation's highest energy costs. Climate change in Alaska will affect hydro-power generation, mining, fishing, and tourism. A University of Alaska Fairbanks report states that "energy production is the main driver of the state's economy, providing more than 80 percent of state government revenue and thousands of jobs. Continuing pressure for oil, gas, and mineral development on land and offshore in ice-covered waters in-creases the demand for infrastructure, placing additional stresses on ecosystems."[46] Alaskans worry about extreme weather events and the increasingly early thawing of lakes.[47] Yet the state's fossil fuel lobbyists continue to insist there is no human cause for global warming.

In Canada, a Liberal government signed – but did not implement – the 1997 Kyoto Protocol. In 2011 the Harper Conservatives walked away from Kyoto altogether. Weirdly, the Harper government seemed to treat global warming mainly as a good-news-for-the-oil-industry story, al-though its representatives did not openly admit that.[48]

On October 19, 2006, Rona Ambrose, the Harper government's first environment minister, introduced the Clean Air Act. She declared por-tentously: "From now on, all industry sectors will have mandatory re-quirements, and we will enforce those requirements."[49] Tailpipe emission standards for vehicles have been jointly imposed by Canada and the United States, and Canada has imposed emission regulations on the coal industry, although those regulations won't be very stringent for quite a while. By 2014, no requirements or regulations had been imposed on the oil-and-gas sector. Leona Aglukkaq, Harper's last environment minister, told a Commons committee: "It is premature to say when they will be ready ... I can't give you a deadline. Work continues. When we're ready, we'll release them."[50] The *Globe and Mail's* Jeffrey Simpson believed that the Canadian Association of Petroleum Producers had successfully lobbied to block any action while Harper was in office.[51] In Yellowknife on August 17, 2006, Harper predicted that the Mackenzie Valley Pipeline would transform the North into "what some call 'the next Alberta.'"[52] By 2016, that pipeline had become a pipe dream and the Alberta economy was tanking. The new federal government, under Justin Trudeau, has been promoting climate action *and* pipelines.

Energy industry spokespersons today generally acknowledge the reality of climate change, but they still reject the idea that it has a human (read "industry") cause. They also question the science that supports human causality. A libertarian minority of deniers describe climate change science as a worldwide con game meant to increase government control of energy markets. Some corporations have been embarrassed by the deniers, but energy companies continue to finance political opponents of climate science.

Bill McKibben, a journalist and founder of the international environmental organization 350.org, often points out the denials made by the energy industry and their allies in the US Congress. "In the last few weeks," he wrote in May 2013,

new data from the CryoSat satellite system have shown that there's only one fifth as much sea ice in the Arctic as there was in 1980 ... The mighty political power of the fossil fuel industry has so far been enough to obliterate reason ... A few countries – notably Germany, which is now supplying 22 percent of its energy needs with renewable sources, and headed for more than 40 percent within a decade – have made good-faith efforts. But in most places the fossil fuel industry has prevailed, both by funding disinformation campaigns and by purchasing the affections of enough legislators to make sure the status quo persists.[53]

On November 5, 2015, New York's attorney general announced that his office had begun investigating whether ExxonMobil had lied to investors and the public about the risks of climate change.[54] The investigation will examine whether company statements to Exxon shareholders accurately reflected the company's own scientific research over the past decade, during which time the corporation subsidized outside interests seeking to throw cold water on climate science. In February 2015, American news outlets reported that Wei-Hock Soon, an externally funded Smithsonian researcher, had received funding from Exxon and other companies to write papers critiquing climate scientists, but had failed to reveal the identities of his funders.[55]

Notwithstanding improvements in general public awareness, educating people about carbon emission levels and their causes has been a challenge. Per Espen Stoknes of the Center for Climate Strategy of the Norwegian Business Institute calls the lack of dissemination of the climate change message the "greatest communication failure of all time," especially given that "the Arctic is a bellwether or 'a canary in the mine shaft.'"[56] In a 2015 Ipsos-Reid poll for *Global News,* only 13 percent of Canadians selected climate change as one of their top three concerns.[57]

Even in the Nordic countries, where governments take global warming more seriously, effective action has taken a back seat. The Sámi complain that the weather is no longer predictable, which has placed their traditional way of life at risk. On February 6, 2015, the Sámi National Day, Sámi political activist Mimie Märak had her hair publicly shorn to show grief for the human ill-treatment of "eanan," or Mother Earth.[58]

Walking the Talk

Few North Americans – or Russians or Scandinavians, for that matter – appreciate how long northern Indigenous peoples have been players in the international arena, nor how aware Indigenous leaders have become of global questions. Since its formation in 1977, the Inuit Circumpolar Council has punched far above its weight on the international stage. As discussed earlier, Inuit diplomacy helped draft the Stockholm Convention of 2001, which curbs the production of persistent organic pollutants (POPs). When faced with change, the Inuit have always been incredibly resilient.[59] They survived hunger and extreme cold for centuries, only to face an even greater existential threat today. Going forward, the Inuit will need devolution, resource revenue-sharing, and genuine respect from national governments. The barriers to Inuit autonomy still seem huge; however, science journalist Alun Anderson wouldn't be surprised if the future of the Arctic includes "Inuit oil millionaires alongside resourceful hunters."[60]

Globally, Inuit leaders continue to be extremely active on climate change issues. But are the Inuit and other northerners "walking the talk" of climate change in their everyday lives? To what extent has Watt-Cloutier's Inuit homeland internalized her urgent message? Not so much, it seems. On cold winter nights, do northerners leave their pickups running while they slip into the coffee shop or bar for an hour or two? Yes, some still do. Does Nunavut's electric utility employ the usual price signals to moderate consumption? No. Are northern communities reducing emissions, cutting line losses, or introducing alternatives to fossil fuels? Not as much as they could.

In 1987, Yukon legislators approved the acquisition of the territorial assets of the federal Crown corporation Northern Canada Power Commission (NCPC) and created a public utility, Yukon Energy Corporation (YEC).[61] Most of YEC's electricity comes from hydro dams, including a large 60 Megawatt plant in Whitehorse. I can still remember when YEC equalized rates at eight cents per kWh for all residential consumers, up to 1,000 kWh per month, and up to 1,500 kWh for small businesses. After that, market prices took effect.

Nunavut's electrical power utility, Qulliq Energy Corporation (QEC), also owned by the territorial government, had a different inheritance.[62]

QEC is the only generator and distributor of electrical power for retail supply in Nunavut. With twenty-six stand-alone diesel plants in twenty-five communities, the corporation serves a population of around 32,000. It is the only public utility in Canada that depends entirely on imported fossil fuels.[63] Nunavut, it is worth noting, has a dramatically high-winter/low-summer fuel consumption pattern.

For a decade, Nunavut has faced huge problems with energy costs. Its government allocates as much as 20 percent of its budget to those costs, a large part of which covers subsidies.[64] In 2014, QEC applied for an across-the-board rate hike that would have sharply increased electricity bills,[65] although after 2020, under a rate-rebalancing proposal, customers in all Nunavut communities, large and small, would pay the same base rates. Various subsidies protect the sizable portion of Nunavut's population who are social housing tenants, and this, according to economists Shakir Alwarid and Laura Prentice, makes power rates essentially meaningless as a conservation tool. As Alwarid and Prentice explained to me, rates are a fiction to most consumers unless they have to pay them.[66] Homeowners and other residential customers in Nunavut receive a subsidy for monthly consumption of up to 700 kWh in the spring and summer, and up to 1,000 kWh in the winter months. The smallest of Nunavut's small businesses – those with gross revenues of $2 million a year or less – may apply for subsidies granted for the same seasonal periods. Larger businesses, such as retail stores, hotels, and airlines, receive no power subsidies and normally pass on such increases to their customers.

There are small hydroelectric sites close to Iqaluit that could be developed, but the territorial government has so far been unable to borrow sufficient funds to advance a hydro project. QEC claims it is improving its cost and fuel efficiencies, but its rates are not structured to foster conservation or to dampen the effects of climate change. The Nunavut government has also set up energy efficiency programs, which are focused mainly on retrofitting older buildings and improving the design of new ones. However, the territory still faces severe energy challenges.

What might be done to remedy all this? At Glencore's Raglan mine, 1,800 kilometres north of Montreal, Quebec's Tugliq Energy Co. and Ontario's Hydrogenics have collaborated on an innovative wind turbine that creates hydrogen, which is used to power the micro-grid, saving millions of litres of diesel fuel.[67] Dozens of diesel-addicted Arctic communities could be rehabilitated with such technology.

Across northern Canada, hydroelectricity has been delivering clean power for a century. Hydro facilities in Yukon and the NWT are already generating more than 130 megawatts of power. However, energy researcher J.P. Pinard is asking Yukoners to take another look at wind power. Yukon currently uses hydro and fossil fuel energy; when energy demand spikes, it resorts to diesel as a backup source. Pinard has proposed that fossil fuels be replaced with a combination of hydro and electrical thermal storage (ETS). ETS stores wind energy as heat; this energy can then be used to warm homes when the wind is blowing. When it isn't, hydro energy is stored instead.

Whitehorse economics writer Keith Halliday points out that currently, 75 percent of Yukon's energy expenditures go for imported fossil fuels, a level that is not sustainable.[68] YEC has demonstrated that at least for now, it has more faith in oil and gas than in renewable energy sources. In 2014 it committed to purchasing liquefied natural gas (LNG) generators, and spent between $38 and 40 million on them before receiving an environmental assessment or public utilities board approval. Ken McKinnon, acting chair of the Yukon Environmental and Socioeconomic Assessment Board, explained that the only alternative at present "is either LNG or new diesel backup, and we just thought ... that the LNG was the better fit at this time."[69] Nevertheless, Piers McDonald, former chair of the YEC board, explained to me that the utility is continuing to examine renewable resource options.

Alaskans worry about what low oil prices and a gas glut (plus high prices at local gas pumps) have done to their regional economy, and state legislators share these concerns. In 2015, for just the first time, a sitting president, Barack Obama, visited Arctic Alaska. Having covered his right flank by approving Shell's offshore drilling program, Obama pleased the left by preaching about the perils of climate change.

Combined wind and diesel generation has worked in Alaska, says David J. Hayes, former deputy secretary and COO of the US Department of the Interior. Hayes thinks it's now time to bring down the cost of the generators through the use of standardized parts and better control systems: "This is an opportunity for the United States to use its technological leadership in renewable energy to bring to the world small-scale renewable options to replace diesel."[70]

The Gordon Foundation's 2015 Arctic public opinion survey, *Rethinking the Top of the World*, found that, unprompted, 26 percent of respondents identified "global warming and climate change" as the greatest threat facing the Arctic region today. When asked how well equipped Canada and the United States were to address climate change, only 19 percent of Canadians and 30 percent of Americans felt their country was "well equipped."[71]

"If there is one place you would imagine people would have to be conscious of climate change, it would be the Arctic, where the temperature is rising around twice as fast as the global average."[72] So commented Irene Quaile of Germany's international broadcaster Deutsche Welle in a story about University of Oregon sociology professor Kari Marie Norgaard. Norgaard spent ten months in the northern Norwegian community of Bygdaby monitoring what she described as an "incredible disconnect between the moral, social, and environmental crisis of climate change and people not realizing it is happening." Quaile's reaction registered her surprise.

Fuelled by human activity, 2016 was the hottest year in recorded history. As journalist Alun Anderson wrote in the *New York Times*: "Everyone is well aware that we may be witnessing the fastest single environmental catastrophe to hit this planet since the rise of human civilization."[73] But Alaskan oil workers, who do not buy into the idea of human-caused climate change, do not see any need to act. If global warming is a natural occurrence, why should humans waste energy fighting it? And, unfortunately, Nunavut has so many problems – income insecurity, overcrowded housing, and economy-sapping energy costs – that perhaps it just cannot prioritize climate change.[74]

Yet as climate change activist Vivian Chan put it to me, "some people are too scared to care." Others try a light-hearted approach: the Yukon Research Centre and the Department of Health and Social Services celebrated Earth Day by distributing condom packages labelled "Stop Dangerous Emissions ... Canada ranks 15th out of 17 countries for greenhouse gas (GHG) emissions per person. You can reduce your own 'dangerous emissions' by turning down the furnace, turning up the heat – and using a condom every time you have sex." At a 2015 Simon Fraser University Carbon Talks event, participants were asked to contribute instant poems. I called my own contribution "Deadpan Frog":

> Did the pot boil over;
> the cook run for cover?
> My whole world was warming
> Without any warning
> I became "hot, hot, hot"
> – then, suddenly, not
> Just a croaking toad
> left legless and cold.

If the nations of the world can strike a deal to reduce carbon emissions, will their leaders live up to it? The annual Arctic Encounter Paris (AEP) symposium was held in Paris, France, in December 2015, during the closing hours of COP21, the UN Convention on Climate Change.[75] Among the symposium attendees were many Arctic luminaries. AEP advertises itself as the only Arctic policy event currently associated with the UN Convention. For the Arctic, where the predations of climate change are overpowering, COP21 was a defining moment.

At the opening of the Indigenous Peoples' Pavilion at COP21, Okalik Eegeesiak, international chair of the ICC, spoke mainly about the shared experiences of the Inuit and the Sámi in a changing Arctic. "The health and well-being of Inuit and Saami are inextricably tied to the Arctic environment and in particular the tundra, the marine environment and the snow and ice," she said. "Inuit and Saami are deeply concerned about the actual and potential impacts of climate change on their cultural, social and economic health and corresponding human rights."[76] High hopes of reaching a climate deal at the UN's Copenhagen Summit in 2009 had crashed and burned, with unhappiness on all sides.[77] Yet after two weeks in Paris in December 2015, negotiators for 195 countries achieved a climate accord. In six years, what had changed?

In 2009, the big players had taken over and pushed aside the small nations. Consequently, "after Copenhagen, many world leaders believed that the United Nations process would no longer work for tackling climate change," Secretary General Ban Ki-moon of the UN told the *New York Times*.[78] But by 2015, three things were different: climate change was now viewed as an imminent danger; China and the United States, the world's greatest polluters, now saw the issue as urgent; and French diplomats made the Paris conference a success by ensuring that every voice was heard. "It was a wonderful surprise that after the incredible disappointment of Copenhagen, these 195 countries could come to an agreement more ambitious than anyone imagined," enthused Jim Yong Kim, president of the World Bank.[79]

As noted, in the run-up to Copenhagen, President George W. Bush had withdrawn from the Kyoto Protocol. His successor, Barack Obama, later introduced a climate bill that was doomed to die on the floor of Congress. China and the United States were playing chicken, each waiting for the other to make the first move on climate change.

But after winning a second term in 2012, President Obama issued a warning to Republicans: "If Congress doesn't act, I will."[80] Meanwhile, China's coal-fired power plants were poisoning its cities, and people were growing angry. On a visit to Beijing in November 2014, Obama and President Xi Jinping of China announced a joint plan of action to reduce their greenhouse gas pollution. That plan became the first draft of the Paris agreement. Nevertheless, China's continued appetite for coal, in tandem with bull-headed opposition from US Republicans and Donald Trump, may undo the deal.

There were signs of change in Canada, too. On the eve of the Paris Summit, Alberta's NDP premier Rachel Notley announced a climate change strategy that included a carbon tax, a cap on Oil Sands emissions, a phasing out of coal-fired electricity, and an emphasis on wind power. The following day, Prime Minister Justin Trudeau met with Notley and the other provincial premiers to discuss a national climate change strategy and the forthcoming Paris conference; Trudeau had invited the premiers to join him there.[81] But even Trudeau was sending mixed signals.

Sheila Watt-Cloutier links high suicide rates among Inuit youth to the deadly effects of climate change. "You have to look at the larger picture of how our hunting culture is not just about going out and killing animals; it is about preparing our young people for everything, challenges and opportunities," she says.[82] Hunting is character-building; it requires patience, courage, the ability to handle stress, and the ability to act with sound judgment. Candis Callison, for her part, has concluded that climate change is a living thing. Northerners can see, hear, and feel its effects, yet they cannot exactly picture the thing itself. It seems like a phantom, a trickster, a ghost.

Northerners are adept at adaption, but can they adapt to climate change? The Gaia Paradigm, the idea that the earth is a living thing, that humans are wearing out their welcome and fouling their own nest, is not something people want to hear. Northerners have achieved a great deal of autonomy, but climate change and globalization could make them feel powerless and threatened once again. Because of the Cold War, the region's economic busts, and the terrors of residential schools, powerlessness is a recurring nightmare for many in the Arctic.

During the summer of 2016, I served as a member of a federal-minister-appointed panel to review the National Energy Board's recommendation on the Trans-Mountain Pipeline expansion. At town hall meetings, the panel heard that both Premier Notley and Prime Minister

Trudeau had stated that a new pipeline would be needed to finance their governments' Climate Action Plans. Alberta embraced that promise. But many citizens speaking at the meetings on the BC coast wondered how Canada could expand the Alberta Oil Sands, build pipelines, and meet even the non-binding commitments of the Paris Accord. Many northerners struggle with the same questions. If President Trump and the US Congress deny the reality of global warming and if Canada builds pipelines from Alberta's Oil Sands, what can tiny Arctic communities do?

Ravens and crows cannot hunt large beasts by themselves. They rely on hunters, foxes, and wolves to find food for them. From far above the herd, the raven finds the path of the caribou. Then, croaking loudly, the raven calls to the hunters and wolves to lead them to the prey. What northern leaders, chiefs, and legislators can do is *lead*. Like the raven, they can point the way and then clean up after the fouling of the Arctic's land, air, and water.

10
Boomers and Lifers
A New Divide

*Welcome the federal bosses to the north, thank them kindly
for visiting, and then bid them farewell.*

As a young Yukon mine worker labouring in 40-below weather,
I could never have imagined "global warming." Yet in May 1970,
after a winter spent working outdoors, I came in from the
cold to learn from CBC Radio that the environment had become an
issue. By now, of course, it is *the* issue. The 2010 Gulf of Mexico oil spill
sharply reminded northerners of the 1989 *Exxon Valdez* disaster, which
dumped millions of gallons of oil into Alaska's Prince William Sound.
Long after the clean-up, Alaskan pickup trucks sported ironic bumper
stickers that read, "Joe Hazelwood for Governor." (Hazelwood was the
captain of the *Exxon Valdez*.) This black humour exposed the "inconvenient truth" that the clean-up had generated more local employment
than had the extraction of Alaska's black gold. Southern debates often
pit environmental voices against economic powers, but most northerners
have long accepted the essential connection between the economy and
the environment.

When the Icelandic Canadian explorer Vilhjalmur Stefansson called
"adventure" a sign of incompetence, he surely had Arctic travel in mind.[1]
We would be wise to take his words as a warning to respect the Far
North's landscapes, waters, and peoples. Many northerners today want
energy and mining ventures to be as non-adventurous as possible –
profitable for the owners while providing safe and rewarding jobs for
locals, paying a fair share of taxes to the regional government, and

having minimal negative impacts on the surrounding environment and society. Northerners now speak less of frontiers and more of homelands, green tourism, and "sustainable mining."

Over three centuries, the Hudson's Bay Company governed much of western and northern Canada, building commercial relationships with Indigenous fur trappers. In 1991, under pressure from animal rights lobbyists, the HBC stopped trading in furs. In the twenty-first century, regional and tribal authorities in the Far North have assumed much of the company's former role in governance. Tourists now cruise north to photograph endangered polar bears, and suddenly the Arctic is everybody's business. In 1967, Glenn Gould composed "The Idea of North," a CBC Radio meditation on being alone in vast landscapes, which reminds us that in an interconnected world, we are all alone together. According to writer Adam Gopnik, "what Gould was after was that ... the true sound of the North is not the sound of one courageous individual but the sound of all these many stories coming together, laid out one on top the other."[2]

Canadians no longer need Jean Sibelius's *Finlandia* or Justice Thomas Berger's Mackenzie Valley Pipeline report to remind them that for thousands of years the Arctic has been not just a "stark and barren" frontier, but a *homeland*.[3] Seventeenth-century philosopher John Locke did not recognize Indigenous homelands, believing that settlers had squatters' rights to America's lands.[4] A century later another thinker, Adam Smith, opined that as communal societies, American Indians could own no land.[5] These convenient notions were the settlers' key to unlocking North America's great wealth, at the cost of massive Indigenous dispossession and poverty. In the nineteenth and twentieth centuries, British law eventually addressed the injustice of the Lockean expropriation of Indigenous property. This has provided Indigenous groups with modest reparations.

Others nations have since improved on North American ideas about reconciliation. In 2003, Norway created a new management regime for the lands and resources of Finnmark County, the ancestral home of Sámi fishers and reindeer herders. In a Nordic version of Canadian co-management, it handed control to a new regional body run jointly by representatives of the Sámi Parliament and Finnmark County. Before achieving home rule in 1979, Greenland experienced Danish and Norwegian colonization, threats of German occupation, and American hegemony. In 2009, Greenlanders achieved self-government and the power to manage their mineral resources and environment; Greenland may be on its way to becoming a nation-state. In 2016, the residents of Girjas, a Swedish Sámi village inside the Arctic Circle, won a thirty-year legal battle for control over hunting and fishing rights on their traditional territory.[6]

Everywhere in the Arctic, climate change is damaging traditional hunting and fishing grounds by shifting wildlife populations off familiar habitats. The treeline is moving northward at rates of approximately 100 metres per year.[7] In *The World in 2050*, geographer Laurence C. Smith predicts that climate change will cause the wholesale northward movement of Western societies.[8] Because the Inuit once lived on the sea ice, the shrinking ice cap is a human rights issue, as Sheila Watt-Cloutier and others have made clear.

Novelist Hugh MacLennan famously called Canada's English and French communities the "two solitudes."[9] Aboriginal and non-Aboriginal populations have long constituted the Arctic's twin solitudes; however, decades of treaty negotiations have given all northern Canadians a deeper appreciation of one another and of what they share. Along with Stefansson, who mocked England's Arctic "adventurers," northerners honour the memory of explorer Samuel Hearne, who with the Denesuline chief Matonabbee succeeded in reaching the Arctic Ocean by way of the Coppermine River in 1771. In that venture, the Aboriginal leader and the colonist "co-managed" their exploration.

Both/And

In June 2011, as the last-minute substitute speaker at the Kingston Conference on International Security (KCIS), I used a popular television show, *Battlestar Galactica*, to speak about the changing Arctic. What does this science fiction series have to do with discussions among military strategists, political scientists, and Arctic experts? Well, for a start, the *Battlestar Galactica* saga begins with a surprise attack reminiscent of Pearl Harbor or 9/11. With no warning, the Cylon army nukes the humans' home planet and kills billions. Several thousand survivors escape by jumping into outer space aboard a ragtag fleet led by the *Galactica*, an intergalactic aircraft carrier. The cybernetic Cylons – a race of robots built by humans, who have evolved to become their creators' mortal enemy – relentlessly pursue *Galactica's* convoy and the remnants of human civilization. As conceived by its writers and producers, the story resonated with echoes of the Cold War, brainwashed Communists, and the "War on Terror" against unfathomable Muslim "extremists," as well as the conquest and colonization of the Americas, not least the Arctic.

Between 2004 and 2009 my son Tahmoh appeared as Karl "Helo" Agathon in the *Battlestar Galactica* series. Tahmoh's character was a young military officer who grew into the role of moral compass for the *Galactica's* crew. A brave and decent warrior, Helo refused to commit war crimes or surrender his humanity. Indeed, he was the only officer to resist genocidal action against the Cylons.

Battlestar Galactica launched Tahmoh's career on American television. In addition, its scripts had special meaning for him as a Yukon-born northerner. The world he grew up in was distant and sharply different from the neon-lit cities where he now works. His childhood territory's population of around 30,000 was isolated and divided, much like that of the 50,000 survivors in the *Galactica's* fleet. Over the five years that *Battlestar* was on the air, Tahmoh played in several episodes that highlighted "northern" colonial and human security issues, from the environment and energy to economic and social divides.

In *Battlestar Galactica's* version of the Hearne/Matonabbee story, Helo survives on Caprica's radiated desert with the help of a Cylon humanoid model he knows as Sharon. After she has provided him with life-saving help, Helo's shipmates rape and torture her and threaten her with execution. As Sharon's colleague and spouse, Helo suffers considerable prejudice as a "Cylon lover." Those conflicts could well have brought back painful memories for my son. As noted earlier, although he does not look "Indian," Tahmoh proudly claims membership through his mother Lu in the White River First Nation, a Tanana Dene community whose traditional territory straddles the border of Alaska and Yukon. Always extremely sensitive to racism, Tahmoh never hesitates to describe himself as a child of two cultures: Indigenous American and immigrant European. I recently gave him a copy of Peter Wohlleben's book, *The Hidden Life of Trees,* about the communications that happen across forests' networks of roots. "Nelnah used to talk about that," Tahmoh responded. His Dene grandmother was not a scientist but a trapper. Here's what the Canadian government and the eight Arctic states on the Arctic Council seem not to notice. Like his sisters, dozens of cousins, and thousands of northerners, Tahmoh is neither *Indigenous* nor *settler*; he is *both*.

Canada proudly proclaims itself to be bilingual and multicultural. Aboriginal–settler reconciliation has added another dimension. As one instance, the University of Victoria law school now teaches this country's *three* legal traditions: English, French, and Indigenous. In *A Fair Country,* John Ralston Saul goes so far as to argue that Canada is, in unacknow-ledged fact, a Métis nation.[10] This new consciousness has even influenced the world of science.[11] Territorial government policies now require that land management decisions incorporate the traditional knowledge of Indigenous elders. Problems of translation persist, however; in 2013 a well-known European scientist told me bluntly that "Eskimos" know nothing about polar bears. In 2015, Inuvialuit wildlife co-management agencies released a new study, "Inuvialuit and Nanuq: A Polar Bear Trad-itional Knowledge Study," which reported that climate change had re-duced the bears' habitat on the ice. Polar bears are thinner now, but they appear to be adapting by hunting on the land.[12]

Southern Canadians have been slow to learn the Far North's lessons: respect Arctic lands and waters, accept the political leadership of north-ern peoples on northern issues, work together, co-manage, and thrive.

With regard to politics, all of the northern realities of my youth have changed, along with the Arctic's social and economic dimensions.

One of *Battlestar Galactica*'s themes was the ongoing power struggle between military and civilian authority – the opposing forces of autocracy and democracy. On a smaller scale, this same tension is evident in Canadian debates over Ottawa's colonial inclinations and in Aboriginal and northern legislators' demands for "provincial" jurisdiction. Franklyn Griffiths has gone further by offering the "secure community" model, which might operate both at the Arctic hamlet level and in the emerging Arctic "community" as a whole.[13] Community is the foundation of the Arctic's future.

On the scorched landscape of Caprica, Helo and Sharon conceived an interspecies child, and in *Battlestar*'s finale, Helo and Sharon rescue their daughter Hera from the Cylon base ship. This treasured child seems to offer new hope that the new world's two founding species will reconcile. The recognition, reconciliation, and renaissance analogies apply in the evolution of Arctic governance as well.

A "Harper Is a Cylon" political button worn by a Simon Fraser University student sparked my idea to use the sci-fi trope for the Kingston conference. The button poked fun at the Canadian prime minister's image as a cold, calculating, and controlling autocrat whose critics howled about his manner of governing, the way he centralized all power in his office, and his top-down, mean-spirited, gutter-partisan administration of the country, including the Canadian Arctic. On the subject of climate change, southerners jeered that Harper was a creature from another planet. Not only had his administration pulled Canada from the Kyoto Accord and gutted fisheries regulations, it had also tried to fast-track the approval processes for pipelines and other megaprojects in defiance of Aboriginal concerns and environmental standards. Harper packed the federal courts with right-wing judges, and as Canada's crime rate fell, federal Conservatives built new prisons.[14] Harper bragged that he was the best prime minister northern Canada had ever had, yet many northerners saw his government as the worst they'd ever had. To put that complaint in perspective, consider what the North has gone through over the past fifty years.

The Arctic of my youth was a distant colony. The North seemed at the time to be ruled by a great white father with two faces. Facing one way was the Indian affairs minister, who exercised the legal powers of the Indian Act; all Indian bands, chiefs, councils, lands, and band members fell under his authority. Facing the other way, the same politician, acting now as northern affairs minister, enjoyed power over territorial lands, mines, minerals, and resources.

Northerners have travelled far from the days when the territories were federal satrapies. In retrospect, the big political events in North America's Arctic region have transpired with astonishing speed. Yet for those involved, fighting for positive change felt like an endless uphill struggle. Moving from the Alaska land claims settlement in 1971 to Home Rule in Greenland, from the purchase of NCPC assets by the NWT and Yukon governments in 1987 to the creation of Nunavut in 1999 and the devolution of land and minerals management to Yukon and then the NWT, has been an exhausting journey.

The long march towards political development took the North in unexpected directions, away from the paths planned by Ottawa. For a while in the 1970s and 1980s, entropy seemed to be the only constitutional law in effect. Canada wrestled with separatist forces in Quebec, the West's alienation, and Aboriginal "nationalism" as the National Indian Brotherhood renamed itself the Assembly of First Nations; all the while, a series of first ministers' constitutional conferences took us nowhere. But while all this was unfolding, Yukon and the NWT were getting their acts together. They no longer operated as "settler" administrations; Indigenous leaders were now well represented in territorial caucuses and cabinets, from which, just a few years earlier, they had been notably absent.

As SFU School of Public Policy professor Doug McArthur wrote: "Canada's North is changing, and some of the most significant changes are in governance."[15] Until the 1990s, Ottawa seemed unwilling to modify the British colonial form of government. Then, slowly, writes McArthur, the feds came to realize that territorial–First Nation administrative partnerships could "overcome barriers, such as scale and costs, to effective Aboriginal governance."[16] In Nunavut, the NWT, and Yukon, McArthur sees the unfolding of a new constitutional settlement, one developed in response to regional political forces rather than as the product of a predetermined federal plan.

Regarding the agreements that Yukon's fourteen First Nations reached with Canada in 1994, after twenty years at the negotiating table, McArthur has this to say:

> In many respects, the Yukon agreements are quite remarkable. They establish new territory-based governments by partitioning land into First Nations settlement lands and general Yukon lands. This is often called the land selection model. They also create First Nation citizenship for members of each First Nation, allowing Aboriginal people to enjoy status as citizens of a First Nation and citizens of Canada.[17]

As one of their authors, McArthur continues to believe that the Yukon self-government agreements carry significance far beyond the territory's borders – that they are innovative enough to act as models for other negotiations across the country. But can we really count the Yukon treaties, land claims settlements, and self-government agreements as success stories?[18] Because their full implementation may be decades away, it is too soon to tell. Certainly the treaties have already improved the lives of many residents of Yukon's First Nations communities. But as with every solution, problems will arise, and among these may be a failure on Ottawa's part to fully and faithfully implement the treaties. To measure the progress in implementing a self-government agreement, it is useful to consider the number of intergovernmental agreements the First Nation in question has with other governments – Aboriginal, municipal, territorial, and federal or in other words, to look at the distance the Indigenous community has put between itself and the paternalism of the old INAC–Indian Band relationship.

One day, when the parties have fully implemented Yukon treaties and self-government agreements, Yukoners may look at all of their new institutions and conclude that they are seriously overgoverned. At that point, Indigenous and non-Indigenous leaders may begin a public dialogue to decide exactly which entity – Indigenous, municipal, or territorial – should provide which service, and who should pay for what. However that conversation proceeds, one fact is clear: the federal–provincial–local hierarchy that may have made sense in the era of the horse and buggy does not work anymore.

Adam Galinsky and Maurice Schweitzer in *Friend and Foe* write that

> Steve Jobs understood the tension between voice and hierarchy ... In the companies he ran, Jobs tried to reduce hierarchy structurally. While at Pixar, he designed its headquarters to promote encounters across the rungs of the company; the front doors, stairs, corridors, all led to a central atrium that also contained the café and mailboxes. Contrast this with General Motors' headquarters, the Renaissance Center, in which executives had a separate elevator that also connected to their own private parking garage.[19]

During the 1970s, like other Whitehorse residents, I went downtown every weekday to the postal boxes at the federal building to collect my mail. The postal boxes acted like a community watering hole where we bumped into our friends and neighbours.[20] Then one day Ottawa decided that Whitehorse residents should have door-to-door mail delivery, and contractors tore out the postal boxes. But when the government tried the same thing in the NWT capital, Yellowknifers refused to let go of their beloved boxes. Hierarchy may hurt community, but communities can always resist.

As noted earlier, Yukon now exercises most "provincial" powers, and Yukon First Nations have won self-government over their lands and communities – a significant modernization.

In the NWT, despite initial resistance from Ottawa, Aboriginal negotiators crafted governance innovations to meet their particular circumstances, including hybrid Aboriginal–municipal structures. The Inuit and the Gwich'in seemed committed to a blended form of self-government and public government at the community level, while the Sahtu favoured public government for some purposes and Aboriginal community self-government for others. The Tlicho Agreement provided a more regional approach, with certain community powers "entrenched" in territorial legislation that could only be amended with the consent of the Tlicho government. Bernard Funston notes that First Nation governments in Yukon may occupy certain legislative fields and so "displace" the Yukon legislature's laws. The situation is different in the NWT, he says: "In general, self-government negotiations and agreements in the NWT contemplate concurrent law-making powers. Therefore, community and regional governments established by self-government agreements could have overlapping jurisdiction with the Legislative Assembly on a significant range of matters."[21]

In *You Will Wear a White Shirt*, former premier Nick Sibbeston outlines the problem NWT negotiators faced:

> Since the territorial government came into the North, they had established settlement councils in many of the Dene communities, often in competition and conflict with chiefs and band councils. Would that policy and approach change? ... In some places, such as Fort Good Hope, the two bodies did come together, merging into a charter community with its own constitution; in others, conflicts between bands and municipalities continue to this day.[22]

The 2003 Tlicho Final Agreement became the first NWT accord to address self-government. The agreement establishes four distinct geographic areas owned and/or used by the Tlicho: one is for traditional use, another is for resource management, a third is owned by the nation, and a fourth has cultural significance.[23] A novel Indigenous–municipal hybrid unlike anything elsewhere in Canada emerged from Tlicho negotiations. A Grand Chief is elected by Tlicho citizens. There are also four chiefs who represent Behchoko, Gameti, Whati, and Wekweeti respectively. Two representatives from each community serve as councillors. The seat of the assembly rotates among the four communities, and the assembly meets at least four times a year. The Tlicho government's laws are made by the Tlicho Assembly.

The Dehcho, located in the southwestern corner of the NWT, have proposed something similar to the Tlicho agreement. They want a new Denendeh territory with a public government and full citizenship rights for all residents.

Since 1978, Yukon has operated on the British parliamentary model, and all three federal parties (Conservatives, Liberals, and NDP) have governed the territory at one time or another. Territorial ministers now sit with their provincial colleagues at national-level interprovincial meetings. Across the mountains in the NWT, the legislature uses a form of consensus more familiar to its Aboriginal population than to the British party system. Doug McArthur asserts that with the founding of Nunavut in 1999, the three "territorial governments now occupy an accepted and settled constitutional space that is no longer vulnerable to parliamentary termination."[24]

None of this came easily. The bureaucratic machinery of governments, federal and territorial, can be slow, but when they wish, politicians can move with lightning speed. Shortly after the NDP came to power in Yukon in 1985, I met as government leader with our MP, Erik Nielsen, in his capacity as Brian Mulroney's deputy prime minister. Nielsen told me that he favoured privatizing the Yukon assets of NCPC, the federally owned hydroelectric utility.

"Our government believes in public utilities," I replied. Nobody had heard of Enron at the time, but I raised the spectre of some foreign owner jacking up Yukon consumers' power rates.

"That's free enterprise," Nielsen responded.

We looked at each other in silence for a few moments. I knew that, as a lawyer, Erik had represented for many years the small Alberta-owned diesel utility that operated in several Yukon communities. I also knew that the Yukon public service did not have the capacity to manage a hydro utility at the time.

"Could you live with public ownership *and* private management?" I asked.

Nielsen nodded.

And that was the deal. Of course, it took lawyers and public servants months to close it. Afterwards, the owners of the private utility kept trying to buy us out, and we had to address that problem in Yukon's constitutionally protected land claims settlement by giving Yukon First Nations the right of first refusal, if ever a future government privatized the energy utility. Fed up with the covetous private manager, Liberal premier Pat Duncan eventually cancelled the Alberta utility's management contract. By that time, Yukoners were perfectly capable of managing Yukon Energy's operations.

Not until both legislators and public servants are fully socialized northerners do autonomy and democracy take root. Bureaucrats and politicians tend to speak different languages – at least, until they start to spend way too much time together. Bureaucrats, by nature, are risk averse. When they stand for public office, politicians become risk-takers and often short-term thinkers. The rarest and most precious of public servants are the entrepreneurial bureaucrats. As a politician, those were the people I wanted leading my project teams.

During the NDP's time in leadership in Whitehorse, most senior territorial officials were schooled in the ways of the federal bureaucracy, while those who had been elected were more attuned to the ways of their communities. This led to communication problems. Senior bureaucrats once handed our cabinet some recommendations from Yukon's judicial council regarding the appointment of a territorial judge. The document detailed basic facts about the several of the male candidates' qualifications, including their schooling in law and the firms where they had worked, but it contained no politically relevant information. For example, it told us nothing about their wisdom, maturity, or what Americans call a candidate's "judicial character." Cabinet was stumped. How would we decide? Then one of our ministers, a former linebacker for the Queen's University Golden Gaels, pointed to one of the names on the list.

"Is that *the* Heino Lilles?" my colleague asked.

"Who is *the* Heino Lilles?" the rest of us responded.

"Only the greatest running back I ever saw," the minister said. "He has great goddamn hands!"

"Do we know anything important about any of the other candidates?" I looked around the room. "No. Then I guess the judge's job goes to the one with great goddamned hands."

As it turned out, this proved to be an inspired choice. Queens University professor Heino Lilles became a Yukon judge in 1987, and he served twenty years on the Yukon bench with great distinction.

Formula Financing

While all three territories administer and collect various taxes, they are still financially dependent on federal transfer payments – though not happily so. The Territorial Formula Financing (TFF) transfer is the largest of these payments. The amount is determined by a combination of the territory's expenditure needs and its revenue capacity. The TFF is designed to allow the territories some autonomy in reducing taxes or increasing spending without penalty.[25] Our minority NDP government, elected in May 1985, became the first Yukon administration to benefit from the TFF arrangements. The territory was a deeply divided place at the time, with all of its mines shut and land claims negotiations derailed. The TFF provided the capital needed for us to start a Keynesian program of infrastructure building, reopen the territory's largest mine – the lead-zinc operation at Faro – and purchase the NCPC Yukon assets of the federal hydroelectric utility.

Since our government was not sure that formula financing would last, we decided that instead of pumping up program expenditures we would invest in capital projects: a college, school buildings, and roads, all with the view to improving operating efficiencies and lowering energy costs. The capital portions of most provincial government budgets amount to only a single-digit percentage of total expenditures. By contrast, the first two Yukon NDP administrations invested over 20 percent of their total budget in infrastructure. It seems that even now, Yukon's capital expenditures exceed national norms.

After Canada transferred province-like powers over land, forests, minerals, onshore water, and resource management to Yukon, the territory cooperated with First Nations to start regulating oil and gas on public lands.[26] Neither in Yukon nor the NWT would devolution proceed without the consent of Aboriginal communities.

In the NWT, the territorial government and Aboriginal governments eventually agreed to share the net fiscal benefit the Canadian government transferred to the territorial government. But fiscal relations between Ottawa and First Nations are not yet satisfactorily settled.[27] Ottawa continues to cap the territorial government's share of resource revenues; this is fundamentally unfair, and stands in sharp contrast to Denmark's revenue-sharing deal with Greenland.

Some people question the northern territories' continued dependence on federal transfer payments. Regardless, the new North is here to stay, affirms Doug McArthur: "Its implementation is far from complete, but its architecture is identifiable ... It has been shaped and developed through much effort and great perseverance on the part of Northerners. The voice of the south – the federal government – has had to change and adapt to realities that would have been unthinkable 25 years ago. The result is indeed a new constitutional settlement in form and substance."[28] Arctic communities have taken the "road less travelled," a path leading away from federal preferences. But, as detailed, it wasn't until land claims talks began in the 1970s that Indigenous and settler representatives began meeting regularly across the negotiating table.[29] Only then did the long process of political maturation and reconciliation between chiefs and legislators, the two solitudes of northern society, really begin to take hold.

Indigenous Internationalism

As noted in previous chapters, the Inuit homeland extends into four Arctic states, as does the Sámi territory. Inuit and Sámi north-to-north "internationalism" has already contributed to Arctic security, the POPs Convention, and climate change debates. Although the Cold War once divided these ancient communities, for years now they have been talking together across state, cultural, and ideological boundaries. Like the Inuit and the Sámi, the Dene have obvious international interests; in Canada, both the Dene and the Inuit air concerns about trans-boundary bird, caribou, reindeer, fish, and whaling issues.[30] On the Arctic Council, the six permanent participants sit at the same table as the eight Arctic states, trying to reach consensus on the great Arctic policy questions.

Former Alaska governor Steve Cowper points to the confluence in Alaska of a land claims settlement, oil development, and the growing political power of Indigenous peoples. He suggests that "the other thing to ponder is the effectiveness of Native legislators when the big money arrived, starting in 1969. They sent their brightest and their best to Juneau. Though nominally of both parties, the Natives effectively functioned as a third party. Neither Republican nor Democrat majorities could do anything without making a deal with the Native caucus."[31]

In Alaska, Yukon, and the NWT, chiefs and legislators cemented their working relationship as democratically elected members of regional legislatures. In the NWT, several "chiefs" – Richard Nerysoo, Nellie Cournyea, Steve Kafkwi, Jim Antoine, and Floyd Roland – became legislators, and then premiers, before returning to their home communities as sub-regional leaders.

With the rapid changes in the North, the emergence of new kinds of Arctic governance has been of great interest to all Arctic states. As outlined earlier, numerous structures exist to govern the Arctic, from global agreements such as the UN Convention on the Law of the Sea (UNCLOS) to the legally binding rules for shipping developed by the International Maritime Organization (IMO). In 2009, the Heinz, Oak, and Gordon Foundations funded the Arctic Governance Project (AGP), an unofficial initiative that brought together northern researchers, Indigenous thinkers, and policy-makers.

Led by American Arctic expert Oran Young, the AGP team in 2010 published *Arctic Governance in an Era of Transformative Change: Critical*

Questions, Governance Principles, Ways Forward.[32] Were existing governance bodies "sufficient to meet the needs for governance arising in the wake of the watershed change now taking place in the Arctic?" the report asked.[33] One positive example given was the 1920 Spitsbergen Treaty, which "features an ingenious arrangement under which the parties recognize Norway's sovereignty over the Svalbard Archipelago in return for commitments by Norway to demilitarize the area."[34] The AGP also cited the 1987 agreement between Canada and the United States to establish the International Porcupine Caribou Herd Board as an international co-management instrument of governance.

The AGP report found that due to the interacting impacts of Arctic events over the past few decades – climate change and globalization, as well as commercial shipping, oil and gas development, mining, fishing, and tourism booms – the Arctic has emerged as a governance barometer, a region that raises questions about the adequacy of measures protecting the health of its environment and its inhabitants.[35] Acknowledging the difficulty of disentangling Cold War relationships, the report reminded readers of the importance of nation-states before adding: "But it is essential to recognize that numerous other actors will play increasingly important roles in meeting this challenge. These include intergovernmental organizations, indigenous peoples' organizations, multinational corporations, environmental non-governmental organizations, and sub-national units of government, to name a few."[36]

Among its specific recommendations for policy-makers, the AGP report included the following comment:

> Good governance in the Arctic will be best served, at least for now, by honoring, implementing, and enhancing existing treaties among nation states, e.g. the United Nations Convention on the Law of the Sea (UNCLOS) and the United Nations Framework Convention on Climate Change (UNFCCC), other intergovernmental agreements, treaties and other arrangements between States and indigenous peoples, and relevant practices that together constitute a living network of relationships designed to promote sustainability, environmental

protection, social justice, and responsible economic development in
the Arctic and to recognize the rights of indigenous peoples to participate in decision-making.[37]

Rather than a fixed hierarchy or pyramid of power in the Arctic,
the AGP report imagines a network of networks: interlocking circles
that connect villages and international organizations, cities and virtual
communities.[38]

The North as a Laboratory

To the three familiar metaphors for the far North – frontier, homeland,
and wilderness – Bernard Funston adds that the North has become a
laboratory – and not just because some Indigenous groups have been
studied to death.[39] (An old northern joke described a typical Inuit family
as a father, a mother, four children, and an anthropologist.) Among the
happier experiments Funston identifies are formula financing, responsible government, and resource revenue sharing.[40] The Arctic is also a
laboratory in the sense that northerners themselves are great innovators.
Along with resilience, flexibility, and adaptability, inventiveness has been
a necessary Arctic and Subarctic survival skill.

In the 1980s, territorial judge Barry Stuart borrowed from Indigenous
practice to institute sentencing circles in rural Yukon communities.
These allowed elders to hear from victims and offenders before advising
the court on appropriate sentences. Former judge Heino Lilles sings the
practice's praise: "As a model of restorative justice, circle sentencing is
unique because it requires a partnership between the community and
the formal justice system."[41]

After the 1985 election, the new Yukon NDP government developed
a bottom-up planning exercise called Yukon 2000. For two years, Yukon
2000 moved towards a broad consensus through a series of public conferences, sector workshops for forestry, fishing, mining, tourism, and
agricultural interests, and community meetings. At the first "values"
conference organized as part of the Yukon 2000 process, two hundred

people gathered at Faro to discuss and define Yukon's shared values. The group reached a consensus on four:

> The *option to stay in the Yukon*: Yukoners see our territory as a desirable place to live, work, learn and raise a family. We want it to stay that way, but we also want to be able to earn a living in our chosen place. Development must offer us the chance to support ourselves and our families, within the territory and within our communities. *Control of the Future*: Yukoners want more control over the economic future of the territory. The keys to greater control are more regional and local decision-making, increased authority for communities, and a higher level of Yukon ownership. *An Acceptable Quality of Life*: Yukoners want development to preserve and enhance the quality of Yukon life. We want wages, business opportunities and public services comparable with the rest of Canada. But we are not prepared to sacrifice either the potential for living off the land or the unspoiled natural environment that surrounds us. *Equality*: Development should ensure an equal economic chance for all Yukoners, including those who do not currently have equal opportunity.[42]

Our government followed up with a Conservation Strategy as a second part to the Yukon 2000 process.

There were two dissenters at the 1986 values conference, both anti–land claims prospectors, and they got all the headlines. The media were observing their usual "no conflict, no story" rule, but the Yukon 2000 exercise was different. Unlike the binary code of public life that pits "prosecution" against "defence" in the courts and "government" against "opposition" in legislatures, the economic and conservation strategies resulting from the Yukon 2000 process were based on a foundation of *agreement*, not disagreement. Overall, participants found the discussions incredibly refreshing. Placer miners and conservation activists discovered shared interests in things like fishing and hiking. In mining towns, the company and the union had never before met except in conflict situations. Likewise, many First Nations and neighbouring municipalities had never had contact except during a crisis, such as fire in the Indian village. I well remember such a meeting in 1977 between the Whitehorse Indian Band, as it then was known, and Whitehorse City Council. Although the band and the city coexisted in the same geographic space, people on both sides had no idea what to say or how to fill the awkward silences. The experience was telling and memorable.

In most cases with Yukon 2000, people found real joy in sitting together to talk about things on which they might agree. In a territory where the Aboriginal tradition of consensus politics lives on, this constructive and sensible form of communication seemed perfectly natural. In this context, the verbal violence of parliamentary conflict can be seen as a perversion, not the norm; the heckling and petty nastiness of legislative combat is often distasteful for neighbourly people from small communities. For a few weeks, a new kind of politics seemed possible. Such consultations are exhausting, though, and hard to facilitate. Open communication is hard to maintain. But it was one of our government's better ideas, and while the Yukon 2000 process was under way, the territory's economy improved and land claims negotiations resumed.

Small innovations worked during our time in government as well. By agreeing to increase the amount of the territorial government funds on deposit, we got CIBC – Robert Service's former employer – to bring banking services back to rural Yukon communities. By taking back the air mile points that civil servants earned through government travel, we were able to pay for emergency medical evacuations. We also contracted with local cabinet makers to design and build suites of desks, bookcases, and typing tables for government buildings. The first sets, beautifully constructed of local woods, were displayed in the foyer of the main government building, where younger Yukoners came to marvel at them. Their grandparents would have taken local crafts and local materials for granted; for many young viewers the display counted as a discovery. My proposal for a larger-scale "local materials" building strategy did not fare so well. Local architects expressed interest in the idea that the maximum sustainable use of local materials (wood, stone, etc.) in Yukon government construction projects might reduce the massive leaks normal in northern economies, besides increasing local employment. The staff in the responsible government department were less keen, however, and some project managers continued their love affair with imported aluminum siding right to the end of my political life.

In the same innovative spirit, Piers McDonald, who became Yukon premier after the NDP was re-elected in 1996, once wittily suggested that the Yukon Hansard, the record of the legislative debate, record only truly original thoughts. Other northern jurisdictions have embraced innovation as well. The NWT founded its Water Act on Aboriginal cultural traditions, and bright young people in the NWT created Dechinta, a land-based "bush university."[43] At a time when Ottawa was increasingly centralizing power in one office, Nunavut decentralized services so that all communities could benefit from public sector employment opportunities. The University of Alaska Fairbanks made itself a "research-focused" centre, and to that end, it committed itself to expenditures of over $140 million.[44]

One of my favourite ideas arose from a Glassco Northern Fellows gathering in August 2016 at Iqaluit. In a response to a news story about a conference on Aboriginal peoples at which all the speakers seemed to be non-Indigenous academics, a group of young northerners, all between twenty-five and thirty-five years, proposed that they organize a conference on "White People" and invite only Indigenous speakers.

During my time as Yukon premier, Alaska legislators outlawed private meetings for politicians, with the consequence that I once sat in the governor's office talking on and on and on about the weather until the TV news reporters in attendance finally got bored and left. Only then did the governor and I get down to business.

Under federal pressure to become officially bilingual, each of the three territories has responded in its own way. The NWT wrote a law endorsing English/French bilingualism but also sanctioning nine "official" Aboriginal languages, all of which may be used in the NWT legislature. Nunavut wrote a language law to respond to the unique educational and employment needs of its Inuktitut-speaking youth. Yukon skirted official bilingualism but negotiated a deal with federal authorities to provide equal funding for both Aboriginal and French-language services.[45]

Federal Involvement

To his critics, Stephen Harper was a control freak. Despite his best-prime-minister-for-the-Arctic boast, however, he could not control his Arctic agenda; the icebreakers, deep-water ports, and beefed-up search-and-rescue he promised during his time in office failed to materialize. Bernard Funston does document some of Harper's achievements: the Geo-mapping for Energy and Minerals (GEM) program to support increased exploration of natural resources and to improve land use decisions; the RADARSAT Constellation Mission, which has a planned launch in 2018 and will cover Canada's vast land mass, oceans, and Arctic coastline under all weather conditions; and a new Canadian High Arctic Research Station at Cambridge Bay, Nunavut.[46]

Older northerners remember the contributions of earlier prime ministers. John Diefenbaker had a compelling northern vision. The Trudeau government invented formula financing and returned to treaty negotiations. Brian Mulroney settled some big land claims, including Nunavut and Yukon. After axing expenditures as finance minister, Prime Minister Paul Martin wanted to invest in ending Aboriginal poverty. Each of them could be seen as a North-friendly national leader.

As discussed, Yukon signed a devolution agreement in 2003 that transferred management of public lands and resources to the territorial government. Ten years later, the federal government reached a devolution agreement with the energy- and diamond-rich NWT. Today, every Canadian province and territory manages its own lands and resources – except for Nunavut.

Doug McArthur suggests that there will be no turning back on Arctic constitutional development, but can we be sure? Could Ottawa undo everything that northerners have achieved over the past fifty years? Could the forces of globalization, climate change, and recolonization combine to turn back the constitutional clock? It isn't impossible. Few

Canadians have ever been to the Far North, so they do not know this place of Indigenous people and settlers, of ice shores and snowy mountains. Why should they care? They *should* care, as I've argued, because the Arctic and Subarctic represent 40 percent of the land mass of their country. In this region, only northerners "stand on guard for thee."

Asserting that Arctic policy means more than oil rigs and polar bears, Alaska legislator Bob Herron of Bethel has pleaded for the US government to include Alaskans at every level in policy-making. "We believe that Northerners are Arctic experts," he says. Unfortunately, Washington is now a one-party government, and Alaska is not considered that newsworthy. US politics today seems to be the business of billionaires, and home-state voters believe they will benefit more from their senator's seniority than from his or her policies. In Alaska, even Democrats voted for the late Republican senator Ted Stevens in the belief that his position as chair of the Senate Appropriations Committee would bring significant benefits to the state.

In Canada, it used to be thought that when a Member of Parliament was appointed to the cabinet, his or her ability to deliver political goodies to constituents was enhanced. But it ain't necessarily so. Each Canadian territory has only one MP and one unelected senator in a Parliament controlled by a leader who may govern with the support of as little as 39 percent of the vote. Though Yukon and the NWT have devolution agreements, they are not provinces and may never be; that makes them terribly vulnerable to federal decrees, climate change, and global economic forces. The territories have few votes in Parliament and (unlike the provinces) no vote under the amending formula for the Canadian Constitution.

Sometimes their grievances against the national capital can make people in the North feel utterly powerless. Everything that northerners have achieved politically over the past few decades was undertaken in an attempt to address this insecurity. But time and time again, Ottawa has shown that it can break its promises on devolution and on measures to address climate change, underfund the implementation of treaties, and unilaterally alter formula financing arrangements over the protests

of Aboriginal and northern governments. Although the territories' remarkable achievements have proved to be influential around the circumpolar North, they may be far more fragile than they appear.

McArthur still firmly believes that the foundations for a new northern
order have been set: "As these arrangements fall into place, the system
of governance in the North is taking a shape that differs from that
in the rest of Canada."[47] The conventional wisdom is that Canadians
dislike constitutional change, but McArthur begs to differ, arguing
that "a new constitutional settlement is in the making, and it will ...
endure."[48] He may be correct, since the democratic institutions created
in the Eastern and Western Arctic over the past generation are remarkable and unique. Nowhere else in Canada is there so much ac-
commodation between Indigenous and settler governments. With the
implementation of land claims and self-government, federal "boxes" –
such as band and disc numbers, and Status, non-Status, or "C-31 A, B,
and C" Indians – should collapse like cardboard garbage in meltwater
channels. Having Tanana or Tlicho, Inupiaq or Inuvialuit, Finnish or
French ancestry might still matter to an individual, but not the colonial
categories.

But even at this late date, unrepentant reactionaries may succeed in
destroying the work of a generation, undoing everything positive and
progressive that Indigenous people and settlers together have constructed over the past fifty years. Here's one example.

The Yukon Environmental and Socio-economic Assessment Board
(YESAB) is a child of both the land claims treaty and the Yukon 2000
bottom-up planning process; it came to fruition after years of consultation involving all parts of the community. Besides providing expeditious
go/no-go decisions for development projects, supported by whatever
technical reports might be required, the Yukon NDP government designed what became the Yukon Environmental and Socio-economic
Assessment Act (YESAA) to guarantee a voice for communities.

As a requirement of Chapter 12 of the Umbrella Final Agreement,
YESAA came into force on May 13, 2003 – one month after the new
Yukon Act took effect and the territory gained law-making authority

with respect to the vast majority of its natural resources. As intended by the original land claims negotiating parties, YESAA applies throughout the territory as a unified, neutral, arm's-length assessment process for all development projects. In 2008, a mandatory five-year YESAA review considered a set of legislative amendments, which ought to have gone first to the House of Commons. Canada's ruling Conservatives, however, chose to bring them in the back door through the country's unelected Senate.[49]

In March 2015, Yukon's Conservative senator Dan Lang introduced Bill S-6. The bill contained seventy changes – agreed to by all parties to the consultation – designed to streamline the YESAA board's regulations. But in drafting his bill, Lang snuck in four more clauses based on a "secret consultation" with insiders (the Prospectors and Developers Association of Canada, the Mining Association of Canada, the Yukon Chamber of Mines, the Canadian Association of Petroleum Producers, and the Canadian Energy Pipeline Association) that would have injected federal influence into regional resource development decisions and bypassed First Nations. For the four secret clauses, Lang chose not to invite comments from ordinary citizens, Yukon's official opposition, communities, environmentalists, or representatives of resource industry workers. This was the very opposite of a "people's agenda."

Already alarmed by the Tories' evident passion for industry-friendly deregulation and by their recklessness on environmental issues, northern critics denounced Lang's initiative. Yukon opposition leader Liz Hanson charged that the changes violated the collaborative spirit and procedural balance of YESAA.[50] Regional Assembly of First Nations (AFN) chief Mike Smith believed that Lang's bill, which would subject an independent board to direction from a federal minister, would chop the limbs off the arm's-length regulatory body, end its independence, and offend the spirit of the Yukon land claims treaty. "We want to protect the land, we want to protect the air and we want to protect it for future generations," Smith said.[51] Three Yukon First Nations filed court challenges against the law. (In April 2016, the Liberal government would announce the repeal of the bill.)[52]

First Nation chiefs had good reason to mistrust Lang and Harper. Lang had fought against the Yukon land claims the whole of his legislative career, and Harper was a Reform Party MP when that party tried to block northern land claims treaties in Parliament. When enacting the NWT devolution agreement in Parliament, the Harper Conservatives had abolished the existing treaty-based land management boards and introduced, without consultation, a centralized "superboard."[53] NWT Aboriginal leaders were enraged; the Sahtu and Tlicho are currently suing Ottawa for violating their treaty rights.[54]

No turning back in the North? We shall see. Northerners cannot be entirely confident that formula financing will endure, that Nunavut will ever get to negotiate devolved jurisdiction over its lands *and* seabed resources, or that land claims and self-government agreements will be faithfully implemented. For almost a decade, Stephen Harper did nothing to advance Nunavut devolution or settle land claims implementation disputes. Then, with his blessing, in the run-up to the 2015 general election, devolution talks resumed and a $255 million out-of-court settlement of Nunavut Tunngavik Inc.'s billion-dollar lawsuit was reached.[55]

On October 19, 2015, the people of Canada elected a new Liberal government under Justin Trudeau. The Liberals took all three northern seats. But how much will actually change? Trudeau promised great change, but history has shown that while the Liberals usually campaign on the left, they generally govern on the right. In the Canadian context, the Liberals are a centre party, one that manages both to support pipeline megaprojects and to court the opponents of those projects. What might the new government do about Arctic issues? Time will tell.

Boomers and Lifers

Fishing Branch River (Ni'iinlii Njik) in northern Yukon, within the traditional territory of the Vuntut Gwich'in First Nation, is one of my favourite places. As the river comes around Bear Cave Mountain it goes underground for a stretch, then re-emerges as a body of water that never freezes, even in 60-below winters. This warm water hosts a population of chum salmon that feeds grizzlies before the bears go to their dens in the mountain. When visiting there one winter day with my colleagues Maurice Byblow and Art Webster, we met three Gwich'in men, Peter Josie, Kenny Tetlichi, and Isaac Thomas, who were counting the chum salmon.

The six of us watched a bull moose sleeping on the riverbank only metres away from a fishing grizzly bear. The scene, which seemed to represent an Arctic Eden, reminded me of the apocalyptic vision of the Bible's Book of Isaiah: "The wolf also shall dwell with the lamb, and the leopard shall lie down with the kid ... And the cow and the bear shall feed; their young ones shall lie down together."

Thanks to climate change, globalization, and land claims agreements, the divide between northern Indigenous and settler communities has shifted, and a new fault line has appeared in Arctic and Subarctic politics. As a consequence, the two sides of the new northern character might more accurately be labelled "boomer" and "lifer." Boomers are adventurers who come north to make a killing, waving goodbye as their booms turn into busts. Lifers are competent folk who stay in the North to make a living in their homeland, working, hunting and fishing, and adapting to climate change as they build and rebuild their communities. Forget political party labels and the old divisions between Indigenous and settler: the future of the North could well end up being decided by these two new contending mentalities, with Indigenous voices joining settler spokespersons on both sides of the debate. The lifer may be the better half of the northern character, but national political leaders have generally been more sympathetic to boomers. Audrey McLaughlin may be as close as we ever come to having a lifer as a national leader.

Of course, there is no such thing as a conflict-free society. If northerners want to govern their territories wisely, then boomers and lifers will need to debate their issues at the dinner table, in coffee shops, and after hockey games. Both sides should quit threatening to cut short the conversation by playing either the federal ace or the judicial trump card;

it is far better for northerners to talk things through in their legislatures and on the airwaves. Boomers and lifers must sit down and do the
hard work of democracy together: articulate shared visions, cooperate
to realize them, and demand that national capitals partner with Arctic
populations on their own ground. These debates will both inform and
continue to form the northern character. The great Canadian philosopher Charles Taylor teaches that humans do not create their identities
by themselves. Our identities are shaped through dialogue as we struggle
to recognize one another and build relationships.[56]

The federal state has loosened its control of Arctic peoples, and it
needs now to cede the political stage to new, hybrid Indigenous/settler
forms of government. For northerners, the most effective response to
attempts at Arctic recolonization by Ottawa, American energy giants,
or Chinese state mining moguls will be to continue the work of decol-
onizing themselves, ridding their minds of the remnants of attitudes
about their inferiority – attitudes imposed on them over centuries of
colonial rule. Against the insecurity wrought by globalization, building
healthy democratic Arctic communities may be the only defence, the
only way northerners can realize the social peace that good government brings. As chiefs and legislators learn to govern together, the feds
should step aside so that the northern character can emerge from their
shadow.

Acknowledgments

H undreds of conversations and much reading went into the writing of this book. It would be impossible to list every contributor, but I must name a special few.

Hunting the Northern Character began as drafts for a series of talks given at a graduate seminar while I was a Fulbright Chair in Arctic Studies at the University of Washington's Henry M. Jackson School of International Studies in Seattle. Nadine Fabbi, Vincent Gallucci, and Resat Kasaba, also Monick Keo, made me feel very much at home there, and my students were great teachers.

My serious education in Arctic issues began during my years as a Yukon legislator and continued after I returned to real life. As a Canadian representative on the Arctic Governance Project, my mentors were the other Steering Committee members: Oran Young, Else Grete Broderstad, Hans Corell, Robert Correll, Udloriak Hanson, Paula Kankaanpää, Jacqueline McGlade, Annika Nilsson, Stanley Senner, and Nodari Simoniya. The tutelage of my colleagues Tom Axworthy, John English, and Sara French on the Munk-Gordon Arctic Security Program was also priceless. Through this activity and subsequent events, including Arctic Circle Assemblies, Canada–UK Colloquia, and Polar Lar Symposia, I benefited from the wisdom of Arctic scholars: Lawson Brigham, Michael Byers, Candis Callison, Alexey Dudarev, Peter Harrison, Rachael Lorna Johnstone, Timo Koivurova, and Gosia Smieszek, among others. As well, my work has been enriched by frequent engagements with Arctic diplomats, especially Inuuteq Holm Olsen, Mary Simon, and Anton Vasiliev.

Naturally, I have also learned from colleagues and friends, especially Alaskans Nils Andreassen, Steve Cowper, William Demmert, Dalee Sambo Dorough, and Drue Pearce; NWT thinkers Jim Antoine, Joanne Barnaby, Bernard Funston, and John B. Zoe; Nunavut associates William Mackay, Letia Obed, David Omilgoitok, Madeleine Redfern, and John Walsh; plus the Yukoners whom I count as early influences: Alfred Berger, Julie Cruikshank, Joyce Hayden, Dave Joe, Margaret Joe, Mary Jane Jim, Norma Kassi , Jennifer Mauro, David Porter, Margaret Scopick, Barry Stuart, and Lindsay Staples. The political actors who made indelible impressions on my youthful thinking about the North include Thomas R. Berger, Gro Harlem Bruntland, Mauno Koivisto, Finn Lynge, Olaf Palme, and Thorvald Stoltenberg. Others, in particular my sadly missed friend Terry Fenge, I honour in the text with a citation or two.

My greatest debt, though, goes to editor Barbara Pulling, who made this book readable, and to Darcy Cullen of UBC Press, who liked it enough to publish it.

Notes

Chapter 1: Who, What, Where?

1 EKOS Research Associates, "Rethinking the Top of the World: Arctic Public Opinion Survey, Vol. 2," Gordon Foundation, 2015, http://gordonfoundation.ca/publication/789. Published January 25, 2011. With support from the World Wildlife Fund, 414 surveys were completed with respondents around the state of Alaska.
2 Statistics Canada, "Labour Force Survey: Employment by Class of Worker, Northwest Territories, 2001 to 2012."
3 Stefansson, "The Royal Road to Humdrum," 135.
4 Quoted in Motaal, *Antarctica*, 34.
5 Gopnik, *Winter*, 89.
6 Smith, *The World in 2050*, 174.
7 Moore, "Presentation and Remuneration."
8 Arctic Climate Impact Assessment, *Impacts of a Warming Arctic*.
9 Lopez, *Arctic Dreams*, 15.
10 National Snow and Ice Data Center, "Introduction: What Is the Arctic?" http://nsidc.org/cryosphere/arctic-meteorology/arctic.html.
11 Smith, *The World in 2050*, 204–5.
12 *Alaska's Constitution: A Citizen's Guide*, Sec. 1, Statement of Policy. Web.
13 Olga Kravets, "Murmansk: The city where the sun doesn't rise for 40 days – in pictures," *The Guardian*, December 17, 2017.
14 http://travel.nationalgeographic.com/travel/countries/canada-facts.
15 "Agreement reached in Port of Churchill's potential sale," *Western Producer*, January 5, 2017.
16 *Canada's Northern Strategy*, Ottawa, 2009, http://www.northernstrategy.gc.ca/cns/cns.pdf.
17 US Government, *National Strategy for the Arctic*, May 2013, https://obamawhitehouse.archives.gov/sites/default/files/docs/nat_arctic_strategy.pdf.

18 Kryukov, "Patterns of Investment."
19 Durfee and Johnstone, *The Arctic in the 21st Century*, Ch. 3.
20 "Norwegian-Americans," Norway.org, http://www.norway.org/News_and_events/Embassy/Norwegian-American-Organizations/Norwegian_Americans/#.WG6vLldEzBI.
21 http://uis.unesco.org/en/country/IS.
22 EKOS, "Rethinking the Top of the World."

Chapter 2: Pawns

1   Fred Langan, "Canada's cruise missile debate flares up, but Trudeau keeps cool," *Christian Science Monitor*, March 29, 1983.
2   Ibid.
3   Young, *Arctic Politics*, 211.
4   Wade Davis, "How we misunderstood the Canadian North, Arctic Circle Panel," *Globe and Mail*, January 20, 2014.
5   Golovnev and Kan, "Indigenous Leadership."
6   Megan Petersen, "UAS brings spotlight to Aleut internment camps," *Ketchikan Daily News*, December 1, 2014.
7   National Park Service, "Evacuation and Internment." Web.
8   *Villages of Widows: The Story of the Sahtu Dene and the Atomic Bomb*, DVD, Peter Blow, Gil Gauvreau, and Gary Farmer (Peterborough: Lindum Films, 1999).
9   Stone, *The Changing Arctic Environment*, 67, 68.
10 George Orwell, "You and the atomic bomb," *Tribune*, October 19, 1945.
11 Winston Churchill, "The Sinews of Peace" [speech], Westminster College, MO, March 5, 1946.
12 Emmerson, *The Future History of the Arctic*, 101.
13 Stefansson, "The North American Arctic."
14 Clearwater, *US Nuclear Weapons in Canada*, 104–5.
15 Lopez, *Arctic Dreams*, xxiv.
16 Michael Ignatieff, "America's Melancholic Hero," *New York Review of Books*, March 6, 2014, 18–19.
17 McGrath, *The Long Exile*.
18 Grant, *Polar Imperative*, 248, 318–19.
19 Andrew Friesen, "'Human flagpoles': Dark story behind Inuit scene on $2 bill: Musician Lucie Idlout says the discontinued bank note reflects a dark time for Canada's Inuit," *CBC News*, 2014.
20 Chance, *The Iñupiat and Arctic Alaska*, 142–46.
21 Nathan Vanderkliffe, "The Crash, the Inuit, and the Bomb," *Up Here Magazine*, October 20, 2012, http://uphere.ca/articles/crash-inuit-and-bomb.
22 Kissinger, *Nuclear Weapons and Foreign Policy*.
23 von Clausewitz, *On War*, 55–56.
24 Mikhail Sergeevich Gorbachev, "The Speech in Murmansk at the ceremonial meeting on the occasion of the presentation of the Order of Lenin and the Gold Star

Medal to the city of Murmansk," October 1, 1987 (Moscow: Novosti Press Agency, 1987), 24.

25 Ibid., 28.

26 Tom S. Axworthy, "Changing the Arctic Paradigm from Cold War to Cooperation: How Canada's Indigenous Leaders Shaped the Arctic Council," paper prepared for the Fifth Polar Law Symposium Arctic Centre, Rovaniemi, Finland, September 6–8, 2012, 40.

27 English, *Ice and Water*, 127.

28 Mark MacKinnon, "Russian bombers over Channel raise stakes," *Globe and Mail*, January 30, 2015.

29 Perry, *My Journey at the Nuclear Brink*.

Chapter 3: Born in the Northern Bush

1 See, generally, Mitchell, *Take My Land, Take My Life*.

2 Hensley, *Fifty Miles from Tomorrow*, 4, 137.

3 Locke, "Of Property," Ch. 5, no. 30.

4 See, generally, Parkman, *The Conspiracy of Pontiac*, vol. 2.

5 Hereafter referred to as "Aboriginal title," as defined by the Supreme Court of Canada in *Delgamuukw v. British Columbia*, 1997 3 SCR 1010. See also *Tsilhqot'in Nation v. British Columbia*, 2014 SCC 44, 26 June 2014, docket 34986.

6 Coulthard, *Red Skin, White Masks*, 7.

7 Treaty Commissioner Alexander Morris's promise in Treaty Six negotiations at Fort Carlton, 1876.

8 King, *The Inconvenient Indian*, 134.

9 Cardinal, *The Unjust Society*.

10 Prime Minister Pierre Trudeau's speech at Seaforth Armoury in Vancouver on August 8, 1969, is found in Cumming and Mickenburg, *Native Rights in Canada*.

11 Joseph Trutch, *Report on the Lower Fraser Indian Reserves*, August 28, 1867. Available in Joseph Trutch Papers, Manuscripts and Typescripts, UBC Library Special Collections (hereafter cited as *Report*). Also in British Columbia, Papers Connected with the Indian Land Question, 1850–75, Victoria, 75, 41–43.

12 Smith, *Our Home or Native Land*, 79.

13 Flanagan, *First Nations? Second Thoughts*, 195.

14 Joseph Gosnell, Proceedings of the Standing Senate Committee on Aboriginal Peoples no. 4, Evidence, February 22, 2000, Parliament of Canada. http://www. parl.gc.ca/Content/SEN/Committee/362/abor/04eva-e.htm?Language=E&Parl=3 6&Ses=2&comm_id=1. Commenting on the Supreme Court of Canada decision in *Calder. v. Attorney-General of British Columbia*, 1973 S.C.R. 313, January 31, 1973.

15 Government of Canada, *Justice Laws*, http://laws-lois.justice.gc.ca/eng/const/page -16.html.

16 See McPherson, *New Owners in Their Own Land*, 144–48.

17 "Indian claims stir Yukon racism," *Toronto Star*, October 20, 1975.

18 Ibid.

19 Sue Ellerton, "Yukon Women," https://youtube/-hEQEkU19jE.

20 Philippe Morin, "Yukon First Nation could negotiate land claim outside Umbrella Final Agreement," CBC News, April 13, 2017.

21 "S.I. Hiyakawa in the news," *LA Times*, http://articles.latimes.com/keyword/s-i -hayakawa.

22 Section 35 recognized Métis rights, but not until April 2016 did Canada's Supreme Court rule that Métis have the same constitutional status as First Nations. Canadian Press, "Metis, off-reserve Natives win Indian Status in Supreme Court ruling," *Huffington Post*, April 14, 2014.

23 See Reports-Canada, "3.0 The Indian Reserve Land Base in Canada," Aboriginal Affairs and Northern Development Canada, https://www.aadncaandc.gc.ca/eng/ 1100100034846/1100100034847#THE_INDIAN_RESERVE_LAND_BASE_IN_ CANADA.

24 McArthur, "The Changing Architecture," 215.

25 Nisga'a Final Agreement, prepared by Mary C. Hurley, Law and Government Division, February 9, 1999, Rev. September 24, 2001.

26 Aboriginal Affairs and Northern Development Canada, April 24, 2014, http://www. aadnc-aandc.gc.ca/DAM/DAM-INTER-HQ-AI/STAGING/texte-text/mprm_pdf_ modrn-treaty_1383144351646_eng.pdf.

27 Among those I met at that Anchorage assembly were delegates from a jurisdiction unknown to me, the Jewish Autonomous Republic, which sat on the Russia–China border, a mountainous area with hot summers and cold winters much like the Western Arctic. We had lots to discuss, but their "land" issues were quite different from northern Canada's.

28 Torvald Falch, Per Selle, Kristin Strømsnes, "The Sámi Parliament: Territorial vs. Non-territorial Authority in Norway," paper presented to ECPR General Conference, Montreal 2015, August 26–29, 2015, S29 – Indigenous Politics in Comparative Perspective.

29 Sámediggi president Sven-Roald Nystø (1997–2005) said this about the right to self-determination in his lecture "Sámediggi, Democracy, and Governance," given at the Politics: Aspects of Power and Democracy conference in Tromsø on October 3–5, 2002.

30 UN Declaration on the Rights of Indigenous Peoples, resolution adopted by the UN General Assembly, March 2008, 13.

31 UN General Assembly, Human Rights Council, Twenty-Seventh Session, agenda item 3, "Promotion and Protection of All Human Rights, Civil, Political, Economic, Social and Cultural Rights, including the Right to Development," Report of the Special Rapporteur on the Rights of Indigenous Peoples, James Anaya: Addendum: "The Situation of Indigenous Peoples in Canada." See also Zi-Ann Lum, "Canada Is the Only UN Member to Reject Landmark Indigenous Rights Document," October 2, 2014. Web.

32 Ibid.

33 United Nations Economic and Social Council, "Continuing Session, Speakers in Permanent Forum Call upon Governments to Repeal Oppressive Laws, Practices

that Encroach on Rights of Indigenous Peoples," United Nations meeting coverage, May 10, 2016, https://www.un.org/press/en/2016/hr5299.doc.htm.

34 Territory Map, *Canada's Arctic: Nunavut*, http://www.nunavuttourism.com/images/guides/mapnunavut.pdf.

35 *Nunatsiaq Online.*

36 "Guide for the Management of Dispute Resolution Mechanisms in Modern Treaties," *Aboriginal Affairs and Northern Development Canada.* Web.

37 Nunavut Tunngavik, "Summary of the 2015 Settlement Agreement." Web.

38 "Interim Report: Honouring the Spirit of Modern Treaties: Closing the Loopholes," *Standing Senate Committee on Aboriginal Peoples*, May 2008, 55.

39 Ibid.; *Mikisew Cree First Nation v. Canada (Minister of Canadian Heritage)*, 2005 SCC 69, 3 SCR 388.

40 "Interim Report," 55.

41 Mills and Irlbacher-Fox, "Living Up to the Spirit of Modern Treaties?" 233.

42 *Cherokee Nation v. Georgia*, 30 US 1 (1831).

43 Gutiérrez Vega, "The Municipalization of the Legal Status."

44 See "Study on Treaties, Agreements and Other Constructive Arrangements between States and Indigenous Populations," UN Commission on Human Rights Sub-commission on Prevention of Discrimination and Protection of Minorities, 1999. Web.

45 http://www.justice.govt.nz/tribunals/waitangi-tribunal.

46 Thomas, *Rivers of Gold.*

47 *Cherokee Nation v. Ga*, 30 35US 1 (1831).

48 Thompson, *Buffalo Days and Nights*, 237.

49 Mitchell, *Take My Land, Take My Life.*

50 Thomas R. Berger, *Village Journey: The Report of the Alaska Native Review Commission* (October 1985), 155. Web.

51 Mitchell, *Take My Land, Take My Life.*

52 Strommer, Osborne, and Jacobson, "Placing Land into Trust in Alaska," 508–36.

53 Ibid., 508.

54 Penikett, "A 'Literary Test' for Indigenous Government?," 32–35.

55 Quote from McArthur, "The Changing Architecture."

56 Nisga'a Final Agreement, Nisga'a Lisims-Ca, April 27, 1999, Ch. 1. Web.

57 *Campbell et al. v. British Columbia*, 2000 B.C.S.C. 1123. The Nisga'a Final Agreement, prepared by Mary C. Hurley, Law and Government Division, February 9, 1999, revised 24 September 2001.

58 "BC treaty referendum," CBC News Online, July 2, 2004.

59 Elections BC, "Report of the Chief Electoral Officer on the Treaty Negotiations Referendum," 2002. Web.

60 Heather Pringle, White River Ash: *The Ancestral Journey of the Navajo.* Web.

61 Navajo Nation Government. Web.

62 White River First Nation. Web.

63 Debra Hanuse, "Brainstorming Governance," panel discussion at the Morris J. Wosk Centre for Dialogue, July 2, 2003, in Penikett, "An Unfinished Journey," 1127.

64 Erdrich, *The Round House.*
65 Borrows, "Aboriginal and Treaty Rights and Violence against Women," 707.

Chapter 4: No Settler Need Apply

1 Axworthy, "Cold War to Cooperation."
2 English, *Ice and Water,* 127.
3 Ibid.
4 Stone, *The Changing Arctic Environment,* 301.
5 Ibid., 130
6 Ibid., 112
7 Roots, "Cooperation in Arctic Science," 136.
8 English, *Ice and Water,* 139.
9 Mulroney, *Memoirs,* 415.
10 Bob Overvold, quoted in English, *Ice and Water,* 216.
11 State of Alaska, Division of Elections, http://www.elections.alaska.gov/statistics/vi_vrs_stats_party_2015.04.03.htm.
12 Axworthy, "Cold War to Cooperation," 2.
13 Ottawa, September 19, 1996. Retrieved from English, *Ice and Water,* but based on Parliament of Canada, "Entrenching Circumpolar Internationalism: Making the Arctic Council Work." Web.
14 Fenge, "The Arctic Council."
15 English, *Ice and Water,* 218.
16 Tennberg, *The Arctic Council.*
17 Axworthy, "Cold War to Cooperation," 26.
18 English, *Ice and Water,* 129.
19 Ibid., 190. See also Nuuk Declaration. Web.
20 Graczyk and Koivurova, *A New Era in the Arctic Council's Polar Record.*
21 Fenge, "The Arctic Council."
22 Graczyk and Koivurova, *A New Era.*
23 Fenge, "Canada and the Kiruna Mandate of the Arctic Council."
24 Jim Gamble, "The Arctic Council at Twenty: Permanent Participants, Arctic Policy in Canada and the United States, and Stewardship," University of Washington–Seattle, November 20, 2015.
25 Young, Kim, and Kim, "Introduction and Overview."
26 "Regional Governments in International Affairs: Lessons from the Arctic," September 18, 2015, Munk School of Global Affairs, University of Toronto, Conference Transcripts, Emily Tsui. http://hosting2.desire2learncapture.com/MUNK/1/Watch/764.aspx.
27 Ibid.; Fenge, "The Arctic Council," 15.
28 Mandela, *Long Walk to Freedom,* 94
29 Fenge, "The Arctic Council: Past, Present, and Future Prospects," http://journals.sfu.ca/nr/index.php/nr/article/download/282/279. See also Minna Turunen and

Paula Kankanpaa, "Visibility of the Arctic Council," University of Lapland, Arctic Centre Report no. 37, 2002.

30 Ibid.; Fenge, "The Arctic Council," 15.

31 Heather Exner-Pirot, "Arctic Council: The Evolving Role of Regions in Arctic Governance," *Alaska Dispatch News*, January 9, 2015.

32 Munk-Gordon Arctic Security Program, the Walter and Duncan Gordon Foundation, http://gordonfoundation.ca/north/munk-gordon-arctic-security-program.

33 The Walter and Duncan Gordon Foundation, press release: "Secure, Sustainable Funding for Indigenous Participation in Arctic Council a Key Priority: Report," May 29, 2012. Web.

34 Helga Haftendorn, "The Case for Arctic Governance: The Arctic Puzzle," Institute of National Affairs, University of Iceland, 2013, 19.

35 "Canada's Second Chairmanship of the Arctic Council." Address by Minister Leona Aglukkaq at Arctic Frontiers Conference, Tromsø, Norway, January 21, 2013. http://www.international.gc.ca/media/arctic-arctique/speeches-discours/2013/01/23a.aspx?lang=eng.

36 Jerald Sabin, interview with John English in *Northern Public Affairs* 2, 1 (September 2013), 27.

37 EU President José Manuel Barroso, letter to Prime Minister Harper dated May 8, 2013.

38 Arctic Council, *Arctic Council Observer Manual*, 2013, https://oaarchive.arctic-council.org/handle/11374/939.

39 Keynote speech by Vice Foreign Minister Zhang Ming at the China Country Session of the Third Arctic Circle Assembly, October 17, 2015, http://www.fmprc.gov.cn/mfa_eng/wjbxw/t1306858.shtml.

40 The Walter and Duncan Gordon Foundation, press release: "Eyeing Resources." http://gordonfoundation.ca/press-release/438.

41 Marie Schram, First Secretary, Swedish Embassy, Singapore, March 20, 2013, "Singapores ansokan om observatorsstatus vid arktiska radet," MFA/EUR/00771/2013.

42 Sabin, interview with John English..

43 Lam, "Beijing's Aggressive New Foreign Policy."

44 Personal communication, Rachael Lorna Johnstone, September 2, 2014.

45 Roseth, "Russia's China Policy in the Arctic," 78.

46 Oran R. Young, "Strengthening the Arctic Council," synopsis response to *The Arctic Council at Twenty* policy report, December 21, 2015, Bren School of Environmental Science and Management, University of Calfornia–Santa Barbara.

47 Käpylä and Mikkola, "The Global Arctic."

48 Michael Byers, "The (Russian) Arctic is open for business," *Globe and Mail*, August 12, 2013.

49 Heather Exner-Pirot, "The Canadian Arctic Council chairmanship: Lots of leadership, no followers," *Alaska Dispatch*, July 2, 2014. This story is posted on *Alaska Dispatch* as part of Eye on the Arctic, a partnership between public and private circumpolar media organizations. Web.

50 Fenge, "Arctic Council vs. Arctic Economic Council."

51 Lloyd Axworthy and Mary Simon, "Is Canada undermining the Arctic Council?," *Globe and Mail*, March 4, 2015.

52 Young, "Strengthening the Arctic Council."

Chapter 5: What You Eat and Where You Live

1   Brody, *Maps and Dreams*.

2   Sam Adams, "From kings of the American plains to piles of sun-bleached bones: How mass slaughter by hunters nearly wiped out the buffalo," *Daily Mail*, January 25, 2013.

3   James Daschuk, "When Canada used hunger to clear the West," *Globe and Mail*, July 19, 2013.

4   Daschuk, *Clearing the Plains*.

5   Daschuk, "When Canada used hunger to clear the West."

6   Mosby, "Administering Colonial Science."

7   Fry, *How a People Die*.

8   Lori Townsend, "Sugar creates genetic trouble for coastal Alaska Natives," APRN, January 28, 2015.

9   Emmerson, *The Future History of the Arctic*, 170.

10 Gray, *Gold Diggers*, 141.

11 Food and Agriculture Organization of the United Nations, "Food Security Statistics," http://www.fao.org/economic/ess/ess-fs/en/.

12 Council of Canadian Academies, "Aboriginal Food Security in Northern Canada: An Assessment of the State of Knowledge." Web.

13 Hon. Carolyn Bennett, "Missing the mark," *Northern Public Affairs: Nutrition North*, Fall 2012, 75.

14 "Feeding my family: An interview with Becky Toretti," *Northern Public Affairs: Nutrition North*, Fall 2012, 72–74.

15 Video: "Leona Aglukkaq Reads Newspaper, Ignores Questions," December 1, 2014. Web.

16 Josh Visser, "Leona Aglukkak apologizes for reading newspaper in House during debate about food crisis in her northern riding," *Canadian Politics*, December 4, 2014.

17 Stone, *The Changing Arctic Environment*, 80.

18 Ibid., 111.

19 Duradev, "Dietary Exposure to Persistent Organic Pollutants."

20 Action Canada Public Dialogue, "Country Food: Improving Food Security in Nunavut through Better Access to Country Food," Asia Pacific Hall, Morris J. Wosk Centre for Dialogue, Vancouver, November 22, 2013.

21 Wade Davis, "How we misunderstand the Canadian North," *Globe and Mail*, January 20, 2014.

22 Smith, *The World in 2050*, 4.

23 Joaqlin Estus, "Climate Change and Alaska Natives: Food," KNBA, December 9, 2014. Web.

24 Ibid.

25 Ibid.

26 According to the State of Alaska's statistical analysis, http://dhss.alaska.gov/dph/
Chronic/Documents/Publications/assets/ChroniclesV1-4.pdf

27 "Food Insecurity in Alaska," 2016, http://map.feedingamerica.org/county/2013/
overall/alaska.

28 Loring and Gerlach, "Food, Culture, and Human Health in Alaska."

29 Shady Grove Oliver, "Anaktuvuk Pass garden gets a boost with high tunnel expansion," *The Arctic Sounder*, March 25, 2016.

30 Cooperative Extension Service, "Food for Thought," April 20, 2011, https://www.
uaf.edu/ces/districts/juneau/food-security-emergency-p/food-for-thought.

31 Ibid.

32 Jimmy Thomson, "Late re-supply barges send food prices soaring in northern
N.W.T. communities," CBC News, August 11, 2016.

33 Action Canada, "People: 2013/2014 Fellows." Web.

34 Action Canada, *Improving Food Security in Nunavut through Better Access to Country
Food*, 2013.

35 Kirk Johnson, "In a tough place to farm, discovering lots to love," *New York Times*,
August 31, 2014.

36 Inuit Circumpolar Council, "Kitigaaryuit Declaration," Inuvik, July 21–24, 2014,
5-6. Web.

37 NDP News, "Auditor general agrees to performance audit on Nutrition North
Program," July 30, 2013. Web.

38 CBC Radio, "Amazon Prime offers an alternative for Canada's North," *Spark with
Nora Young*, September 11, 2016. Web.

39 Qikiqtani Truth Commission, Final Report: "Achieving Saimaqatigiingniq," Iqaluit,
2010. Web.

40 Mark Edwards, "Alaska Economic Update – Part 4," Alaskanomics.com, February
25, 2016.

41 Chuck Tobin, "City's housing market is rebalancing," *Whitehorse Daily Star*, May
18, 2012.

42 "Whitehorse house prices up over 2014," CBC News North, December 30, 2015.

43 CMHC, "Northern Housing Report," 2016, https://www.cmhc-schl.gc.ca/odpub/
esub/65446/65446_2016_A01.pdf?fr=1471045264034.

44 "Is Yellowknife housing affordable?," *Above All, Yellowknife*, February 16, 2011.

45 Ibid.

46 CMHC, "Northern Housing Report," 2016.

47 John Thompson, "Life on Iqaluit's mean streets," *Nunatsiaq News*, November 10, 2006.

48 *Homelessness in the Territorial North*, report prepared for the Housing and Homelessness Branch, Human Resources and Social Development Canada, October 26,
2006. Web.

49 Government of Nunavut (Nunavut Housing Corporation) and Nunavut Tunngavik
Inc., "Nunavut Ten-Year Inuit Housing Action Plan: A Proposal to the Government
of Canada," September 2004, 1–22. Web.

50 Right Hon. Adrienne Clarkson, "Speech from the Throne," February 2, 2004.
51 Steve Ducharme, "Action on Nunavut housing shortage stalled: NHC president," *Nunatsiaq Online,* June 14, 2016.
52 Anna Mehler Paperny, "Ten years in, Nunavut gets failing grade," *Globe and Mail,* October 20, 2009.
53 Ibid.
54 "Nunavut is facing a severe housing crisis," Housing Corporation's Appearance before the Standing Senate Committee on Aboriginal Peoples, March 23, 2016. Web.
55 Ducharme, "Action on Nunavut housing shortage stalled."
56 Paperny, "Ten years in, Nunavut gets failing grade."
57 Ducharme, "Action on Nunavut housing shortage stalled."
58 Senate of Canada, "Proceedings of the Standing Senate Committee on Aboriginal Peoples – Issue 4 – Evidence," March 23, 2016, http://www.parl.gc.ca/content/sen/committee/421/APPA/04EV-52459-E.HTM.
59 Department of Finance Canada, "Federal Support to Provinces and Territories," https://www.fin.gc.ca/fedprov/mtp-eng.asp.
60 Paperny, "Ten years in, Nunavut gets failing grade."
61 Janet Davidson, "Renovator and Holmes on Homes host offers easy fixes for First Nations housing crisis," CBC News, December 3, 2011.
62 Ibid.
63 Assembly of First Nations, Atikameksheng Anishnawbek, the Holmes Group, "First Nations Sustainable Development Standards," 2013. Web.
64 Darren McDonald, "New First Nations housing standard better than a building code," *Northern Ontario Business,* July 14, 2014.
65 Suzanna Caldwell, "New 'Super Insulated' homes in Arctic Alaska," *Alaska Dispatch News,* January 4, 2015.
66 Munk–Gordon Arctic Security Program, "Rethinking the Top of the World: Arctic Public Opinion Survey, Vol. 2," 2015. Web.
67 Tony Penikett, "Arctic security means more than Arctic sovereignty," *Globe and Mail*, January 26, 2011.
68 Canadian foreign minister Lloyd Axworthy, September 1996, 51st General Assembly and in an address of April 1997. Quoted in Dhanapala, Harriss, and Simons, *Arctic Security in the Twenty-First Century Conference Report,* 56.
69 Griffiths, "Not That Good a Fit?," 57.
70 Ibid.
71 Ibid., 57.
72 Young and Einarsson, "A Human Development Agenda for the Arctic," 241.

Chapter 6: Knowing Yourself

1 Carmen Chai, "How much is your doctor making? What you need to know about Canada's physician workforce," Global News, August 23, 2016.
2 Canadian Institute for Health Information, "Supply, Distribution and Migration of Physicians in Canada 2014," September 2015. Web.

3 André Picard, Social Policy in Ontario, "Canadian medical profession is facing major upheaval," *Globe and Mail*, August 23, 2013.

4 Yukon Health Care Review, 61, http://www.hss.gov.yk.ca/pdf/yukon_health_care_review.pdf.

5 Canadian Institute for Health Information, "National Health Expenditure Trends, 1975 to 2015," 2015. Web.

6 Yukon Health Status Report, 2009. Web.

7 Gaye Hanson, Teri Lindsay, Kheyawk Louise Parke, and Lisa Taylor, "First Nation Health Programs at Whitehorse General Hospital Review 2008–2009," Final Report prepared for Rhonda Holway-McIntyre, Director First Nations Health Programs, 5 Hospital Road, Whitehorse, Yukon, March 31, 2009.

8 Ibid.

9 Ibid.

10 Gary Geddes, "Aboriginal health continues to be a national shame: Review of Boyer, *Moving Aboriginal Health Forward*," *Vancouver Sun*, December 27, 2014.

11 Boyer, *Moving Aboriginal Health Forward*.

12 Ibid.

13 "Circumpolar Health Comes Full Circle," proceedings of the 15th International Congress on Circumpolar Health, August 5–10, 2012, Fairbanks, ed. Neil Murphy, Alan Parkinson, and Kue Young. For statistical data, visit the Circumpolar Health Observatory at http://circhob.circumpolarhealth.org.

14 Kue Young, in ibid.

15 Young, "Circumpolar Health: What Is Next?"

16 Ibid.

17 Ibid.

18 Raffan, *Circling the Midnight Sun*, 421.

19 Lisa Demer, "In rural Alaska, a new approach to fighting suicide emerges," *Alaska Dispatch*, December 5, 2015.

20 English, *Ice and Water*, 254.

21 Griffiths, "Not That Good a Fit?" 55–60.

22 Jack Hicks (Ilisimatusarfik and Carleton University), "Elevated Rates of Historical Trauma in Inuit Communities: The Evidence, an Explanatory Hypothesis, and the Implications for Suicide Prevention Measures Targeting Inuit Children and Youth" (abstract), International Association for Suicide Prevention World Congress, Montreal, June 16–20, 2015.

23 Chandler and Lalonde, "Cultural Continuity."

24 Ibid.

25 Natan Obed, President of Inuit Kanatami, presentation: "Inuit Perspectives on National Policy Issues," Museum of Nature, Ottawa, February 5, 2016.

26 "Our Stories of Residential Schools in Yukon and Canada: Seeking Understanding – Finding Our Way Together," First Nations Programs and Partnerships, Department of Education, Yukon Government, 2016–17.

27 King, *The School at Mopass*, 65.

28 Ibid.

29 Sibbeston, *You Will Wear a White Shirt*, 27–28.

30 Mark Kennedy, "'Simply a savage': How the residential schools came to be," *Ottawa Citizen*, May 22, 2015.

31 Wade Davis, "How we misunderstand the Canadian North," *Globe and Mail*, January 20, 2014.

32 John Paul Tasker, "Residential schools findings point to 'cultural genocide,' commission chair says," CBC News, May 29, 2015.

33 Justice Murray Sinclair, Chair, Truth and Reconciliation Commission of Canada, *What Is Reconciliation?* YouTube.

34 Emile Therien, "The national shame of Aboriginal incarceration," *Globe and Mail*, July 20, 2011.

35 This section draws heavily from that report.

36 J. Prentice, Standing Committee on Aboriginal Affairs and Northern Development, 1st Session, 39th Parliament, evidence, May 29, 2007.

37 Ungerleider, *Failing Our Kids*.

38 Mendelson, "Improving Education on Reserves." Web.

39 Richards, Hove, and Afolabi, "Understanding the Aboriginal/Non-Aboriginal Gap," C.D. Howe Institute, 2008. Web.

40 Darrick Baxter, "How Technology Is Saving Native Tribe Languages," TEDx Winnipeg. Youtube.

41 Assembly of First Nations, "A Portrait of First Nations and Education," paper delivered at Chiefs Assembly on Education, October 1–3, 2012.

42 Mendelson, "Aboriginal Peoples and Postsecondary Education in Canada." Web.

43 Mendelson, "Improving Primary and Secondary Education in Canada," 2–3.

44 Taylor, *The Language Animal*.

45 Demmert, *Improving Academic Performance*.

46 Moses Hernandez, Nina Larsson, Jessie MacKenzie, and Itoah Scott-Enns, Denendeh Fellowship Team, Glassco Fellows Consulting Company, April 2015.

47 Thomas R. Berger, Conciliator's Final Report: "The Nunavut Project" (2006), 21–22, http://www.tunngavik.com/index.php?iDocCat=19.

48 Bainbridge, "A Response to Kelly Gallagher–Mackay," 763.

49 Berger, Conciliator's Final Report, 36.

50 Bainbridge, "A Response to Kelly Gallagher–Mackay," 765.

51 Richards, Hove, and Afolabi, "Understanding the Aboriginal/Non-Aboriginal Gap."

52 RCAP Report, 1996. Web.

53 Santa Fe Indian School. Web.

54 Kinew, *The Reason You Walk*, 125.

55 Nancy A. Morgan, "Legal Mechanisms for Assumption of Jurisdiction and Control over Education by First Nations," prepared for the First Nations Education Steering Committee, 1998, http://www.fnesc.ca/publications/pdf/legalmechanisms.pdf.

56 Wherrett, *Aboriginal Self-Government*. Web.

57 Mendelson, *Improving Primary and Secondary Education in Canada*.

58 Ibid., 5.

59 "First Nations' education: Failure is no longer an option" (editorial), *Globe and Mail*, April 19, 2014, F9.

60 Gloria Galloway, "AFN national Chief Atleo quits over on-reserve education," *Globe and Mail*, May 3, 2014.

61 Jorge Barrera, "Budget 2016 falls short on Trudeau's First Nation education promise," *APTN National News*, March 22, 2016.

62 English, *Ice and Water*, 265.

63 Gordon and White, "Indigenous Educational Attainment in Canada."

Chapter 7: Underfoot

1 Anne Lewis and Kathleen Smith, "Yukon's first underground miner: Janeane MacGillivray," *Yukon News*, May 6, 2016.

2 In 1981, Laura Sky filmed a documentary, *Moving Mountains* (26m, English), about women coal miners in Canada's Rocky Mountains. Visit skyworksfoundation.org.

3 Einarsson, Larsen, Nilsson, and Young, *Arctic Human Development Report*, 69–71.

4 Andrew Topf, "Controversial BC Coal Mine Greenlighted with Conditions," Mining. com.

5 Richard Gilbert, "Union Report Challenges Ownership Claims of Chinese Mining Company," *Journal of Commerce*, January 8, 2013.

6 "Chris Alexander says Canada's doors still open to rich Chinese," CBC News, February 14, 2014.

7 Charles Burton, "China's leadership entrenches: This cannot bode well," *Globe and Mail*, March 6, 2014.

8 Sophie McBain, "China's billionaire politicians quadruple their wealth," *New Statesman*, March 6, 2014.

9 Bill Curry, "Ottawa poised to ease rules for temporary foreign worker program," *Globe and Mail*, August 10, 2016.

10 "China sees coal mine deaths fall, but outlook grim," Reuters, January 11, 2007.

11 Sharon Lafraniere, "Graft in China covers up toll of coal mines," *New York Times*, March 11, 2009.

12 Ian Johnson, "The Chinese Invade Africa," *New York Review of Books*, September 25, 2014.

13 Michael S. Schmidt and David E. Sanger, "5 in China army face US charges of cyber-attacks," *New York Times*, May 19, 2014.

14 Nunavut Land Claims Agreement, Article 26; see also FAQ, Baffinland, http://www.baffinland.com/people-careers/faq/?lang=en.

15 Anderson, *After the Ice*, 259.

16 "A mine is a hole in the ground with a liar on top" is usually attributed to Mark Twain. Pyne, *A Hole in the Ground*, 285.

17 "Yellowknife's giant mine cleanup costs to double," CBC News, March 27, 2013.

18 Jonah Bromwich, "How Do You Move a City? Ask Kiruna, Sweden," May 20, 2016. Web.

19 Arctic Athabaskan Council, "Kets of Russia and Athabaskan Peoples of North America." Web.

20 Sophie Hohmann and Marlène Laruelle, "Former gulag mining centre looks to immigrant Siberia far north frontier town," *Le Monde Diplomatique*, August 2016.

21 James Munson, "Cost of Faro's toxic tomb to top $450 million," *Yukon News*, February 9, 2009.

22 Nunavut Lands and Resources Devolution Negotiation Protocol. Web.

23 "Brainstorming Governance," panel discussion, Morris J. Wosk Centre for Dialogue, Vancouver, July 2, 2003.

24 Goldenberg and Penikett, "The Right to Devolution in Nunavut."

25 Goldenberg and Penikett, "Closing the Citizenship Gap in Canada's North," 1.

26 Conley, "Commentary," in *The Arctic in World Affairs*, 79.

27 Mary Janigan, "On the rocky road to national energy strategy," *Globe and Mail*, December 1, 2012.

28 Government of Canada, Government of Nunavut, and Nunavut Tunngavit Incorporated, *Nunavut Lands and Resources Devolution Negotiation Protocol*, http://www.eia.gov.nu.ca/PDF/Devolution%20Protocol_eng.pdf.

29 "Minister Duncan appoints Mr. Dale Brown as chief federal negotiator for Nunavut Devolution," (press release), Aboriginal Affairs and Northern Development Canada, May 18, 2012.

30 Ibid.

31 Mary Simon, Seventh Annual Symons Lecture on the State of the Confederation, Charlottetown, PEI, November 3, 2009.

32 Goldenberg and Penikett, "Closing the Citizenship Gap," 34.

33 "Nunavut premier wants devolution talks," CBC News, January 27, 2011. Web.

34 Paul Mayer, "Mayer Report on Nunavut Devolution," 2007. Web.

35 Goldenberg and Penikett, "Closing the Citizenship Gap," 65.

36 Ibid., 50.

37 "Multibillion-dollar iron mine approved for Baffin Island," CBC News, September 15, 2012. See also Pav Jordan, "Baffinland sees silver lining in scaling back Mary River project," *Globe and Mail*, January 25, 2013; Jane George, "Baffinland lets NIRB look at plan for Mary River lite," *Nunatsiaq News*, June 17, 2013.

38 Guy Quenneville, "Nunavut Inuit group shows its members the mining money," CBC News, May 23, 2016.

39 Young, *Arctic Politics*, 43.

40 Peter, "Inuit Use and Occupation," 47.

41 Steve Cowper, personal communication, November 6, 2013. "I think at bottom what Nunavut needs is leverage."

42 Haftendorn, *The Case for Arctic Governance*," 9.

43 English, *Ice and Water*, 299.

44 Terry Macalister, "Greenland government falls as voters send warning to mining companies," *The Guardian*, March 15, 2013.

45 Ania Swiatoniowski, "Advancing a World Class Zinc-Lead Deposit," Selwyn Chihong Mining Ltd., February 28, 2014.

46 Anthony Speca, "Nunavut, Greenland, and the Politics of Resource Revenues," May
    2012. http://archive.irpp.org/po/archive/may12/speca.pdf.
47 Ibid.
48 Ibid., 62.
49 NANA Regional Corporation, Inc. NANA was one of thirteen Alaska Native
    Regional Corporations created under the Alaska Native Claims Settlement Act of
    1971 (ANCSA).
50 Matthew Price, "Norway: Is the world's largest sovereign wealth fund too big?"
    BBC News, September 12, 2013.
51 Budget Address, 2014–15, Northwest Territories, Hon. J. Michael Miltenberger,
    Minister of Finance, Fifth Session of the Seventeenth Legislative Assembly, February
    6, 2014.
52 Legislative Assembly of the Northwest Territories, *Hansard*, February 11, 2014,
    http://www.assembly.gov.nt.ca/hansard/hansard-february-11-2014?keyword
    =#221034.
53 Emmerson, *The Future History of the Arctic*, 230.
54 Smith, *The World in 2050*, 328.
55 Rob Huebert, "Applying Lessons from Canadian History in the Development of
    Public Policy for Northern Canada: An Action Canada Public Dialogue," Asia
    Pacific Hall, Morris J. Wosk Centre for Dialogue, Vancouver, November 22, 2013.
56 Emmerson, *The Future History of the Arctic*, 180–81.
57 Shawn McCarthy, "Canada raises liability for offshore oil spills to $1-billion," *Globe
    and Mail,* June 18, 2013.
58 Yereth Rosen. "With shell gone from the Arctic, US official fears fading attention
    to the region," *Alaska Dispatch News*, May 18, 2016.
59 Emmerson, *The Future History of the Arctic*, 227.
60 The Arctic Sunrise Arbitration (*Netherlands v. Russia*), Permanent Court of Arbi-
    tration (PCA), on October 4, 2013; Steven Lee Myers, "Russia releases Greenpeace
    ship," *New York Times,* June 6, 2014.
61 Shaun Walker and Sam Jones, "Arctic activists denied bail: Russian charges against
    Greenpeace's team could take months to be heard," *Guardian Weekly*, October 25,
    2013.
62 H.P. Rajan, Arctic Security Conference, School for International Studies, Simon
    Fraser University, Vancouver, April 11–12, 2008, 62–66.
63 Ibid., 62.
64 Byers, *International Law and the Arctic*, 29.
65 Levon Sevunts, "Why Canada can't have the North Pole," *Radio Canada Inter-
    national*, May 8, 2016.
66 "Far East bonanza: Resource-rich Sea of Okhotsk all Russian, UN confirms," *RT*,
    March 15, 2014. Web.
67 Byers, *International Law and the Arctic*, 1.
68 Arctic Athabaskan Council, "AAC Calls upon the Minister of Foreign Affairs to
    include Arctic Indigenous Peoples in Arctic Summit," February 12, 2010. Web.
69 Ibid.

70　Saul, *A Fair Country*, 2009.

71　Ibid.

72　Re Pebble, the best coverage is from Bloomberg: Bradford Wieners, "Why miners walked away from the planet's richest undeveloped gold deposit," Bloomberg, September 30, 2013.

73　Lisa Demer, "Risk to salmon," *Alaska Dispatch News*, January 15, 2014.

74　Suzanne Goldenberg, "Anglo American pulls out of Alaska mines project," *The Guardian*, September 16, 2013.

75　Edward S. Itta, "In the Arctic, it's not Natives who are restless," *Alaska Dispatch News*, April 24, 2014; Inga Turi, "Commentary"; Kirsi-Marja Korhonen, Regional Director, Lapland Metsahallitus Forestry Ltd, Finland reports that Sámi make effective use of GPS and other electronic devices in managing forests and reindeer. Plenary Session, "Sustainable Economic Development of Arctic and Northern Regions," Arctic Circle Forum, Quebec City, December 13, 2016,

76　Alex DeMarban, "Arctic Ocean may be next as Alaska officials seethe over ANWR move," *Alaska Dispatch News*, January 26, 2015.

77　Maura Forrest, "Researchers ponder conundrum of disappearing Arctic caribou," *UPI.com*, March 23, 2017.

78　Alaska Fisheries Science Centre, "The Convention on Conservation of Pollock in Central Bering Sea," http://www.afsc.noaa.gov/REFM/CBS/Docs/Convention%20on%20Conservation%20of%20Pollock%20in%20Central%20Bering%20Sea.pdf.

79　Lopez, *Arctic Dreams*, 172.

80　Kryazhkov, "Development of Russian Legislation," 140–55.

81　Ibid.

82　Ibid.

83　Dr. Florian Stammler, University of Lapland, Finland, "Community Perspectives on Extractive Industries in the Arctic," 2015 Arctic Energy Summit Executive Summary, https://www.institutenorth.org/assets/images/uploads/attachments/Executive_Summary2015_web_fin_fin_%281%29.pdf.

84　Young, *Arctic Politics*, 85.

85　Ibid., 183.

86　Emmerson, *The Future History of the Arctic*, 99–100.

87　Doug Saunders, "We spent even more than we earned," *Globe and Mail*, December 20, 2014.

88　Emmerson, *The Future History of the Arctic*, 258. On Svalbard, Alun Anderson found dissenters from this view who believed that "Norway is really run by StatoilHydro ... [and] is a petrostate just like Saudia Arabia." *After The Ice*, 129.

89　Young, *Arctic Politics*, 110.

90　Ibid., 116.

91　Emmerson, *The Future History of the Arctic*, 258.

92　Hodge, "Towards Contribution Analysis."

93　Elena Dybtsyna "The Blue Future of the Arctic," High North Dialogue conference report, Nord University, 2016.

94 Soliman, "Fisheries Governance and How It Fits within the Broader Arctic Governance," 1234.

Chapter 8: Arctic Security

1 EKOS Research Associates, *Rethinking the Top of the World.*
2 Bomber Command Museum of Canada, "Bomber Command's Losses," http://www.bombercommandmuseum.ca/commandlosses.html.
3 Freeman Dyson, "How to Dispel Your Illusions," *New York Review of Books*, December 22, 2011.
4 Rob Huebert, "The myth of Arctic sovereignty: Do we really need to defend the North?" *Globe and Mail*, January 22, 2014.
5 Griffiths, Huebert, and Lackenbauer, *Canada and the Changing Arctic*, 4.
6 Territorial Sea Geographical Coordinates (Area 7) Order: S.O.R./85-872. The regulation was enacted pursuant to the Territorial Sea and Fishing Zones Act, R.S.C. 1970, c.T-7, as amended.
7 Michael Byers, "At least the Russian Arctic is open for business," *Globe and Mail*, August 12, 2013.
8 Griffiths, Huebert, and Lackenbauer, *Canada and the Changing Arctic*, 186.
9 Morton, "Providing and Consuming Security."
10 Huebert, "Canadian Arctic Sovereignty and Security," 4.
11 Grant, *Polar Imperative.*
12 The Simons Foundation, "Ernie Regehr." Web.
13 Kuptana, "The Inuit Sea."
14 Huebert, "Canadian Arctic Sovereignty and Security," 17.
15 Rolf Ekéus, *Arctic Security in the 21st Century Conference Report*, School for International Studies, Simon Fraser University, Vancouver, April 11–12, 2008, 38, http://www.jayanthadhanapala.com/content/Arctic_Security_Conference.pdf
16 Stone, *The Changing Arctic Environment*, 51.
17 Department of National Defence, *Defining a Comprehensive Approach*, 6.
18 On the Cold War, see Emmerson, *The Future History of the Arctic*, 120–21.
19 Munk Gordon Arctic Security Program, "Canada as an Arctic Power: Recommendations for the Canadian Chairmanship of the Arctic Council." Munk School of Global Affairs, 2012.
20 Huebert et al., *Climate Change and International Security.*
21 Huebert, "The Myth of Arctic Sovereignty: Do We Really Need to Defend the North?," Arctic Circle Panel, January 22, 2014.
22 Munk-Gordon Conference 2013, *Arctic Peoples and Security*, Walter and Duncan Gordon Foundation.
23 Nuuk Declaration, Web; Arctic Council, "Agreement on Aeronautical and Maritime Search and Rescue in the Arctic," May 12, 2011. Web.
24 Paul Berkman, "Preventing an Arctic Cold War," *New York Times*, March 12, 2013.
25 Huebert et al., *Climate Change and International Security.*

26 Steve Chase, "Ottawa rebukes Russia for military flights in Arctic," *Globe and Mail*, February 28, 2009.

27 Byers, *International Law and the Arctic*, 189–90.

28 Tamnes, quoted in Emmerson, *The Future History of the Arctic*, 121.

29 Lawson W. Brigham, reply to Huebert in *Foreign Policy*, Letters, "True North," November 2010, http://www.foreignpolicy.com/articles/2010/10/11/true_north.

30 Sergei Lavrov and Jonas Gahr Støre, "Canada, take note: Here's how to resolve maritime disputes," *Globe and Mail*, September. 21, 2010.

31 Canada's Northern Strategy, "Exercising Our Arctic Sovereignty," http://www.northernstrategy.gc.ca/sov/index-eng.asp.

32 Emmerson, *The Future History of the Arctic*, 68.

33 Randy Boswell, Canwest News Service, "Canada non-committal over U.S. position on Beaufort Sea dispute," *Gazette* (Montreal), March 9, 2010.

34 Byers, *International Law and the Arctic*, 60

35 Arctic Council, *Arctic Marine Shipping Assessment 2009 Report*, Table 2.3, 21, https://www.pmel.noaa.gov/arctic-zone/detect/documents/AMSA_2009_Report_2nd_print.pdf.

36 Ibid.

37 Young, "Arctic Politics in an Era of Global Change."

38 Kuptana, "The Inuit Sea."

39 Tom Bell, "Sen. Angus King pursues funding to add icebreakers in Arctic," *Portland Press Herald*, December 8, 2015.

40 Michael Byers, "Polar Law: Arctic Shipping Breakout Session," paper presented at Arctic Circle, Reykjavik, October 31, 2014.

41 Alexander A. Khramchinin, "Cold War spreads over Arctic," *Independent Military Review*, February 17, 2012.

42 Griffiths, Huebert, and Lackenbauer, *Canada and the Changing Arctic*, 205.

43 Kim Mackrael, "Canada, Denmark closer to settling border dispute," *Globe and Mail*, November 29, 2012.

44 Laakuluk Williamson Bathory, "We are a nation of lovers," *Up Here*, February 1, 2015.

45 Osthagen, *Arctic Perils*.

46 Department of National Defence, Defence Science Advisory Board, *Defining a Comprehensive Approach to Canadian Arctic Theatre of Operations*, 2, 72.

47 United States Department of Defense, "Arctic Strategy, November 2013," https://www.defense.gov/Portals/1/Documents/pubs/2013_Arctic_Strategy.pdf.

48 The Arctic Yearbook, "The Arctic Coastguard Forum: A Welcome and Important Step," http://www.arcticyearbook.com/commentaries2015/169-the-arctic-coast-guard-forum-a-welcome-and-important-step.

49 Ernie Regehr, The Simons Foundation, Briefing Paper: "The Arctic Coast Guard Forum: Advancing governance and cooperation in the Arctic," November 12, 2015. Web.

50 Ibid.

51 British Antarctic Survey, *The Antarctic Treaty* (1959). Web.

52 Griffiths, Huebert, and Lackenbauer, *Canada and the Changing Arctic*, 190.
53 James Homes, "America's Airsea Battle, Arctic Style," *Indian Strategic Studies*, March 23, 2013.
54 Chris Westdal, Arctic Security Conference Report, School for International Studies, Simon Fraser University, April 11–12, 2008, 28.
55 Amy Knight, "Putin's Downhill Race," *New York Review of Books*, September 26, 2013, 57.
56 "The Future of Europe: Interview with George Soros," *New York Review of Books*, April 24, 2014.
57 Michael Ignatieff, "The New World Disorder," *New York Review of Books*, September 25, 2014.
58 Paul Berkman, "US-Russia reset and the first Arctic head-of-state summit," *Alaska Dispatch News*, December 7, 2016.
59 "Canada to skip Arctic Council meeting in Moscow," CTV News, April 15, 2015.
60 Jessica Mathews, "The Road from Westphalia," *New York Review of Books*, March 19, 2015.
61 Griffiths, Huebert, and Lackenbauer, *Canada and the Changing Arctic*, 191.
62 UN, Oceans and Law of the Sea, "Chronological Lists of Ratifications of, Accessions and Successions to the Convention and the Related Agreements." Web.
63 Griffiths, Huebert, and Lackenbauer, *Canada and the Changing Arctic*, 39.
64 EKOS Research Associates, *Rethinking the Top of the World*, 21.
65 Arctic Council, *Agreement on Aeronautical and Maritime Search and Rescue* (2011), ss. 2–3.
66 Thomas S. Axworthy and Vanessa Gastaldo, "Working Together: The Case for Increased Canada-US Cooperation for Arctic Emergency Preparedness," *Northern Public Affairs*, July 2014.
67 Cacciaguidi-Fahy, "The Law of the Sea and Human Rights," 1; quote from UNHCR, "Rescue at Sea, Stowaways and Maritime Interception," *United Nations High Commissioner for Refugees*, December 2011, 12.
68 Nuuk Declaration. Web.
69 Peter Varga, "Auditor General of Canada urges upgrades to Northern search and rescue," *Nunatsiaq Online*, May 7, 2013.
70 "Iqaluit Coast Guard office maintains pan-Arctic vigil," *Nunatsiaq Online*.
71 Ernie Regehr and Michelle Jackett, "Circumpolar Military Facilities of the Arctic Five – Updated," July 15, 2016. Web.
72 Government of Norway, Ministry of Transportation, "National Transport Plan 2014–2023," *Government of Norway*. Web.
73 Axworthy and Gastaldo, "Working Together."
74 Mickey McCarter, "Coast Guard reactivates heavy icebreaker Polar Star," *Homeland Security Today*, December 7, 2012.
75 Assessment based on a quote by Rear Admiral Thomas Ostebo, in Mark D. Miller, "Arctic military policy discussed," *Juneau Empire*, February 15, 2013. Ostebo oversees CG activities for all of Alaska.
76 O'Rourke, *Changes in the Arctic*, 41.

77 Lt.-Col. John St. Dennis, Munk-Gordon Emergency Preparedness roundtable, Whitehorse, Yukon, December 11, 2013.

78 See Defence Science Advisory Board, "Defining a Comprehensive Approach to the Canadian Arctic Theatre of Operations."

79 "Body of missing Tulita, N.W.T., teen found," CBC News, July 15, 2012.

80 "Tourists, hunters near Arctic Bay get chopper rescue," CBC News, June 26, 2013.

81 Bernard Funston, "Emergency Preparedness in Canada's North: An Examination of Community Capacity," background paper for National Roundtable on Arctic Emergency Preparedness, Ottawa, February 25–26, 2014. A shorter version of this paper appeared in *Northern Public Affairs* 2, 3 (July 2014): 48–51.

82 Auditor General of Canada, "Marine Navigation in the Canadian Arctic." Web.

83 Lawson Brigham, comment at "Arctic Encounters Symposium," Seattle University Law School, February 7–8, 2014.

84 Nicole Mortillaro, "Crystal Serenity's journey through Northwest Passage draws excitement, climate change fears," Global News, August 29, 2016.

85 Scoresby, *The Arctic Regions*.

86 Christopher P. Knight, "NORDREG now Mandatory within the Northwest Passage," Fraser Milner Casgrain LLP, November 8, 2010, http://www.fmc-law.com/upload/en/publications/2010/1010_Focus_On_Transportation.pdf.

87 Peter Varga, "Iqaluit Coast Guard office maintains pan-Arctic vigil," July 26, 2013. Web.

88 Concerns about pollution from dumping have been addressed internationally by the Convention for the Prevention of Pollution from Ships (MARPOL). See International Maritime Organization, "History of MARPOL." Web.

89 William Yardley, "A new race of mercy to Nome, this time without sled dogs," *New York Times*, January 9, 2012.

90 John McGarrity and Henning Gloystein, "Northwest Passage crossed by first cargo ship, the Nordic Orion," *National Post*, September 27, 2013.

91 David "Duke" Snider, quoted. in Laursen, "Making and Breaking the Polar Code," *MarineLink*, July 14, 2014.

92 Eric Haun, "Polar code will force big operator investment," *MarineLink*, October 16, 2015.

93 Steven Chase, "New deal nears on 'polar code' to regulate Arctic shipping," *Globe and Mail*, January 27, 2014.

94 Brigham, "The challenges and security issues of Arctic marine transport," 21.

95 James Holmes, "America's AIRSEA Battle, Arctic Style," *The Diplomat*, March 23, 2013.

96 "Mission to rescue doctor reaches South Pole," CNN.com, April 24, 2001.

97 Ray Lilley, "Plane takes off on Antarctic rescue," Associated Press, April 24, 2001.

98 Galinsky and Schweitzer, *Friend and Foe*, 80–81.

99 Griffiths, Huebert, and Lackenbauer, *Canada and the Changing Arctic*, 107.

100 Staff Sgt. Anna-Marie Wyant, "Rescue airmen partner with Canadians for search-and-rescue training," Aviation.ca, August 9, 2012.

101 "RI-based Coast Guard cutter heads to Arctic," Globe Newspaper Company, August 8, 2012.

102 Griffiths, Huebert, and Lackenbauer, *Canada and the Changing Arctic*, 59.

103 Yukon, Northwest Territories, and Nunavut Governments, "A Northern Vision: A Stronger North and a Better Canada," May 28, 2009, http://www.anorthernvision.ca/documents/newvision_english.pdf.

104 Griffiths, Huebert, and Lackenbauer, *Canada and the Changing Arctic*, 87.

105 Yukon, Northwest Territories, and Nunavut Governments, "A Northern Vision."

106 Funston, "Emergency Preparedness in Canada's North."

107 Griffiths, "Not That Good a Fit?" 60.

108 Bell, "Sen. Angus King pursues funding."

109 Anderson, *After The Ice*, 121.

110 Steve Rennie, "Facility will have no functional use during winter, says briefing note," Canadian Press, September 8, 2014.

111 Ernie Regehr, The Simons Foundation, "Fighter aircraft and Arctic sovereignty" (occasional paper), May 14, 2013. Web.

112 Ibid.

113 Lee Berthiaume, "Coast guard's new icebreaker to cost twice as much as originally estimated," *Ottawa Citizen*, November 13, 2013.

114 Griffiths, Huebert, and Lackenbauer, *Canada and the Changing Arctic*, 112

115 Canadian Coast Guard, "Icebreaking – Levels of Service," *Government of Canada*, 2013, http://www.ccg-gcc.gc.ca/Performance-Targets#A3.

116 Stewart Webb, "Ottawa is buying the wrong boat to defend the Arctic," *iPolitics*, October 30, 2014. Web.

117 Griffiths, Huebert, and Lackenbauer, *Canada and the Changing Arctic*, 106.

118 Murray Brewster, "Airbus chosen to build Canada's new search planes, ending 12-year procurement odyssey," CBC News, December 8, 2016.

119 176th Wing Alaska Air National Guard. Web.

120 Department of Defense, "Report to Congress on Arctic Operations and the Northwest Passage," May 2011, 23.

121 Ibid., 25.

122 Benjamin Burditt, "The Future of Search and Rescue in the US and Canadian Arctic," course paper for "Arctic Insecurities," JSIS 482A/582B, University of Washington, Seattle, 2013, 13.

123 Department of National Defence, DSAB Report 1001, 9ii.

124 Ibid.

125 Auditor General of Canada, *Report of the Commissioner of the Environment and Sustainable Development*.

126 "Irving shipbuilding commits $2M in funding for research in Canada's North," *Canadian Defence Review*, September 6, 2016.

127 Government of Canada, "Defence Policy Review," http://dgpaapp.forces.gc.ca/en/defence-policy-review/index.asp.

Chapter 9: Hungry Ghost

1 Lopez, *Arctic Dreams*, 111.
2 Arctic Council, "Barrow Declaration," October 13, 2000, http://www.arctic-council. org/index.php/en/document-archive/category/5-declarations; Arctic Climate Impact Assessment, "Impacts of a Warming Arctic," 2004. Web.
3 International Arctic Research Center, University of Alaska–Fairbanks.
4 Aboriginal Affairs and Northern Development Canada, "Arctic Climate Impact Assessment," September 15, 2010. Web.
5 Michelle Ma, "Rivers, lakes impact ability of forests to store carbon," *UW Today*, December 21, 2015.
6 Ibid.
7 Callison, *How Climate Change Comes to Matter*, 68.
8 Eric Reguly, "No climate-change deniers to be found in the reinsurance business," *Globe and Mail*, November 28, 2013.
9 Callison, *How Climate Change Comes to Matter*, 69.
10 Ibid.
11 Cruikshank, *Do Glaciers Listen?*
12 Callison, *How Climate Change Comes to Matter*.
13 Ibid., 76.
14 Nunatsiaq News, "NDP seeks emergency commons debate on Arctic Sea ice decline," *Nunatsiaq Online*, March 23, 2015; Callison, *How Climate Change Comes to Matter*, 63.
15 Ibid., 65
16 Ibid.
17 Ibid., 57.
18 Ibid., 44–45.
19 Chris Mooney, "The Arctic is thawing much faster than expected, scientists warn," *Washington Post*, February 11, 2016.
20 English, *Ice and Water*, 280.
21 Lopez, *Arctic Dreams*, 79.
22 Sheila Watt-Cloutier, "Petition to the Inter-American Commission on Human Rights Seeking Relief from Violations Resulting from Global Warming Caused by Acts and Omissions of the United States," December 7, 2005, 14, http://www.ciel. org/Publications/ICC_Petition_7Dec05.pdf.
23 Callison, *How Climate Change Comes to Matter*, 92. See also "The Big Melt," a series of articles published in the *New York Times* in 2005.
24 Callison, *How Climate Change Comes to Matter*.
25 T. Koivurova, "International Legal Avenues to Address the Plight of Victims of Climate Change," December 27, 2007. Web.
26 Ibid., para. 3.
27 IPCC, "Fourth Assessment Report," 2007, http://www.ipcc.ch/report/ar4.
28 James Astill, "The Melting North," *The Economist*, June 16, 2012.

29 NASA Earth Observatory, "Key Science Points from the 2013 IPCC Report," September 27, 2013. Web.
30 IPCC, "Fourth Assessment Report," 2014, http://www.ipcc.ch/report/ar5.
31 Astill, "The Melting North," 4.
32 IPCC, "Summary for Policymakers," "Fifth Assessment Report," 2013, http://www.climatechange2013.org/images/report/WG1AR5_SPM_FINAL.pdf.
33 Justin Gillis, "Climate efforts falling short, U.N. panel says," *New York Times*, April 13, 2014.
34 Ibid.
35 Robert Correll, quoted in Callison, *How Climate Change Comes to Matter*, 79.
36 Alun Anderson, "Get ready for the Inuit oil millionaires," *New Scientist*, 24 September, 2008.
37 Jennifer Francis, quoted in "The battle for the Arctic," *The Week*, November 30, 2013.
38 Rob Huebert, Heather Exner-Pirot, Adam Lajeunesse, and Jay Gulledge, "Climate Change and International Security: Arctic as Bellwether," Center for Climate and Energy Solutions, May 2012. Web.
39 University of Calgary Centre for Military and Strategic Studies, "Arctic Security," 2014. Web.
40 Thomas Homer-Dixon, "Climate Change, the Arctic, and Canada: Avoiding Yesterday's Analysis of Tomorrow's Crisis," in *Securing Canada's Future in a Climate-Changing World* (Ottawa: 2008), 89. Paper prepared for the 20th Anniversary Conference of the National Round Table on the Environment and the Economy, Ottawa, October 30, 2008. Homer-Dixon is CIGI Chair of Global Systems at Balsillie School, Waterloo Centre for Environment and Business, University of Waterloo.
41 Justin Gillis, "Short answers to hard questions about climate change" *New York Times,* November 28, 2015.
42 David Kaiser and Lee Wasserman, "The Rockefeller Family Fund vs. Exxon," *New York Review of Books*, December 8, 2016.
43 English, *Ice and Water*, 281.
44 Ibid.
45 Kaiser and Wasserman, "The Rockefeller Family Fund."
46 National Oceanic and Atmospheric Administration (US), *Arctic Peoples and Ecosystems: U.S. Climate Resilience Toolkit,* https://toolkit.climate.gov/regions/alaska-and-arctic/arctic-peoples-and-ecosystems.
47 "Arctic lakes thawing earlier each year," University of Southampton, December 19, 2016. Web.
48 Jeffrey Simpson, "Canadian politics: Still waiting for those emissions regulations," *Globe and Mail*, December 7, 2013.
49 Ibid.
50 Canadian Press, "No timeline for oil and gas regulations, Aglukkaq says," CBC News, November 28, 2013.
51 Jeffrey Simpson, "Still waiting for those emissions regulations," *Globe and Mail*, December 7, 2013.

52 Scott, *Stories Told,* 15.
53 Bill McKibben, "Some Like It Hot!," *New York Review of Books,* May 9, 2013.
54 Justin Gillis and Clifford Kraus. "Exxon Mobil investigated for possible climate change lies by New York attorney general," *New York Times,* November 5, 2016.
55 Smithsonian, "Smithsonian Statement: Dr. Wei-Hock (Willie) Soon," February 26, 2015. Web.
56 Irene Quaile, Deutsche Welle, "Is the Arctic in climate change denial?" *Alaska Dispatch News Ice-Blog,* January 24, 2014; English, *Ice and Water,* 275.
57 Leslie Young, "Climate change a low priority for most Canadians: Ipsos poll," Global News, November 15, 2015.
58 https://twitter.com/350Europe/status/563722641958526977/photo/1.
59 Anderson, *After the Ice,* 40.
60 Quoted in Callison, *How Climate Change Comes to Matter,* 96.
61 Yukon Energy, "The History of Power in Yukon," February 26, 2009. Web.
62 Qulliq Energy Corporation, 2013, http://www.nunavutpower.com.
63 Qulliq Energy Corporation, "About Us," http://www.qec.nu.ca/about.
64 Laura Prentice, personal communication, November 15, 2013.
65 "Nunavut power utility files 5.1 per cent rate hike scheme," *Nunatsiaq Online,* November 4, 2013.
66 Personal correspondence, Shakir Alwarid and Laura Prentice, November 15, 2013.
67 Sima Sahar Zerehi, "'We're already doing it': Quebec company touts wind power in Canada's Arctic," *CBC News,* September 20, 2016.
68 Yukoners spend around $150 million per year on fossil fuels, including business and government. This is according to the Yukon Bureau of Statistics and various other sources.
69 Sandi Coleman interview with Dave Porter, CBC Radio Special Report, June 12, 2014. Web.
70 Liz Ruskin, "How Should US Lead in the Arctic?," *Eye on the Arctic,* September 30, 2014. Web.
71 Gordon Foundation, *Rethinking the Top of the World: Arctic Public Opinion Survey,* vol. 2. Web.
72 Quaile, "Is the Arctic in climate change denial?"
73 Reuters, "British Data Echoes U.S. Climate Report," January 26, 2015. Web.
74 Arctic Eider Society, "IK-Map." http://arcticeider.com/map.
75 Arctic Encounter Paris (AEP 2015), December 11–12, 2015.
76 Victoria Herrmann, "COP21 and the Arctic: Adaptation, Damage, and the Work to Be Done," *The Arctic Institute.* Web.
77 Coral Davenport, "A climate deal 6 fateful years in the making," *New York Times,* December 13, 2015.
78 Ibid.
79 Ibid.
80 Suzanne Goldenberg, "Barack Obama pledges to bypass Congress to tackle climate change," *The Guardian,* June 25, 2013.

81 Canadian Press, "Trudeau, first ministers meet Monday ahead of UN climate talks," CBC News, November 22, 2015.
82 Callison, *How Climate Change Comes to Matter*, 58.

Chapter 10: Boomers and Lifers

1   Stefansson, "The Royal Road to Humdrum," 135.
2   Gopnik, *Winter*, 87.
3   Zadie Smith, "Windows on the Will," *New York Review of Books*, March 10, 2016.
4   Locke, *Second Treatise of Civil Government*, Ch. 5.
5   Smith, "Private Law," 459–60.
6   David Crouch, "Sweden's indigenous Sami people win rights battle against state," *The Guardian*, February 3, 2016.
7   Carey Restino, "Arctic treeline advance not as fast as previously believed," *Alaska Dispatch News*, September 17, 2016, https://www.adn.com/arctic/article/arctic-treeline-advance-not-fast-previously-believed/2012/03/19/.
8   Smith, *The World in 2050*.
9   MacLennan, *Two Solitudes*.
10 Saul, *A Fair Country*.
11 For much more on polar bears' history and fate in a changing climate, see Andrew Revkin, "Recording the polar bear's view of its changing environment," *New York Times*, June 10, 2014.
12 Wildlife Management Advisory Council, "Inuvialuit and Nanuq: A Polar Bear Traditional Knowledge Study," 2015. Web.
13 Griffiths, "Not That Good a Fit?" 55–60.
14 Richard Viguerie, "A conservative case for prison reform," *New York Times*, June 9, 2013.
15 McArthur, "The Changing Architecture of Governance."
16 Ibid., 188.
17 Ibid., 196.
18 Department of National Defence, Defence Science Advisory Board, *Defining a Comprehensive Approach*.
19 Galinsky and Schweitzer, *Friend and Foe*, 85.
20 After Justin Trudeau was born on December 25, 1971, at a time when his father Pierre Trudeau's government was thought to be in danger in the upcoming 1972 federal election, I remember Flo Whyard, editor of the *Whitehorse Star* and a tireless Tory campaigner, standing by the mailboxes, chanting, "Just in time. Just in time. Just in time."
21 Funston, "Canada's North and Tomorrow's Federalism," 141.
22 Sibbeston, *You Will Wear a White Shirt*, 55.
23 McArthur, "The Changing Architecture of Governance," 202.
24 Ibid., 207.
25 Ibid., 211.

26 Ibid., 217.
27 Ibid., 227.
28 Ibid., 29.
29 See map, "Yukon: Traditional Territories of First Nations and Settlement Areas of Inuvialuit and Tetlit Gwich'in," Yukon Department of the Environment, Whitehorse. Web.
30 See, for example, Gwich'in Comprehensive Land Claim Agreement, Article 12.6, "Management of Migratory Species." Web.
31 Personal correspondence with Steve Cowper, July 26, 2014.
32 Arctic Governance Project, "Arctic Governance in an Era of Transformative Change: Critical Questions, Governance Principles, Ways Forward," April 14, 2010. Web.
33 Ibid.
34 Ibid.
35 Arctic Governance Project, "Indigenous Governance in the Arctic." Web.
36 See Gwich'in Comprehensive Land Claim Agreement.
37 Ibid., 17.
38 Habermas, *The Lure of Technocracy*.
39 Funston, "Canada's North and Tomorrow's Federalism," 91.
40 Ottawa transferred $3 billion to the three Arctic territories in the fiscal year 2010–11 – an increase of 26 percent over the past five years. See Department of Finance Canada, "Federal Support to Provinces and Territories," http://www.fin.gc.ca/fedprov/mtp-eng.asp.
41 Heino Lilles, Territorial Judge (Whitehorse), "Circle Sentencing: Part of the Restorative Justice Continuum," plenary speaker's talk given at "Dreaming of a New Reality," Third International Conference on Conferencing, Circles, and other Restorative Practices, August 8–10, 2002, Minneapolis.
42 Yukon Economic Strategy, 2000, http://yukondigitallibrary.ca/Publications/Yukoneconomicstrategy/Yukon%20Economic%20Strategy.pdf
43 Andrea Woo, "Learning from the land in the North," *Globe and Mail*, June 1, 2014. See also Dechinta Centre for Research and Learning. Web.
44 University of Alaska Fairbanks, "UAF Facts and Figures," 2016. Web.
45 Smyth, "Colonialism and Language in Canada's North."
46 Funston, "Canada's Arctic Policy," 120.
47 McArthur, "The Changing Architecture of Governance," 190–91.
48 Ibid., 190–91.
49 Standing Senate Committee on Energy, The Environment, and Natural Resources Evidence. Ottawa. September 23, 2014: Examination of Bill S-6, An Act to amend the Yukon Environmental and Socio-economic Assessment Act and the Nunavut Waters and Nunavut Surface Rights Tribunal Act.
50 Christopher Reynolds, "AFN joins call for Senate public hearings," *Whitehorse Daily Star*, September 22, 2014.
51 Ibid.
52 Nancy Thomson, "Contentious Bill S-6 amendments to YESAA to be repealed," CBC News, April 8, 2016. Web.

53 Linda Leon, "Dear Ryan: Protect the Peel River Watershed!" Rabble.ca: Blogs, July 17, 2014.
54 Anthony Speca, "Devolution in the Northwest Territories: Progress or Poison?" *Arctic Yearbook* 2014 (Commentary). Web.
55 "Ottawa to pay Nunavut Inuit $255M in settlement," CBC News, May 4, 2015.
56 Taylor, *The Malaise of Modernity*, 45–46.

Bibliography

Anderson, Alun. *After the Ice: Life, Death, and Geopolitics in the New Arctic.* Washington, DC: Smithsonian, 2009.

Arctic Climate Impact Assessment. *Impacts of a Warming Arctic.* Cambridge: Cambridge University Press, 2004. http://www.amap.no/documents/doc/impacts -of-a-warming-arctic-highlights/792.

Arctic Governance Project. *Arctic Governance in an Era of Transformative Change: Critical Questions, Governance Principles, Ways Forward,* April 14, 2010.

Auditor General of Canada. *Report of the Commissioner of the Environment and Sustainable Development.* Ottawa: 2014.

Axworthy, Thomas S. "Cold War to Cooperation: How Canada's Indigenous Leaders Shaped the Arctic Council." *Yearbook of Polar Law,* September 6–8, 2012.

Bainbridge, J. "A Response to Kelly Gallagher-Mackay." *Canadian Journal of Education* 31, 3 (2008): 761–66.

Blow, Peter. *Villages of Widows: The Story of the Sahtu Dene and the Atomic Bomb.* DVD, Peter Blow, Gil Gauvreau, and Gary Farmer. Peterborough: Lindum Films, 1999.

Borrows, John. "Aboriginal and Treaty Rights and Violence against Women." *Osgoode Hall Law Journal* 50, 3 (2013): 699–736.

Boyer, Yvonne. *Moving Aboriginal Health Forward.* Saskatoon: Purich Publishing, 2014.

Brigham, Lawson. "The Challenges and Security Issues of Arctic Marine Transport." In *Arctic Security in an Age of Climate Change,* edited by James Kraska, 20–32. Cambridge: Cambridge University Press, 2013.

Brody, Hugh. *Maps and Dreams: Indians and the British Columbia Frontier.* Vancouver: Douglas and McIntyre, 1988.

Byers, Michael. *International Law and the Arctic.* Cambridge: Cambridge University Press, 2013.

Cacciaguidi-Fahy, Sophie. "The Law of the Sea and Human Rights." *Panoptica* 1, 9 (2007): 1–20.

Callison, Candis. *How Climate Change Comes to Matter*. Durham, NC: Duke University Press, 2014.

Canadian Coast Guard. "Icebreaking Levels of Service." *Government of Canada*. 2013. http://www.ccg-gcc.gc.ca/Performance-Targets#A3.

Cardinal, Harold. *The Unjust Society*. Vancouver: Douglas and McIntyre, 1999.

Chance, Norman A. *The Iñupiat and Arctic Alaska: An Ethnography of Development*. Fort Worth: Holt, Rinehart and Winston, 1980.

Chandler, Michael, and Christopher Lalonde. "Cultural Continuity as a Hedge against Suicide in Canada's First Nations." *Transcultural Psychiatry* 35, 2 (1998): 191–219.

Chapin, F.S., III, S.F. Trainor, P. Cochran, et al. *Climate Change Impacts in the United States: Third National Climate Assessment*. Fairbanks: University of Alaska Fairbanks, 2014.

Clearwater, John. *US Nuclear Weapons in Canada*. Toronto: Dundurn Press, 1999.

Conley, Heather A. "Commentary." In proceedings of the 2014 North Pacific Arctic Conference, *The Arctic in World Affairs*, edited by Oran R. Young, Jong Deog Kim, and Yoon Hyung Kim. Seoul: Korean Maritime Institute, East-West Centre, 2014.

Coulthard, Glen Sean. *Red Skin, White Masks: Rejecting the Colonial Politics of Recognition*. Minneapolis: University of Minnesota Press, 2014.

Cruikshank, Julie. *Do Glaciers Listen? Local Knowledge, Colonial Encounters, and Social Imagination*. Vancouver: UBC Press, 2005.

Cumming, Peter, and Neil Mickenburg. *Native Rights in Canada*, 2nd ed. Toronto: Indian-Eskimo Association/General Publishing, 1972.

Daschuk, James. *Clearing the Plains: Disease, Politics of Starvation, and the Loss of Aboriginal Life*. Regina: University of Regina Press, 2013.

Demmert, William. *Improving Academic Performance among Native American Students: A Review of the Research Literature*. Charleston: ERIC Clearinghouse on Rural Education and Small Schools, 2001.

Department of National Defence, Defence Science Advisory Board. DSAB Report 1001, *Defining a Comprehensive Approach to Canadian Arctic Theatre of Operations*, Ottawa, April 2012.

Dhanapala, Jayantha, John Harriss, and Jennifer Simons. *Arctic Security in the Twenty-First Century Conference Report*. Vancouver: Simon Fraser University, School for International Studies, 2008.

Duradev, Alexey. "Dietary Exposure to Persistent Organic Pollutants and Metals among Inuit and Chukchi in Russian Arctic Chukotka." *International Journal of Circumpolar Health*, July 10, 2012. https://www.ncbi.nlm.nih.gov/pmc/articles/PMC3417677.

Durfee, Mary, and Rachael Lorna Johnstone. *The Arctic in the 21st Century*. Lanham: Rowmann and Littlefield, forthcoming.

Einarsson, Níels, Joan Nymand Larsen, Annika Nilsson, and Oran R. Young. *Arctic Human Development Report*. Stefansson Arctic Institute, 2002–04.

EKOS Research Associates. *Rethinking the Top of the World: Arctic Security Public Opinion Survey* (Final Report). Toronto: Munk-Gordon Arctic Security Program, 2011.

Emmerson, Charles. *The Future History of the Arctic*. New York: Public Affairs, 2010.

English, John. *Ice and Water: Politics, Peoples, and the Arctic Council*. London: Allen Lane, 2013.

Erdrich, Louise. *The Round House*. New York: HarperCollins, 2012.

Fenge, Terry. "The Arctic Council: Past and Future History and the Prospects with Canada in the Chair from 2013 to 2015." *Northern Review* 37 (Autumn 2013): 8–35.

–. "Arctic Council vs. Arctic Economic Council." *Arctic Athabaskan Council Newsletter,* Summer 2014. http://www.arcticathabaskancouncil.com/aac/files/newsletters/AAC_Summer_2014.pdf.

–. "Canada and the Kiruna Mandate of the Arctic Council." *Northern Public Affairs* (August 2013): 43–46.

Flanagan, Thomas. *First Nations? Second Thoughts*. Montreal and Kingston: McGill-Queen's University Press, 2000.

Fry, Alan. *How a People Die*. Pender Harbour: Harbour Publishing, 1970.

Funston, Bernard. "Canada's Arctic Policy." In proceedings of the 2014 North Pacific Arctic Conference, *The Arctic in World Affairs*, edited by Oran R. Young, Jong Deog Kim, and Yoon Hyung Kim. Seoul: Korean Maritime Institute, East-West Centre, 2014.

–. "Canada's North and Tomorrow's Federalism." In *Constructing Tomorrow's Federalism: New Perspectives on Canadian Governance*, edited by Ian Peach, 115–55. Winnipeg: University of Manitoba Press, 2007.

Galinsky, Adam, and Maurice Schweitzer. *Friend and Foe*. New York: Crown Business, 2015.

Goldenberg, Adam, and Penikett, Tony. "Closing the Citizenship Gap in Canada's North: Indigenous Rights, Arctic Sovereignty, and Devolution." *Michigan State International Law Review* 22, 1 (2013): 23–66.

–. "The Right to Devolution in Nunavut." *Michigan State University College of Law Journal of International Law*, August 30, 2013, https://papers.ssrn.com/sol3/papers.cfm?abstract_id=2318312.

Golovnev, Andrei V., and Sergei Kan. "Indigenous Leadership in Northwestern Siberia: Traditional Patterns and Their Contemporary Manifestations." *Arctic Anthropology* 34, 1 (1997): 149–66.

Gopnik, Adam. *Winter: Five Windows on the Season*. CBC Massey Lecture Series. Toronto: House of Anansi Press, 2011.

Gordon, Catherine E., and Jerry P. White. "Indigenous Educational Attainment in Canada." *International Indigenous Policy Journal* 5, 3 (2014). http://doi.org/10.18584/iipj.2014.5.3.6.

Graczyk, Piotr, and Timo Koivurova. *A New Era in the Arctic Council's Polar Record.* Cambridge: Cambridge University Press, 2013.

Grant, Shelagh D. *Polar Imperative: A History of Arctic Sovereignty in North America.* Vancouver: Douglas and McIntyre, 2010.

Gray, Charlotte. *Gold Diggers.* Toronto: Phyllis Bruce Books, 2011.

Griffiths, Franklyn. "Not That Good a Fit? 'Human Security' and the Arctic." In *Arctic Security in the 21st Century: Conference Report,* edited by Jayantha Dhanapala, John Harriss, and Jennifer Simons, 55–60. Vancouver: Simon Fraser University, School for International Studies, 2008.

Griffiths, Franklyn, Rob Huebert, and P. Whitney Lackenbauer. *Canada and the Changing Arctic: Sovereignty, Security, and Stewardship.* Waterloo: Wilfrid Laurier University Press, 2011.

Gutiérrez Vega, Pablo. "The Municipalization of the Legal Status of Indigenous Nations by Modern (European) International Law." *Law and Anthropology* 12, 17 (2005): 17–54.

Habermas, Jürgen, *The Lure of Technocracy.* Cambridge: Polity, 2015.

Haftendorn, Helga. *The Case for Arctic Governance: The Arctic Puzzle.* Reykjavik: Institute of National Affairs, University of Iceland, 2013.

Hensley, William L. Iggiagruk. *Fifty Miles from Tomorrow.* New York: Picador, 2009.

Hermann, Victoria. "COP21 and the Arctic: Adaptation, Damage, and the Work to Be Done." The Arctic Institute, December 2, 2015.

Hodge, Anthony R., "Towards Contribution Analysis" [draft title]. In *Extractive Industries and the Development of Low-Income Economies.* Oxford: Oxford University Press, forthcoming.

Huebert, Rob. "Canadian Arctic Sovereignty and Security in a Transforming Circumpolar World." In *Foreign Policy for Canada's Tomorrow,* no. 4, Canadian International Council, July 2009.

Huebert, Rob, Heather Exner-Pirot, Adam Lajeunesse, and Jay Gulledge. *Climate Change and International Security: The Arctic as Bellwether.* Arlington: Centre for Climate and Energy Solutions, 2012

Inga Turi, Ellen. "Commentary." In proceedings of the 2014 North Pacific Arctic Conference, *The Arctic in World Affairs,* edited by Oran R. Young, Jong Deog Kim, and Yoon Hyung Kim. Seoul: Korean Maritime Institute, East-West Centre, 2014.

Käpylä, Juha, and Harri Mikkola. "The Global Arctic: The Growing Arctic Interests of Russia, China, the United States, and the European Union." Finnish Institute of International Affairs, Briefing Paper 133, 2013.

Kinew, Wab. *The Reason You Walk.* Toronto: Viking, 2015.

King, Alfred Richard. *The School at Mopass: A Problem of Identity.* New York: Holt, Rinehart and Winston, 1967.

King, Thomas. *The Inconvenient Indian: A Curious Account of Native People in North America.* Toronto: Anchor Canada, 2013.

Kissinger, Henry A. *Nuclear Weapons and Foreign Policy.* Garden City: Doubleday, 1957.

Knight, Christopher P. "NORDREG Now Mandatory within the Northwest Passage." Fraser Milner Casgrain LLP, November 8, 2010.

Koivurova, Timo. "International Legal Avenues to Address the Plight of Victims of Climate Change: Problems and Prospects." *Journal of Environmental Law and Litigation* 22 (December 2007): 267–99.

Kryazhkov, Vladimir A. "Development of Russian Legislation on Northern Indigenous Peoples." *Arctic Review on Law and Politics* 4, 2 (2013): 140–55.

Kryukov, Valeriy A. "Patterns of Investment in the Russian Onshore Arctic: An Area of Stable Growth?" In proceedings of the 2014 North Pacific Arctic Conference, *The Arctic in World Affairs*, edited by Oran R. Young, Jong Deog Kim, and Yoon Hyung Kim. Seoul: Korean Maritime Institute, East-West Centre, 2014.

Kuptana, Rosemarie. "The Inuit Sea." In *Nilliajut: Inuit Perspectives on Security, Patriotism, and Sovereignty*, edited by Scott Nickels et al. Ottawa: Inuit Qaujisarvingat – Inuit Knowledge Centre and Munk-Gordon Arctic Security Program, 2013.

Lam, Willy. "Beijing's Aggressive New Foreign Policy and Implications for the South China Sea." *China Brief* 13 (2011): 11.

Locke, John. "Of Property." In *Two Treatises of Government*. 1689. Indianapolis/Cambridge: Hacket Publishing Company, 1980.

–. *Second Treatise of Civil Government*. 1690. Indianapolis/Cambridge: Hackett Publishing Company, Indianapolis and Cambridge, 1980.

Lopez, Barry. *Arctic Dreams: Imagination and Desire in a Northern Landscape*. Toronto: Bantam Books, 1986.

Loring, Philip A., and S.C. Gerlach. "Food, Culture, and Human Health in Alaska: An Integrative Health Approach to Food Security." *Environmental Science and Policy* 12, 4 (2009): 466–78.

MacLennan, Hugh. *Two Solitudes*. Toronto: Macmillan, 1945.

Mandela, Nelson. *The Long Walk to Freedom: The Autobiography of Nelson Mandela*. New York: Little, Brown, 2008.

McArthur, Doug. "The Changing Architecture of Governance in Yukon and the Northwest Territories." In *Northern Exposure: Peoples, Powers, and Prospects in Canada's North*, edited by Frances Abele, Thomas J. Courchene, F. Leslie Seidle, and Francis St-Hilaire. Montreal and Kingston: McGill–Queen's University Press, 2009.

McGrath, Melanie. *The Long Exile: A Tale of Inuit Betrayal and Survival in the High Arctic*. London: Fourth Estate, 2006.

McPherson, Robert. *New Owners in Their Own Land: Minerals and Inuit Land Claims*. Calgary: University of Calgary Press/Arctic Institute of North America, 2003.

Mendelson, Michael. "Aboriginal Peoples and Postsecondary Education in Canada." Ottawa: Caledon Institute of Social Policy, July 2006.

–. "Improving Education on Reserves: A First Nations Education Authority Act." Ottawa: Caledon Institute of Social Policy, 2008.

–. "Improving Primary and Secondary Education in Canada." Ottawa: Caledon Institute of Social Policy, 2006.

Mills, Stephen J., and Stephanie Irlbacher-Fox. "Living Up to the Spirit of Modern Treaties? Implementation and Institutional Development." In *Northern Exposure: Peoples, Powers, and Prospects in Canada's North*, edited by Frances Abele, Thomas J. Courchene, F. Leslie Seidle, and Francis St-Hilaire. Montreal and Kingston: McGill–Queen's University Press, 2009.

Mitchell, Donald. *Take My Land, Take My Life: The Story of Congress's Historic Settlement of Alaska Native Land Claims, 1960–1971*. Fairbanks: University of Alaska Press, 2001.

Moore, Carolyn Anne. "Presentation and Remuneration: White Women Working in the Klondike Gold Rush (1897–1899) and the Decade Following (1900–1910)." Master's thesis, University of Toronto, 1994.

Morton, Desmond. "Providing and Consuming Security in Canada's Century." *Canadian Historical Review* 81, 1 (2000): 1–28.

Mosby, Ian. "Administering Colonial Science: Nutrition Research and Human Biomedical Experimentation in Aboriginal Communities and Residential Schools, 1942–1952." *Histoire sociale/Social History* 46, 91 (2013): 145–72.

Motaal, Doaa Abdel. *Antarctica: The Battle for the Seventh Continent*. Santa Barbara: Praeger, 2013.

Mulroney, Brian. *Memoirs*. Emblem Additions, 2008

O'Rourke, Ronald. *Changes in the Arctic: Background and Issues for Congress*. Washington, DC: Congressional Research Service, 2013.

Osthagen, Andreas. *Arctic Perils: Coast Guards as an Arena for Defense Collaboration* [Draft II]. Oslo: Norwegian Institute for Defence Studies, 2014.

Parkman, Francis. *The Conspiracy of Pontiac and the Indian War after the Conquest of Canada*. Vol. 2. Lincoln: University of Nebraska Press, 1994.

Penikett, Tony. "A 'Literary Test' for Indigenous Government?" *Northern Public Affairs: Governance* (Spring 2012): 32–35.

–. *Reconciliation: First Nations Treaty Making in British Columbia*. Vancouver: Douglas and McIntyre, 2006.

–. "An Unfinished Journey: Arctic Indigenous Rights, Lands, and Jurisdiction." *Seattle University Law Review* 37 (2014): 1127–56

Penikett, T., C. Ungerleider, and S. Oldford. *The Possibilities and Limitations of New Governance Arrangements for the Education of First Nations Learners on Reserve*. Ottawa: Indian and Northern Affairs Canada, 2009.

Perry, William. *My Journey at the Nuclear Brink*. Stanford: Stanford University Press, 2015.

Peter, Aaju. "Inuit Use and Occupation." In *Nilliajut: Inuit Perspectives on Security, Patriotism, and Sovereignty*, edited by Scott Nickels et al. Ottawa: Inuit Qauji-sarvingat – Inuit Knowledge Centre and Munk-Gordon Arctic Security Program, 2013.

Pyne, Daniel. *A Hole in the Ground Owned by a Liar*. Berkeley: Counterpoint, 2012.

Rachlis, Michael, and Carol Kushner. *Second Opinion: What's Wrong with Canada's Health Care System and How to Fix It*. Toronto: HarperCollins, 1989.

Raffan, James. *Circling the Midnight Sun: Culture and Change in the Invisible Arctic*. Toronto: HarperCollins, 2014.

Richards, John, J. Hove, and K. Afolabi. "Understanding the Aboriginal/Non-Aboriginal Gap in Student Performance: Lessons from British Columbia." Toronto: C.D. Howe Institute, 2008.

Roots, E.F. "Cooperation in Arctic Science: Background and Requirements." In *Arctic Alternatives: Civility or Militarism in the Circumpolar North*, edited by Franklyn Griffiths. Toronto: Science for Peace, 1992.

Roseth, Tom. "Russia's China Policy in the Arctic." *Strategic Analysis* 38, 6 (2014): 841–59 .

Saul, John Ralston. *A Fair Country: Telling Truths about Canada*. Toronto: Penguin Canada, 2009.

Scoresby, William. *The Arctic Regions and the Northern Whale-Fishery*. London: Religious Tract Society, 1820.

Scott, Patrick. *Stories Told: Stories and Images of the Berger Inquiry*. Yellowknife: Edzo Institute, 2007.

Sibbeston, Nick. *You Will Wear a White Shirt*. Vancouver: Douglas and McIntyre, 2015.

Smith, Adam. "Private Law." In *Adam Smith: Lectures on Jurisprudence*, edited by R.L. Meek, D.D. Raphael, and P.G. Sten. Oxford: Clarendon Press, 1978.

Smith, Laurence C. *The World in 2050*. New York: Penguin, 2010.

Smith, Melvin. *Our Home or Native Land: What Governments' Aboriginal Policy Is Doing to Canada*. Victoria: Crown Western, 1995.

Smyth, Steven. "Colonialism and Language in Canada's North: A Yukon Case Study." *Arctic* 49, 2 (June 1996): 155–61.

Soliman, Adam. "Fisheries Governance and How It Fits within the Broader Arctic Governance." *Seattle University Law Review* 37, 4 (2014): 1209–37.

Stefansson, Vilhjalmur. "The North American Arctic." In *Compass of the World: Symposium on Political Geography*, edited by Hans Werner Weigert, Richard Edes Harrison and Vilhjalmur Stefansson. New York: Macmillan, 1949.

–. "The Royal Road to Humdrum." In *As Told at the Explorers Club: More Than Fifty Gripping Tales of Adventure*, edited by George Plimpton. Guilford: Lyon Press, 2003.

Stone, David P. *The Changing Arctic Environment: The Arctic Messenger*. New York: Cambridge University Press, 2015.

Strommer, Geoffrey D., Stephen D. Osborne, and Craig A. Jacobson. "Placing Land into Trust in Alaska: Issues and Opportunities." *American Indian Law Journal* 3, 2 (Spring 2015): 508–36.

Taylor, Charles. *The Language Animal: The Full Shape of the Human Linguistic Capacity*. Cambridge, MA: Harvard University Press, 2016.

–. *The Malaise of Modernity*. Toronto: House of Anansi Press, 1991.

Tennberg, Monica. *The Arctic Council: A Study in Governmentality*. Aldershot: Ashgate, 2000.

Thomas, Hugh. *Rivers of Gold: The Rise of the Spanish Empire, from Columbus to Magellan*. New York: Random House, 2003.

Thompson, Henry. *Buffalo Days and Nights*. Translated by Peter Erasmus. Toronto: Fitzhenry and Whiteside, 1999.

Ungerleider, C.S. *Failing Our Kids: How We Are Ruining Our Public Schools*. Toronto: McClelland and Stewart, 2003.

von Clausewitz, Carl. *On War*. Edited by Anatol Rapoport. Translated by J.J. Graham. New York: Penguin, 1968.

Wherrett, J. *Aboriginal Self-Government*. Ottawa: Library of Parliament, 1999.

Young, Kue. "Circumpolar Health: What Is Next?" *International Journal of Circumpolar Health* 72 (2013): http://doi.org/10.3402/ijch.v72i0.22447.

Young, Oran. *Arctic Politics: Conflict and Cooperation in the Circumpolar North*. Hanover: University Press of New England, 1992.

–. "Arctic Politics in an Era of Global Change." *Brown Journal of World Affairs* 19, 1 (2012): 165–78.

Young, Oran, and Níels Einarsson. "A Human Development Agenda for the Arctic: Major Findings and Emerging Issues." In *Arctic Human Development Report*, edited by Níels Einarsson et al. Tromsø: Arctic Council, 2004.

Young, Oran R., Jong Deog Kim, and Yoon Hung Kim, eds. *The Arctic in World Affairs: A North Pacific Dialogue on the Future of the Arctic*. Seoul/ Honolulu: Korea Maritime Institute/East-West Center, 2013.

Yukon, Northwest Territories, and Nunavut Governments. "A Northern Vision: A Stronger North and a Better Canada." Yellowknife: 2007

Index

Note: AC stands for Arctic Council; ACIA, for Arctic Climate Impact Assessment Report; AEPS, for Arctic Environmental Protection Strategy; AGP, for Arctic Governance Project; ICC, for Inuit Circumpolar Council; INAC, for Indian and Northern Affairs Canada; RAIPON, for Russian Association of Indigenous Peoples of the North; SAR, for search-and-rescue; TFF, for Territorial Formula Financing.

revenues, 121, 173; new negotiations
with Liberal government (2016), 170–
71; Nunavut Lands and Resources
Devolution Negotiation Protocol
(2007), 170; provincial status remote,
168
Nunavut Land Claims Agreement
(1993): federal control over lands
and resources, 164–65, 167; public-
service employment targets for
Inuit, 147–48; resource-sharing
deal, 176; signing, 61
Nunavut resources: development
options, 179; federal control over,
164–65, 167, 268; Mary River iron
ore mine, 172–73; Nunavut Impact
Review Board, 164; Nunavut Lands
and Resources Devolution Negotiation Protocol (2007), 170; Protocol
ignored by government, 170;
Qikiqtani Inuit Association's deal,
172–73; resource-sharing deal with
Ottawa, 175–76
Nunavut Tunngavik Inc. (NTI): in
Land Claims Agreement Coalition,
65; revenues from Inuit-owned lands,
176; settlement of lawsuit against
federal government, 272; Ten-Year
Inuit Housing Action Plan, 119–20;
treaty (1993), 61
Nystø, Sven-Roald, 62

Obama, Barack: Comprehensive
Conservation Plan for Arctic, 184;
efforts to mitigate global warming,
230, 233, 245–46; first president to
visit Alaska, 3, 242–43; on importance of Arctic security, 24–25; support for UN Declaration on Rights
of Indigenous Peoples, 63
Obed, Natan, 138
oil and gas sector: Agreement on Oil
Spill Prevention and Pollution, 82;
in Arctic, 178–80; caribou vs. oil

exploration, 184; climate change
lawsuit against oil companies,
229–30; interest in Arctic oil and
gas declining, 179–80; oil barge
grounding (Kulluk), 214; regulations
lacking in Canada, 237–38; Trans-
Mountain Pipeline expansion, 246–
47; value of oil and gas deposits,
169. See also ExxonMobil
Okalik, Paul, 167, 168
Okpik, Abe, 140
Operation Nanook military exercise,
217–18
Orange, Bud, 15
Osborne, Stephen D., 69
Osthagen, Andreas, 204
Ottawa Declaration (1996), 79–80, 90
Ottawa nation, 46–47
Our Home or Native Land (Smith), 49

Paasio, Pertti, 83
Paix des Braves Agreement, 50, 116
Penikett, John, 126, 194–95
Penikett, Laura, 11
Penikett, Stephen, 11–12, 216–17
Penikett, Tahmoh, 251–52
Penikett, Tony: appointed as Nunavut's
devolution negotiator (2006), 167;
article on desire of North to self-
govern, 170; campaign manager for
W. Firth, 1, 15–16; elected positions
in Yukon, 14, 17; interest in and links
to the North, 3–4; Mad Trapper
movie, 14–15, 17; public policy work
in North, 4; Reconciliation book, 56;
suit against federal government re
Meech Lake Accord, 167; on those
against Aboriginal land claims, 52.
See also Yukon
Penikett v. Canada, 167
Perry, William J., 42
Pinard, J.P., 242
pipeline projects: Kinder Morgan
pipeline, 64; Line 3 pipeline project,

Saganash, Romeo, 109

Sahtu Dene, 31–32, 61, 257, 272

Sambo, Dalee, 87

Sámi people: climate change, problems due to, 239; hunting/fishing rights on traditional territory, 250; international homeland, 261–62; Iron Curtain and, 37, 43; language still in use, 21; pollutants in local foods, 109; Sámi Convention, 62; Sámi Council member of AC; self-government (Finnmark Act, 2005), 62; survival in harsh environment, 21

Sante Fe Indian School (New Mexico), 150–51

Saskatchewan, 127–28, 169, 177

Saul, John Ralston, 183, 252

The School at Mopass (King), 138–39

Schweitzer, Maurice, 217, 256

Scoresby, William, 213

search-and-rescue (SAR): AC's multilateral SAR treaty (2011), 200, 208; Agreement on Co-operation on Aeronautical and Maritime Search and Rescue (AAMSAR), 82, 208–9; Alaska Territorial Guard, 211; Canada's lack of preparation, 209, 212–13; Canada's National Search and Rescue Program, 210–11; Canadian Rangers, 211; charting of Arctic Ocean, 213, 215–16; *Clipper Adventurer* grounding, 212–13; icebreakers, 197, 210, 220–21; IMO Polar Code (mandatory) needed, 213–15; importance of emergency response, 208; knowledge exchange among participants, 212; RCMP's role, 210, 212; resources not equal to growing needs, 209–10; shipping regulations by IMO, 213–15; US aircraft/helicopter fleet, 221

Sears, Robin, 29

Second Opinion (Rachlis and Kushner), 128

Second World War: Denmark responsible for defence of Greenland, 32; destruction by retreating German army in Norway's North, 36–37; human rights abuses in North, 31–32; US soldiers in North, 32

security in the Arctic: "A Northern Vision" report of territorial premiers, 218; Canada's paternalistic approach to northerners, 124; Canadian concern over sovereignty and lack of control, 196–97; Coast Guards' concern re environmental problems, 203; concept includes human, community, economic, environmental security, 195–96, 198; control *vs.* chance in maintaining security, 193–96; emphasis on human security *vs.* military after Cold War, 123–24; framework for (*see* security in the Arctic, framework); Harper's approach to Inuit historic occupancy, 201; major investments necessary, 198; Russian aircraft "buzzing" borders, 200, 201; Russian annexation of Crimea, 201, 206–7; Russia's expansion of Northern Fleet, 200–201; US security programs, 201. *See also* food in the North; housing in the North

security in the Arctic, framework: community dimension, 198–99, 218–20; cooperation dimension, 198–200, 204–8, 216–18; coordination dimension, 198–99, 216–17; coordination in SAR (*see* search-and-rescue (SAR)); investment dimension, 198–99, 218–24; "North First" approach, 223–24

self-government by Indigenous peoples: Aboriginal right under 1982 Constitution, 152; BC Supreme Court on self-government rights, 70; consensus legislatures, 5; Déline

spending per capita, 129; health indicators, 136; legislation re substance abuse, 127; Traditional Diet Program in Whitehorse Hospital, 133. *See also* Yukon Health Act (1990)

Yukon Health Act (1990): accessibility (coverage), 127, 132; accountability, 127, 131; community clinics not implemented, 130–31; cultural sensitivity, 127, 132–34; Health and Social Services Council, 129–30; Health Investment Fund, 128–29; implementation plan lacking, 134; integration of health and social services, 127, 129–30; partnerships and collaboration, 127, 130–31; prevention, supports for, 127–29; Yukon Community Wellness Court, 130; Yukon Health Status Report, 131

Yukon Native Brotherhood, 52, 54

Yukon NDP (New Democratic Party): Aboriginal tradition of consensus politics, 266; all Yukoners represented by legislators in land claims negotiations, 55; appointment of Heino Lilles as judge, 259–60; author's elected positions, 17; campaigns against Mackenzie Valley Pipeline, 16, 52; finalization of land claims negotiations, 54–55; innovative ideas, 266–68; investing TFF transfer payments, 260–61; mine closings and follow-up, 75; negotiation of and public meetings about Yukon Treaty, 57–62; student housing at Ayumdigut Campus, 159;

"values" conference (1986), 264–65; Yukon Environmental and Socioeconomic Assessment Act (2003), 270–71; *Yukon 2000* planning exercise, 42, 264–66; Yukon Umbrella Final Agreement (1990), 57–62, 181

Yukon resources: Bill S-6, court challenges against, 271–72; comanagement of fish and game resources, 71, 111; Faro mine closure, 166; female mine workers, 161–62; job insecurity for northern miners, 161–62; jurisdiction over lands and resources (2001), 170, 171–72; resourcesharing deal with Ottawa (2001), 175; Selwyn Chihong investment in lead/zinc mine, 174–75; uncertainties of resource extraction, 165–66

Yukon Umbrella Final Agreement: agreements with individual First Nations, 61; artificial deadline for completion, 57; Canada's international obligations re conservation, 62–63; development assessment chapter, problems, 57–58; enactment (1993), 60; Indigenous governance re-established, 59, 71, 254–56; scale of treaty, 59; sustainability, stewardship, sharing of power, 59; tools to manage lands and resources, 60, 71; Yukon Environmental and Socioeconomic Assessment Act, 270–71

Yup'ik people, 33, 43, 44

Zhang, Ming, 93